THE COMPLETE

inklings

Columns on Leadership and Creativity

THE COMPLETE
inklings
Columns on Leadership and Creativity

David P. Campbell

Center for Creative Leadership
Greensboro, North Carolina

The Center for Creative Leadership is an international, nonprofit educational institution founded in 1970 to advance the understanding, practice, and development of leadership for the benefit of society worldwide. As a part of this mission, it publishes books and reports that aim to contribute to a general process of inquiry and understanding in which ideas related to leadership are raised, exchanged, and evaluated. The ideas presented in its publications are those of the author or authors.

The Center thanks you for supporting its work through the purchase of this volume. If you have comments, suggestions, or questions about any Center publication, please contact John R. Alexander, President, at the address given below.

Center for Creative Leadership
Post Office Box 26300
Greensboro, North Carolina 27438-6300

Center for
Creative Leadership
leadership. learning. life.

©1999 Center for Creative Leadership

All rights reserved. No part of this publication may be reproduced, stored in a retrieval system, or transmitted, in any form or by any means, electronic, mechanical, photocopying, recording, or otherwise, without the prior written permission of the publisher. Printed in the United States of America.

CCL No. 343

Articles originally appearing in *Leadership in Action*—Volume 17, Numbers 3 and 4; Volume 18, Numbers 1 through 6; and Volume 19, Number 1—are reprinted with permission of Jossey-Bass Inc., Publishers.

Campbell Leadership Index, CLI, Campbell Interest and Skill Survey, CISS, and Campbell Organizational Survey are trademarks owned by David Campbell, Ph.D. Center for Creative Leadership, its logo, CCL, and Leadership Development Program (LDP) are registered trademarks owned by the Center for Creative Leadership.

Library of Congress Cataloging-in-Publication Data
Campbell, David P.
    The complete inklings : columns on leadership and creativity / David P. Campbell.
      p. cm.
    ISBN 1-882197-48-8
    1. Leadership. 2. Creativity in business. I. Title. II. Title: Inklings.
  HD57.7.C358 1999
    658.4'092—dc21   99-23297
                                                                                            CIP

Table of Contents

Foreword ix

Preface xi

For Me To Be More Creative, I Am Waiting For 1

Schizophrenia in Management Excellence, or Why I Am Still Borrowing Money for the Kids' Tuition 5

Leadership or Management? 9

The Type-A Domino Theory 13

Organizational Success Is Easy: Simply Hire Good People and Keep Them 17

Push the Risks Downward 21

Nixon on Leadership: Surprisingly Good 25

Who Will Tend the Butterflies? 29

You're Probably Smarter Than Your Parents, But Lazier, Too 33

Imagination Is Intelligence at Play 35

Where Are You, Mike Wallace, When I Need You? 39

Travel Nonsense from *The Wall Street Journal* 43

Campbell's Travel Tips: Carry a Swiss Army Knife and Put the Rental Car Keys on Top of the Hotel TV 49

Fathers, Sons, and Mutual Respect 55

Risk-taking, or How I Came to Jump Out of a Banquet Cake 59

One Hundred Punch Lines 63

Experience: The New Management Fad 69

Both Ronald Reagan and I Are Growing Older 73

Pink and Blue Test Forms: The Single Greatest PR Mistake in the History of Psychological Testing 77

A Passionate Corrections Officer with Sparkling Eyes 83

Affirmative Action Poker 87

Corporate Taboos and Junk Detectors 93

The CCL Power Eating Plan Diet: If Nobody Sees You Eat It,
It Doesn't Count 99

A Collection of Old Watches: "Time Flies, Never to Return" 103

Who Gets the New Truck? 107

My Life with Industrial/Organizational Psychologists 113

How Can I Stay Out of Their Way Today? 117

Money Can't Buy Happiness, But It Helps If You Look for It in
Interesting Places 121

"ABC—Always Buy Colorado," and Other Nonsense 125

LDP: History's Most Influential Psychological Training Program 129

Sad, Poignant Memories 133

The Normal Memo Is Normally Dull 137

The Leader As Extravert 143

The Average Self-rating on "Ethical Behavior" Is Way Above Average 147

Men and Boys and Their Toys 151

Problem-Makers, Problem-Solvers, and Problem-Finders 157

Seven Ways to Make a Living 161

Some Nuggets of Bureaucratic Gold 165

A Sucker for Enthusiasm 167

Only Art Endures 171

The Genesis of Weirdo Test Items 177

Simulated Foxholes on a New Jersey Beach 181

Some of My Best Friends Manage Hotels, But 187

A Cadre of Colorless Leaders	191
An Internationally Sized Laboratory for Creative Leadership	195
Now, Exactly Where Is Latvia?	199
Life in the Psychological Lane	203
Nature's Way	207
A Case of Etymological Thin Ice	209
Memories of War . . .	213
An Inside Look at the Olympics	219
The Rhythms of Foreign Cultures	223
Civic Art at Sunrise	227
A Mid-Career Leadership Curriculum for High-Potential Leaders	231
Down-to-Earth Life and Leadership	237
Jugando con Palabras en Español	241
Notes from a Road Warrior	245
Are We Connecting?	249
Whatever Happened to the Skyhook?	253
Wall Street Rules That Have Made Some People Rich . . . Sometimes	257
Twenty-five Years—Seemingly Quick as a Heartbeat	261

Foreword

Eighteen years ago, when the Center for Creative Leadership launched its newsletter *Issues & Observations*, the editor, Bill Drath, had an idea for a series of short articles that would complement the research-based pieces anchoring the publication. He envisioned a column, called "Inklings," that would creatively veer off the path of leadership as it is commonly understood to follow clues that imagination hinted might be meaningful.

The challenge was finding someone who could do such a column. It would require an experienced writer (because columns are in general much more difficult to do well than standard articles) with an in-depth understanding of leadership and leadership studies (because readers would have to trust the writer's judgment about what was important). People with such qualifications are rare, but fortunately CCL had one, in the person of David Campbell, at that time our executive vice president. Bill approached David with the idea and, despite numerous commitments, he accepted.

The first Inklings appeared in May 1982, in the second issue of *I&O*'s second volume year. The column was an immediate hit and has been a significant part of the publication's success over the years. So it was with some sadness that I learned that David had decided to bring the column to a close in order to concentrate on his other writing, especially a book in progress. But this also provides us with an opportunity to celebrate David's achievement. We at CCL want to honor him, and treat his readers, by bringing all sixty-one columns together here in one place.

As I re-read these pieces, I am once again reminded of David's gift for writing and his affinity for a good story and a good joke. David has always seen a strong correlation between leadership and humor and is quick to point out that most of us take ourselves (and others) too seriously too much of the time. If ever prose could reflect a twinkle of the eye, it is David's. These essays are indeed labors of love, every one of them.

I am also struck by the many changes that have occurred during Inklings' impressive run. David has taken on the role of Smith Richardson Senior Fellow in Creative Leadership, and he has moved from Greensboro to Colorado Springs, working out of CCL's campus there. *Issues & Observations* is now called *Leadership in Action* and is co-published with Jossey-Bass Publishers in San Francisco. And there are numerous other changes, many of which are discussed in David's final column. I am also struck by how David, throughout it all, has remained true to the initial vision: sometimes looking at leadership directly, sometimes out of the corner of his eye, but always using his imagination as guide.

This has resulted in his writing on an impressive range of topics: risk-taking, father-son relationships, motivation, technology, enthusiasm, decision-making, humor, the perils of travel, civic art, health, and cultural understanding—to name only a few. The current editor, Martin Wilcox, tells me that in his ten years with *I&O/LiA*, he could never predict what an Inklings would be about, but he always knew that, whatever the topic, he would find a unique joy in life, intelligence, humor, and a commitment to learning from experience.

I agree, and I think you will, too.

John Alexander
President, Center for Creative Leadership
Greensboro, North Carolina
May 1999

Preface

When I was invited to write the Inklings column for *Leadership in Action,* I accepted, despite considerable apprehension, for two major reasons. First, like many writers, I often do not know what I think about a given subject until I am forced to put my opinions on paper and I thought it would be a useful exercise to force myself to work through some interesting topics. Second, I wanted to find out if I were capable of writing to a regular deadline. Writing is hard work for me, and the few weeks preceding deadlines—for an important speech or book review or, especially, the occasional book or test manual—were, and are, typically filled with anxiety, guilt, writer's block, and an omnipresent sense of inadequacy.

A typical conversation at such times might be: "Want to go out for a walk, or a movie, or a beer somewhere?"

"I can't. I'm busy."

"But you haven't done anything for two hours but stare out the window and play solitaire on your computer."

"#@*&!...CAN'T YOU SEE I'M WRITING?"

So the column was a real challenge for me, and I had no idea whether I would be able to meet a year's worth of deadlines—much less the seventeen years' worth that it has turned out to be. I will come back to this topic.

I have been asked which of these columns are my favorites. Two come immediately to mind. The first is "For Me To Be More Creative, I Am Waiting For . . ."—which presents 101 excuses for not being creative: such as, [I am waiting for] "the coffee to be ready" or "my subordinates to mature." These have proven to be universal in their applicability, and I have used them, or recommended them to others, as useful explanations for virtually any procrastination—for instance, why the dissertation has not been finished, the patent application filed, the will written, the weight lost, or the smoking stopped. Distressingly, once the idea was conceived, this column was one of the easiest to write. I am stunned at how easy it was to think up 101 reasons for not doing what I should be doing.

The other memorable column for me is the one on father-son relationships and the difficulties of achieving affectionate parity ("Fathers, Sons, and Mutual Respect"). That produced an unusually high number of empathic letters, phone calls, and comments around the water cooler. As I said in the column, most fathers have sons and all sons have fathers, so the dynamics are widespread. I still believe that until the son achieves something of significance valued by both of them, the relationship cannot move forward from parent-child to valued friends.

That column has become more poignant for me because the son who was featured there, who had introduced me to the pleasures of diving unclothed into an icy mountain swimming hole, has since left this particular world, and his departure has forced me to abruptly confront my own ideas of immortality, the afterlife, and some notion of eternity. Writers from all ages—from the Greeks, to Shakespeare, to Ellen Goodman—have noted the unnaturalness of parents having to face a child's mortality before they confront their own, and such an experience leaves one with a slowly softening patina of sadness. I am glad that I wrote that column then; I do not think I could do it now.

In re-reading the pieces in this book, I note with wry interest the absence of topics I have grappled with but have never successfully written columns about. For example, I tried several times to write about the spiritual aspects of leadership. My attempts, however, always seemed corny or hokey. I am not certain, as I yearn to elucidate an elegant philosophy of the spirituality of leadership, that one can ever quite escape having grown up in Iowa. I am ever aware of a cluster of overall-clad, toothpick-chewing neighbors reading over my shoulder, chuckling among themselves, "Who does that Campbell kid think he is anyway?" So I doubt that I will ever be able to express convincingly my notion that leaders must be driven by mystical visions larger than mission statements, staffing tables, budgets, and "actual against plan" spreadsheet columns. Yet, ironically, leaders who do not understand budgets, headcounts, and accountability are not likely to achieve their ethereal agendas.

I would also like to have written a column on the pernicious effects of governmental and military secrecy. For every honest secret compromised, we have probably had ten (or a hundred or a thousand?) undetected Watergates, savings-and-loan cover-ups, weapons-spending overruns, and Iran-Contra fiascoes. A few unfettered C-Span cameras continually wandering the hallways and conference rooms of the White House, Capitol Hill, and the Pentagon would probably protect us from a lot of zealots. "My gosh, David, you mean you think the citizens of this country should be constantly informed about what's going on? Why that's positively un-American!" Strange, how autocratic our democratic leaders can become when their personal span of discretion is threatened.

(Some years ago I sat in on a briefing at the Air Force Academy given by the Academy Chaplain. It was an interesting presentation, showing historical curves of chapel attendance for cadets of different denominations. The Chaplain, a man of considerable charm, began the briefing by noting that his data were classified as "TOP SACRED." My kind of guy.)

Another column I would like to have written is one about the stance our society has taken against physical risks (When was the last time you saw a diving board at a hotel swimming pool or a teeter-totter on a playground?) and the corresponding legal insanity we have wished upon ourselves. I now see earning a law degree as analogous to buying a radar detector: both are preludes to helping someone evade the spirit of the law.

I also wanted to write columns about the relationships between races, and between the sexes, in the workplace but I was too cowardly. Being an aging white male these days is almost ipso facto proof of incorrect thinking, and casual viewpoints that I have, such as that some behavioral patterns are genetically based and are therefore out of reach of the usual environmental programs, take on high-test explosiveness when offered over the lunch table. When I ventured such a conclusion once, in an Oregon fern-tea-and-tofu bar, to my two 1980s Ivy League-educated sons, the temperature quickly soared past incendiary, and we have by tacit agreement avoided further family discussion of that topic.

I would also like to have written an opinion piece pointing out that the sexual repression of the 1950s is returning and that the constraints are probably going to tighten up further during the next decade or so—for example, 1950s-type flirtations are rapidly becoming synonymous with sexual harassment—until another 1960s-type relief explosion inevitably occurs.

Now that I have decided to bring this column to an end, I may have to accept that the above paragraphs will comprise my published writing on these topics—although I suspect that I will have opportunities in other venues.

Looking back on the Inklings column—on the pieces I wrote and the ones I didn't—I am struck by how much has changed at the Center for Creative Leadership in seventeen years. You will find my views on this in the final column.

As to the question raised in my first paragraph (whether I could learn to write to a regular deadline), after seventeen years I still do not have an easy answer. For the most part I have met my deadlines, but always with such anxiety and stress that it seemed that each column must be the last. After finishing each one of them I pushed back from the keyboard with the certain assurance that I would never have another original idea in my life, and the effort was so draining that I have complete empathy for Robert Heinlein's belief that writing is for the most part a socially acceptable activity but you should do it in private and wash your hands afterward.

Colorado Springs, Colorado
May 1999

For Me To Be More Creative, I Am Waiting For . . .

1. Inspiration
2. Permission
3. Reassurance
4. The coffee to be ready
5. My turn
6. Someone to smooth the way
7. The rest of the rules
8. Someone to change
9. Wider fairways
10. Revenge
11. The stakes to be lower
12. More time
13. A significant relationship to (a) improve, (b) terminate, (c) happen
14. The right person
15. A disaster
16. Time to almost run out
17. An obvious scapegoat
18. The kids to leave home
19. A Dow-Jones of 1500
20. The Lion to lie down with the Lamb
21. Mutual consent
22. A better time
23. A more favorable horoscope
24. My youth to return
25. The two-minute warning
26. The legal profession to reform
27. Richard Nixon to be reelected
28. Age to grant me the right of eccentricity
29. Tomorrow
30. Jacks or better
31. My annual checkup
32. A better circle of friends
33. The stakes to be higher
34. The semester to start
35. My way to be clear
36. Black people to be free

37. An absence of risk
38. The Japanese to leave town
39. My uncle to come home from the service
40. Someone to discover me
41. More adequate safeguards
42. A lower capital gains rate
43. The statute of limitations to run out
44. My parents to die
45. A cure for herpes
46. The things that I do not understand or approve of to go away
47. Wars to end
48. My love to rekindle
49. Someone to be watching
50. A clearly written set of instructions
51. Better birth control
52. The ERA to pass
53. An end to poverty, injustice, cruelty, deceit, incompetence, pestilence, crime, and offensive suggestions from my peers
54. A competing patent to expire
55. Chicken Little to return
56. My subordinates to mature
57. My ego to improve
58. The pot to boil
59. My new credit card
60. The piano tuner
61. This meeting to be over
62. My receivables to clear
63. The unemployment checks to run out
64. Spring
65. My suit to come back from the cleaners
66. My self-esteem to be restored
67. A signal from Heaven
68. The alimony payments to stop
69. The gems of brilliance buried within my first bumbling efforts to be recognized, applauded, and substantially rewarded so that I can work on the second draft in comfort
70. A reinterpretation of Robert's Rules of Order
71. Various aches and pains to subside

72. Shorter lift lines
73. The wind to freshen
74. My children to be thoughtful, neat, obedient, and self-supporting
75. Next season
76. Someone else to screw up
77. My current life to be declared a dress rehearsal, with some script changes permitted before opening night
78. Logic to prevail
79. The next time around
80. You to stand out of my light
81. My ship to come in
82. A better deodorant
83. My dissertation to be finished
84. A sharp pencil
85. The check to clear
86. My wife, film, or boomerang to come back
87. My doctor's approval, my father's permission, my minister's blessing, my accountant's acquiescence, or my lawyer's okay
88. Morning
89. California to fall into the ocean
90. A less turbulent time
91. The Iceman to Cometh
92. An opportunity to call collect
93. A better write-off
94. My smoking urges to subside
95. The rates to go down
96. The rates to go up
97. The rates to stabilize
98. My grandfather's estate to be settled
99. Weekend rates
100. A cue card
101. You to go first

Schizophrenia in Management Excellence, or Why I Am Still Borrowing Money for the Kids' Tuition

I have three close friends who have made themselves several million dollars by being superb managers; they all have different personalities, but I have noticed that they do have one mildly schizophrenic trait in common. I know three other self-made millionaires, not nearly as well, but they also seem to have this same trait. While six people is not a sufficient foundation for a new psychological theory, this one consistency among these highly unusual people strikes me as central to their success and may well merit further study.

Let me tell you three anecdotes to illustrate the point.

I was sitting in a hotel bar one afternoon with one of these friends; he was explaining to me his latest venture. The bar belongs to him as part of his network of properties in what he calls "The Hospitality Industry."

My friend has a coiled-spring intensity about him, and he was hunched over a paper napkin rapidly outlining the components of his newest deal. My eyes were semiglazed because he was using numbers with more zeros behind them than I am accustomed to. I listened with fascination as he sketched in his strategy, using terms such as "option-to-buy," "accelerated depreciation," "balloon payments," and "off-setting cash flow," and it occurred to me that he wasn't pushing numbers around on the napkin as much as he was manipulating concepts.

As we were talking, the bartender, cleaning up behind the bar, dropped a glass and smashed it. "Damn," said my friend without raising his head, "another wasted 38¢," and he went right on with his discussion of $75,000 here and $250,000 there.

I sat there thinking, "Worrying about 38¢ in the context of several hundred thousand dollars is weird . . . but that's why he's rich and I'm still borrowing money for the kids' tuition."

The second episode happened when I was sitting in on a meeting of the board of directors of a publicly held printing company where I am acquainted with the CEO. The CEO has a powerful personality, and though he is a better listener than most of the dominant corporate types I have known, he in fact owns enough of the company stock so that the board of directors is guaranteed not to make waves.

One of the items on the board's agenda was "The New Equipment Acquisitions Budget," and an operating manager was making a presentation recommending the purchase of two new presses, one for $180,000, the other for $620,000. He had obviously well researched the situation, had the payback schedules and other facts available, and the CEO clearly supported this acquisition. So the normal perfunctory motion was made and passed. I sat there thinking, "Hey, why didn't they even ask the obvious question, 'What's the difference between these presses? One costs $180,000, the other $620,000. Why?'" But the question didn't come up and they went on to other business, which included a discussion of the salary of the fellow in the mailroom. He had been there a long time and was apparently doing the job well. The issue was that he was making $4.65 an hour, but he had an offer for another job at $5.15 an hour and was thinking of leaving. After a longer discussion on this topic than was conducted on the presses, the CEO said "I know we can fill that job for $4.65 an hour. If he can better himself elsewhere, we'll have to let him go."

I thought to myself, "To worry about 50¢ an hour when you have just spent almost a million bucks on presses is weird . . . but that's why he's rich and I'm still borrowing money . . . etc."

(In writing this now, I cannot recall the context of why such a trivial salary issue reached the board in the first place, but I do remember the discussion vividly.)

The third example occurred when I was being shown around the new building of one of the country's largest mail-order operations. My friend, the owner, was very proud of his completely automated office and centralized computer installation. As I recall, all the computer-related and warehouse equipment cost something over $1 million. While we were wandering through, he said to me, "Have you seen our new catalog yet?" I said no, so he asked one of his passing subordinates to bring him one. A few minutes later, the subordinate caught up with us and handed him two catalogs. My friend took one, handed it to me, and then handed the other one back to the subordinate and said, in distinctly icy tones, "I only asked for one. Please put this copy back in stock." His displeasure at the implied waste was obvious.

I thought once again, "Worrying about a wasted mail-order catalog when you have just bought enough computer equipment to run a good-sized bank is weird . . . but that's why he's rich and I'm still borrowing . . . etc."

These three anecdotes illustrate this peculiar managerial schizophrenia that I have often noted in the behavior of people capable of amassing large sums of money. They revel in the bold move, in the orchestration of hundreds of thousands of dollars of new assets, but they are equally aware of the 38¢ glass, the excessive 50¢ per hour, and the wasted catalog. I suspect it is not the specific waste as much as it is the general concept. "Instinctive thrift" is another important concept to be manipulated, equal in impact to "accelerated depreciation" or "off-setting cash flow." To them, there is no schizophrenia here, just another crucial factor.

A final story documenting the same point came from a man I never met but whose name is prominent in the life of CCL, H. Smith Richardson, Sr. He built the Richardson-Vicks empire and was the founder of the Smith Richardson Foundation, which has supported the Center. One of his long-time subordinates told me the following story.

He and Mr. Richardson were in New Orleans many years ago on a business trip and at the end of the day were relaxing in the hotel lounge. When they were leaving, Mr. Richardson asked for the check; it was for 92¢. He turned to his young colleague and said, "I want to show you something," then asked the waitress, "How much are the drinks?"

"Forty-five cents each," she replied.

"Why is the bill 92¢?"

She answered, "The bill is for two drinks, plus 2¢ tax."

Mr. Richardson asked, "At what point does the tax begin?"

She replied, "At 50¢."

"There's no tax under 50¢?" he asked.

"That's right."

He winked at his protegé and said to the waitress, "Would you please bring us separate checks?"

She brought them separate checks for 45¢ each, a total of 90¢, which they paid, saving 2¢. Mr. Richardson said, as they walked out, "Don't knock the pennies. They may keep you from going broke some day."

Which is why, when he died, he left behind several hundred million dollars . . . and why I'm still borrowing money for the kids' tuition.

Leadership or Management?

He leaned forward—a tall, handsome man—and, from across the coffee table in his huge office suite, fixed me with an engaging smile, warm eyes, and a strong voice. He was personally charismatic, in a powerful administrative post, with a Ph.D. in physics; I knew he had to be intellectually bright. Consequently, I winced when he said, "Tell me, Doctor, you're the expert. What's the difference between leadership and management?"

Ah, God, I thought to myself, I've had this conversation about a zillion times. The fact that he asked the question means that he holds a strong opinion on the issue—and it probably boils down to the belief that leadership is somehow mystical, involving style and tone and white knights on horses while management, in contrast, is something created by bureaucracies demanding accountable, cost-effective solutions to humdrum problems.

"Well, there's not much difference," I said casually, knowing it was going to zing him. "You can play word games if you'd like, and define leadership as something that involves setting organizational goals and management as something that involves carrying them out, but when it comes down to the actual behavior necessary to be either a good leader or a good manager, I think it is mostly the same—at least overlapping: If you can't manage, you can't lead, and if you can't lead, you can't manage."

He smiled; he had me.

He said, "I've known lots of people who were good leaders but not good managers, and lots of managers who were incapable of leadership—they just pushed papers."

"Could be. I just see it differently. The good leaders I have known lasted only a short time in organizations unless they were willing to do the staff work, to get involved in the budgeting process, to worry about the appraisal and feedback systems, to do the behind-the-scene politicking that it takes to build an institution. When you look at the John Woodens and Alfred P. Sloans and George Marshalls of the world, men who have built enduring enterprises, you find a great deal of attention to efficiency and detail. In contrast, the charismatic leader without a management orientation is characterized by the DeLoreans of the world, comets without substance. There's heat and light and deliciously active excitement for awhile, but it goes away when the immediate crisis and media exposure fades. What lasting contribution to world peace has been made by the Pattons and LeMays? They were considered by many to be outstanding leaders, but did their actions truly leave the world safer for their grandchildren, or do we still have to go through round after round of people like that proving they can inspire men to pound the hell out of each other?"

He was, of course, not convinced, and we wandered on, in a pleasant sparring mode, over conversational ground that both of us were familiar with. Questions and replies had an easy, effortless flow, and we thought each other to be brilliant, though misguided.

Leadership, I'm convinced, is recognized by most people only when there is a highly visible crisis or when there is some easily defined technological breakthrough. Without a publicly visible event, without a televisable happening, there is no leadership. Which doesn't mean that good things don't happen. People still manage resources wisely, reward excellence appropriately, communicate with the necessary networks—in general do all of the things called for by good management principles, including, incidentally, planning for the future in ways that prevent crises, thereby eliminating the need for flamboyant, crisis-oriented leadership. But such actions produce few victories, press conferences, or parades.

A case in point: Jonas Salk, the scientist, is usually credited in the public's mind as the man who eradicated polio, and he is thus generally seen as a "leader"; he has a massive reputation, deservedly so. Yet the eradication of other diseases—measles, for example—followed almost exactly the same pattern as did polio, but no "leader" is credited with those achievements. Measles has been managed out of existence by a whole collection of dedicated professionals, but it was management, not leadership. While the desirable outcome was the same, there is no one for the pedestal.

I find it paradoxical that in a society crying out for leadership, the following quote is widely circulated, with a lot of affirmative head-nodding when it is read:

> *A leader is best when*
> *People barely know that he exists.*
> *Of a good leader, who talks little,*
> *When his work is done, his aim fulfilled,*
> *They will say, "We did this ourselves."*
>
> Lao Tse

Leadership or Management?

Most of us want to be led that way—that is, "Give me the resources and then leave me alone"—but it is hard to imagine that approach ever being recognized as leadership. It would be too dull.

The concept of leadership should probably be restricted to wars, diseases, recessions, strikes, riots, artistic productions, and championship games. In contrast, it will be management that takes out the garbage, educates the children, distributes the food, shelters the poor, and protects your pension so that it will be there twenty years from now. Rebuttal?

The Type-A Domino Theory

"I have finally figured out why I work so hard."

(The setting was my favorite coffee shop, and the conversation was with one of those Type-A overachievers that I enjoy so much. The speaker, who was about to launch into a lengthy monologue, was a man who has more money than he needs, along with a sizeable surplus of cars, boats, exotic real estate, tax shelters, and ex-wives.)

"I have finally figured out why I work so hard.

"It's not because I like my work . . . I DO like it, but I like lots of other things, too, like reading and walking on the beach.

"It's not because I make lots of money . . . I do and I like that, but I can think of several ways that I could probably make more.

"It's not because I am contributing to the world . . . I actually believe I do make an important contribution in my own unique way, but I can think of other places where I could do even more good . . . [grinning now] while continuing to do well.

"It's not the fascinating people that I meet . . . I do meet them in seemingly endless arrays, but that is not altogether to the good. They come and go too fast; it would be nice to have a few friends who didn't have to wear name tags."

He continued, "There are lots of other related reasons, and they're all true, but . . . but even collectively, they are inadequate for explaining this passionate drive to press on that I seem to have.

"The other night, while soaking in the hot tub, I hit upon the perfect explanation.

"It's my DOMINO THEORY OF MOTIVATION.

"It goes this way: Let's assume that your goal in life is to knock over dominos, okay? The dominos are arranged in rows ahead of you, each row perpendicular to your line of sight as you look out ahead, with each row twice as long as the previous one: The first row has one domino; the second row has two; the third has four; the fourth, eight; then 16, 32, etc. To knock over a row, you simply reach out and tip over the first one in the row and let the domino action take over.

"Now, a reasonable lifetime goal for a young person might be to knock over 64 dominos at once. That's a good number, let's go with it.

"So you go through your early career, thinking, 'Boy, if I could only knock over 64 dominos, I'd never ask for anything more.' You sweat and strain and strive and connive, and then one day, voilà!, they bring you to the domino table.

"You sit down, compose yourself, straighten your tie, then reach out and knock over the first row, which has one domino in it.

"SPLAT! It's only one domino, but it is your first one, and it makes a very satisfying sound. Then you lean forward a little so you can reach the second row, and flick over the first domino in it. It falls over, taking the other one in its row with it. SPLAT, SPLAT! Great!

"You lean forward more, and knock over the first domino in the third row, and it takes the other three in that row down, and then you're at the fourth row, where there are eight dominos, and as they fall, the noise and action is getting pretty exciting.

"Reaching the fifth row is a little harder, you have to stretch more but, when you do, you get 16 dominos at once! The exhilaration of that success pushes you to the sixth row easily, where you watch gleefully as 32 dominos go down with one flick.

"There you sit, incredulous, only one flick away from achieving everything you have been working for all your life—you are going to be able to knock over 64 dominos. And you do it. You shift your weight forward again, stretch out almost as far as you can, and flick over the first domino in the seventh row. With a very satisfying clatter, down go 64 dominos.

"You are ecstatic! You did it! WOWEE, HUZZAH, AND RUMPLESTILTSKINS!

"Then you know what happens next? You become aware that you are still sitting there, stretched out, leaning forward, straining almost but not quite to your maximum, and you realize that with just a little bit more effort—not much really, relative to what you have already given—you can reach forward a little farther and knock over 128 dominos, TWICE AS MANY AS YOU HAD EVER ASPIRED TO.

"So, of course, you do it. " And BINGO, BANGO, BONGO, down go 128 dominos.

"And what's next—I'm sure you're with me—a row with 256 dominos in it. And then 512, and then 1,024 . . . The immediate possibility of dramatically escalating your achievements seduces you into thinking of nothing else but that next row of dominos . . . and you continue to sit there, absolutely hooked, knocking over more dominos than you ever believed existed just a little while before. Dominos, dominos, dominos, nothing exists but dominos!"

And he continued, more philosophically, "There are lots of implications of this thinking: It explains why my work life is steadily taking over more and more of my energy and enthusiasm. Talent is a wonderful thing to use. How can I tear myself away from an arena where I am demonstrably good—I'm already at the seventh level of skill—and spend my evenings and weekends doing other things where I am still operating down at the short-domino-row level when I could stay at my office, work late, do things I like to do, and be knocking over thousands of dominos at the same time? One more sale, one more speech, one more deal . . . always saying to yourself, 'Just one more.'

"I really like my domino model: It explains to me just why it is that the harder I work, the more I enjoy it . . . and now if you will excuse me, there are about 10-to-the-nth dominos waiting for me this afternoon, and there's a good possibility that a big bunch of them are going to be tax-free . . . "

Organizational Success Is Easy:
Simply Hire Good People and Keep Them

The selection and development of excellent managerial talent is fairly simple in theory but virtually impossible to achieve in practice.

In theory, all you have to do is begin with an organization that has a strong, distinctive culture, one that features optimism and effectiveness and responsibility; make certain that within this culture there are many appropriately sized challenges for managers to tackle at every level as they work their way up the hierarchy—preferably challenges that emphasize new products, programs, or procedures requiring close, continual association with the customer, client, or consumer; set up pay, promotion, and appraisal policies that reward the managers who succeed in these challenges; hire into this system bright, energetic, ambitious people who already have proven track records of achievement in earlier endeavors; and—voilà!—eventually you will have at the top, and at every layer below, a cadre of experienced managers capable of exploiting the opportunities offered to your organization.

There is nothing particularly complicated about any one of those steps, but in practice it is almost impossible to combine them into an integrated system.

A Strong Culture. Well-managed organizations have about them a sense of a strong, permeating culture, one that helps focus the organization's resources on what needs to be done. Within limits, the specific nature of the culture is not important, as long as it features a forward-looking optimism; an efficient, thrifty effectiveness; and a sense of the value of hard work and responsibility. The culture itself can range from the dark-suited/buttoned-down collar/marketing-service orientation of IBM, to the wholesome/Midwestern/steak-and-potatoes/pragmatic efficiency of Caterpillar, to the straight-arrow/research-driven/disciplined/ "many-innovations-to-market" mentality of 3M.

Within a strong culture, ninety percent of the managers know ninety percent of the time what to do, how to do it, what resources they can count on, and where the allowable limits of deviancy are.

Without this strong sense of culture, executives at the top have to keep handling issues that should be handled routinely several layers below them, which means that the lower level managers are deprived of the experience while the higher level managers are kept busy handling brush fires instead of focusing on the larger issues that will determine the organization's future.

Appropriate Challenges. Given the pace of change with which we are surrounded, organizations need to be in a constant mode of self-renewal; simple maintenance is not sufficient. One method of achieving this is to continually have new products, programs, and procedures under development—the routinization of change, if you will. Such projects are excellent training and assessment experiences for managers. For eager, ambitious, and forward-looking managers, they are also fun and stimulating.

The challenge to the organization is how to manage the provision of a series of constant challenges, how to monitor them for effective performance, and how to knit them together into the organization's overall goals without disrupting the stability of ongoing operations. Change for the simple sake of change is not the goal, but rather change within the framework of a long-term strategy.

Pay, Promotion, and Appraisal Policies. Managers tend to spend their time on whatever the organization rewards, or at least on whatever they perceive the organization rewards. If enthusiastic, effective, innovative managers are rewarded, that is the model that young managers, whose antennae are extremely sensitive in this regard, will strive for. If, in contrast, conservative, cautious, and deferential drones survive the winds of change that blow occasionally through all organizations, then that will provide a different set of signals to those managers who are still on their way up.

New Hires. The best prediction of what people are going to do in the future is what they have done in the past. If you want ambitious, effective, forward-looking managers, then you look for people whose track records suggest they are that kind of person. This is a simple conclusion, but it is hard to implement. People who apply for jobs have not all had the same opportunities to excel. Is the record of achievement of a person who has been able to take full advantage of society's blessings necessarily superior to the more modest record of a person who has had few such advantages? Efforts to control for such inequitable social conditions have led to restrictions on employment practices that further complicate the selection of managerial talent.

Knowing what you want to accomplish in new hires is not difficult; knowing how to do it has eluded some of our best thinkers.

The overall concepts for developing excellent managers remain simple: Start with a strong organizational culture characterized by a healthy, effective philosophy. Hire effective, ambitious people with good track records. Provide them with an ever-expanding series of challenges that fit in with the organization's long-range strategies. Reward and promote the successful ones.

It's roughly as simple, and as easy to achieve, as saying that the way to be happy is to stay healthy, work at useful and interesting tasks, stay in love, and avoid war.

Push the Risks Downward

One common feature of training courses on entrepreneurialism, creative management, or innovative problem solving is an emphasis on risk-taking. It is easy to demonstrate from history that the status quo can be deadly. We can invoke the manufacturers of buggy whips, iron lungs, or slide rules and thus argue that the organization seeking renewal needs to venture into new territory where the outcome can never be certain: that is, it needs to take risks.

Without risks, the theory goes, there can be no dramatic progress. Further evidence of the generality of this phenomenon—progress through risks—comes from the research on innovative people; they are indeed risk-takers, they stand out from the pack as being willing to try something new, and they are resilient in the face of failure.

Along with this economic and social science evidence, we have the collective wisdom of well-worn proverbs:

Nothing ventured, nothing gained.
Faint heart never won fair lady.
Behold the turtle; he makes progress only when he sticks his
  neck out.

As with so many other good theories, however, putting a risk-taking approach into practice produces a significant quandary: If you take big enough risks often enough, sooner or later you will fail, and the consequent fallout may be painful, humiliating, disastrous, perhaps even lethal.

Risk-taking can be particularly dangerous within an organization that has a low tolerance for failure, and this includes, in the perception of most of the people within them, most large corporations and government agencies. If the organization cannot tolerate failure, then taking risks is stupid, especially since virtually all organizations do tolerate mediocrity. For the short run, mediocrity is much safer than innovativeness. Nothing ventured, nothing lost.

Let me suggest a way of looking at risk-taking that makes sense in a management environment, a strategy that can produce the benefits of risk-taking without risking a whacking disaster.

For purposes of illustration, let me use an example from your own financial life. Get a number in your head that represents the amount of money that you can personally afford to lose on some new imaginative investment—a hot stock tip, or leasing supermarket shopping carts, or some such thing—where the loss would neither affect your standard of living by creating a vacuum in your monthly cash flow, nor lower your sense of self-esteem by making you feel incompetent.

The number might be $50, $500, $5,000, or $50,000, though it has been my experience that even people who can afford to lose $50,000 feel stupid doing so—which may tell you more about my acquaintances than it does about the psychology of high rollers.

Anyway, get a dollar amount in your head that you could afford to lose without disastrous results.

Now here is the quandary. That number is so modest relative to your lifestyle that winning that amount is not going to make a positive difference in your life any more than losing it would make a negative difference. If you can afford to lose it, then winning by doubling it, even tripling or quadrupling it, is not going to greatly affect your lifestyle or self-esteem either.

The quandary is that winning the risks that you can afford to take is not sufficient to produce much excitement in your life.

But let's consider what would happen if you would delegate that amount of risk downward. Let one of your children, perhaps a teenager interested in the stock market or in old coins, invest that amount of money in a project while you provide the protective umbrella. If they lose it, a significant loss for them, you will back them up. If they win that amount, however, it will be a really big deal for them, expanding their resources notably and building their self-esteem. With a success or two of that magnitude behind them, they can then ratchet themselves up the scale of risk-taking, biting off slightly more each time, with you continuing to provide the protection.

The analogy holds for the managerial world: You can let—indeed encourage—your subordinates to take risks greater than they could afford to take without your backing. If they succeed, they will have moved up a step in their development and will have produced more resources for you to work with; if they fail, it will be on a modest scale where you will be able to cover their losses, both financially and psychologically.

If you have several subordinates, each working at an appropriate level of risk, the odds of one of them hitting it big are improved.

Of course, the first time you allow subordinates to take a risk and then *don't* support them if they fail, your credibility is gone forever. Tolerating failure means just that—tolerating failure.

The alternative to this strategy is either to take all the risks yourself, which is dangerous because sooner or later you are going to lose one, or to insist upon only sure bets within your span of control, an even more dangerous stance over the long run given the pace of change currently challenging all organizations.

Adopting this strategy of pushing the risks downward in an organization means that, at every level, people can be taking risks that are meaningful to them in size, yet not potentially disruptive to the organization because the people above them are providing the umbrella.

Curiously—again from my personal experience—many organizations operate exactly contrary to this strategy; the risks get dragged upward. Managers not only will not allow their subordinates to take risks that they, the managers, can afford to lose; they will not even let the subordinates take risks that they, the subordinates, can afford to lose. The thought of loss of any size is seen as such an obvious failure that "the people upstairs" prohibit even moderate risks.

Perhaps that is true for you too. How would you feel if your teenage child dropped $100 in trading for a rare stamp that turned out to be bogus? Teenagers today can survive such a loss, and you certainly can, but your first inclination might well be to chastise your child for stupidity.

Pursuing this strategy of pushing the risks down in either your family or your organization insures that you are going to be continually surrounded by experimental projects, any one of which could go awry and cause you mild embarrassment. But you also should be in a place to constantly observe a series of small wins that will ultimately be the source of new, invigorating ideas for your organization's future.

You do not have to do this, of course; you can play it safe, which may be the biggest risk you will ever take.

Nixon on Leadership: Surprisingly Good

Here are some quotations on leadership and on leaders that he has known, from the recent writings of Richard Nixon. I think they are surprisingly good.

Management is prose; leadership is poetry.

The successful leader has a strong will of his own, and he knows how to mobilize the will of others. The leaders [discussed here] are ones who succeeded—some more than others—in imposing their will on history. They are men who have made a difference. Not because they wished it, but because they willed it. That distinction is vital in understanding power and those who exercise power. Followers wish. Leaders will.

Power is the opportunity to build, to create, to nudge history in a different direction.

Some people live in the present, oblivious of the past and blind to the future. Some dwell in the past. A very few have the knack of applying the past to the present in ways that show them the future. Great leaders have this knack. As Bruce Catton wrote of Lincoln, "once in a while, for this man, the sky failed to touch the horizon and he saw moving shapes, off beyond."

Politics is compromise, and democracy is politics.

In evaluating a leader, the key question about his behavioral traits is not whether they are attractive or unattractive, but whether they are useful. Guile, vanity, dissembling—in other circumstances these might be unattractive habits, but to the leader they can be essential. He needs guile in order to hold together the shifting coalitions of often bitterly opposed interest groups that governing requires. He needs a certain measure of vanity in order to create the right kind of public impression. He sometimes has to dissemble in order to prevail on crucial issues. Long before he acknowledged it publicly, de Gaulle confided privately that he believed independence was the only answer for Algeria. Roosevelt talked of keeping America out of war while maneuvering to bring it into war.

One reason why it is frequently so difficult to sort out myth from reality in reading about political leaders is that part of political leadership is the creation of myths.

Neither means nor end, in isolation, can be used as the measure of a leader. Unless he has a great cause, he can never be in the front rank. Leadership must serve a purpose, and the higher that purpose the greater the potential stature of the leader. But purpose is not enough. He also has to perform. He has to produce results, and he has to do it in a way that serves that higher purpose. He must not use means that disgrace or undo the purpose. But if he does not produce results, he fails his cause and fails history.

Before the end of the century we will probably elect a woman to the vice presidency and possibly to the presidency.

Over the holidays, I did something that I vowed I would never do; I increased Richard Nixon's wealth. I bought one of his books. Although I enjoy political autobiography, and I really like almost any book that has the I-was-there-and-this-is-what-it-was-really-like flavor, I have successfully resisted buying the Nixon memoirs because I have been so offended by what he almost did to this country and its institutions.

I do, however, work at a center focused on the topic of leadership, and when I saw the *Leaders* book* in a bookstore I thought to myself, I should at least be familiar with it; I'll skim it while standing here in the aisle.

The opening sentence surprised me: "In the footsteps of great leaders, we hear the rolling thunder of history." Well, I thought to myself, I didn't know Richard Nixon was a fluent romanticist, and I flipped to the frontispiece, to see who the ghost writer was.

None was listed.

I skimmed on, and ran across "Management is prose; leadership is poetry." That did it, that was enough. I bought the book and read it in a few evenings.

Leaders (New York: Warner Books, 1984) by Richard M. Nixon.

The book is astonishingly good, especially in its literary qualities. I now have no fear that it was ghost written. It doesn't have the slickness of the professional writer; it does have pungent prose, distinct Nixonian rhythms, and insights too personal to come from secondary sources.

The book is essentially biography, containing chapter-length descriptions of seven leaders who have had dramatic impacts on our contemporary world (Churchill, de Gaulle, MacArthur, Yoshida, Adenauer, Khrushchev, and Zhou Enlai) with another chapter covering more briefly another dozen or so people who have had less impact because they came from smaller countries. The book opens with a short chapter to set the scene and closes with a summing up chapter that is basically an essay on leadership. Most of the quotes above come from the final chapter.

Whatever flaws Richard Nixon has, he is a superb writer.

He also displays here a remarkable breadth of scholarship. He has combined his unparalleled firsthand acquaintance with the leaders of the world over the past twenty-five years with long hours of reading and years of note-taking. The index, which is unusually good, lists over three hundred individuals, the majority of whom Nixon has known at least well enough to gain a quick first impression of, and he weaves his impressions adroitly into his writings. The index also includes a range of other authors—Shakespeare, Kipling, Freud—and Nixon has effectively used quotations from these sources to illustrate important points in his political portraits.

I mean to tell you, I am impressed.

I suppose you are now waiting for an "Even so, he couldn't completely conceal the true Richard Nixon."

That kind of analysis could be done. After all, the book is 365 pages long, and there are some pithy Nixon ideas there. There are at least a half dozen sentences scattered through the book that could be scrunched up together into a mosaic demonstrating Nixon's well-known petulant paranoia with the press, such as the one suggesting that major presidential decisions are often dismissed by the media "with the curl of a commentator's lip."

And surely some of the Nixon staff members howled when they read, "Virtually all of the major leaders I have known were exceptionally skilled in the vanishing art of face-to-face conversation. Leadership is persuasion, and the leader who fails as an interesting, impressive conversationalist is likely to fail as a persuader and therefore as a leader." One of the most common themes in the books written by those close to Nixon was how difficult he was to converse with, especially about anything personal.

Perhaps he didn't wish to stoop. In several places in the book, he argues that these truly great men (and one woman, Golda Meir) were uncommon people, and instinctively knew enough to hold themselves above the masses. Further, Nixon may not have thought particularly well of his own staff. Toward the end of the book, in the summing up chapter, he says,

> In assembling a staff, the conservative leader faces a greater problem than does the liberal. In general, liberals want more government and hunger to be the ones running it. Conservatives want less government and want no part of it. Liberals want to run other people's lives. Conservatives want to be left alone to run their own lives. Academics tend to be liberals; engineers tend to be conservatives. Liberals flock to government; conservatives have to be enticed. With a smaller field to select from, the conservative leader often has to choose between those who are loyal but not bright and those who are bright but not loyal.

How would you feel if you had served on the staff of someone who wrote that? You, too, would probably think he was a lousy conversationalist.

Never mind the small talk, this is an excellent book and no serious scholar of either politics or leadership should ignore it. Nixon's grasp of large events, his acquaintance with world leaders over a twenty-five-year period, his personal energy in drawing the strings together, and his surprising literary fluency have converged to produce an important document. He quotes Churchill as saying, "The best way to make history is to write it." He has done a lot of that here; this book will serve him well.

Who Will Tend the Butterflies?

I would like to list three apparently disparate facts, discuss them, then suggest a unifying deduction.

1. In the summer of 1979 a cloud of Monarch butterflies, thousands and thousands and thousands of them, settled on a tree on the sand dunes of the eastern shore of Lake Michigan.

2. In the high forests of the central Mexican Sierra Madre mountains, population pressure is now leading to deforestation as the local populace cuts the trees for firewood.

3. In 1968 Moses Kiser, Sr., pledged $500 to landscape a city limits sign—"Welcome to Greensboro"—on the eastern edge of the city.

Now let me elaborate.

First, the butterflies. In the summer of 1979 I was working on the staff of a leadership camp for high school students at a place called Camp Miniwanca, about fifty miles north of Muskegon, Michigan. It is one of the loveliest sites in the Midwest, right on the shores of Lake Michigan at a place where the wind and water have created huge sand dunes that are slowly migrating inland, producing a band of dunes hundreds of yards deep and, in places, over fifty feet high. New vegetation has taken hold, and wandering through the shrubs and trees on the dunes is a pleasant way to spend an afternoon.

To wander the dunes in the early evening when the sun is going down over the lake is more than pleasant; it borders on the mystical. The combination of sand, water, evening breeze, sunset, and isolation produces one of those settings in which one ponders what life is all about.

During one such evening, a member of the camp staff, a naturalist by training and by inclination, came running down the beach to gather us up. "There's a Monarch butterfly migration going on," he said excitedly. "You gotta come see this."

Fifty or sixty students and staff trekked over the dunes to where he led us. There we saw one of the most memorable sights of my life: a tree completely covered with brightly colored butterflies. After the initial expressions of glee and amazement, reverence took over, and we just sat on the sand watching and thinking. It was conducive to meditation, and more than one of us thought some version of, "In a world full of miracles like this, my own problems suddenly seem trivial."

I have since learned that these butterflies migrate alone; although they do cluster at times, each year they fly one by one to the high mountains of central Mexico, where they winter.

Which brings me to my second fact: The forests of central Mexico are being depleted by overcutting, and the habitat of the Monarch butterfly is being destroyed. I learned this at a business dinner last week in Mexico; one of my dinner companions was a young Mexican who, with a few others, has taken it upon himself to do something about this problem. Among other things, he has written a book about the Monarch butterfly—complete with dozens of color photographs—to raise the awareness of the world. He is also engaged in various social programs to alleviate the situation, such as finding other employment for those who have been dependent on the firewood as a source of income.

I told him of my admiration for what he was doing, and described the butterfly-covered tree that I had seen five years ago. He smiled and said softly, "Perhaps you can imagine two or three acres of trees like that, with twenty-five to thirty million butterflies per acre."

When I asked him what progress he was making and what funds he had available, he said, "It is a very complex problem, requiring a great deal of coordination. Our problem is not money; the interest is widespread and funds come easily. The basic problem is lack of volunteer talent to get things done. In the States, you are lucky because you have a history of volunteer activity for such programs; there is no similar history in Mexico; we must learn everything as we go. We need talent more than we need money."

Which brings me to my third fact: Coincidentally, the day after I returned home, the *Greensboro News & Record* carried a lengthy article on "Greensboro Beautiful." Since its modest beginning in 1968, this volunteer organization has been responsible for some one hundred thirty-five landscaping projects including thoroughfares, medians, traffic circles, triangles, parks, uptown plazas, memorial tree areas, and the development of a Bicentennial Park—a seven-and-one-half-acre plot containing four hundred trees, nine hundred flowering shrubs, twenty flower beds with twelve thousand annuals and perennials, a fragrance garden for the visually impaired, a wildflower garden, a rose garden, and a sundial with an original sculpture.

Funds have been donated by local businesses, individuals, and garden clubs, and the work has been done mainly by volunteer labor.

The unifying deduction from these three facts is that if we want our children to have experiences of wonder and awe, whether it be the sight of thousands of butterflies, the solitude of unspoiled wilderness, or the presence of the evening star burning brightly in a clean sky, we must learn how to export this volunteer leadership talent. Our exports to the world have included food, guns, music, blue jeans, and television shows. How can we add volunteerism—as it is practiced in garden clubs, neighborhood associations, and Little Leagues—in a way that will raise the quality of life everywhere? Curiously, the spread of volunteerism will almost certainly be done by volunteers, and especially by self-motivated ones who, like my Mexican dinner companion, will not wait to be asked.

The rewards would be satisfying; a few million extra butterflies would be an invigorating legacy.

You're Probably Smarter Than Your Parents, But Lazier, Too

You are probably brighter than your parents, at least in the sense of scoring higher on IQ tests, and you are almost certainly brighter than your grandparents.

On the other hand, you may be lazier.

Evidence to support these conclusions comes from a recent psychological study that likely will become a classic. The study appeared in the journal *Psychological Bulletin* under the title "The Mean IQ of Americans: Massive Gains 1932 to 1978" (January 1984); it was authored by James R. Flynn, who has the unlikely address of the Department of Political Studies, University of Otago, Dunedin, New Zealand.

Flynn argues persuasively with intriguing data that over the forty years prior to 1984 the American population gained 0.3 of a point in IQ each year, or about 14 points over the entire period. He is not certain whether the gain is "real" or "semi-real." (In another context, an example of a "semi-real" gain would be improved heights achieved by a polevaulter as a result of being given a better pole; the athlete would in no sense be different but the performance would be better.) But he is convinced, as am I, that the implications either way are important.

To understand Flynn's analysis, it is necessary to review briefly just how an intelligence test is constructed. There are really only two steps: first, a series of test questions is prepared, and second, a representative sample of the population is tested to use as a comparative base. The average performance (IQ) of this sample is arbitrarily set at 100, and all future scores are compared against this base.

What Flynn has shown is that as tests have been restandardized over the years, this standardization base of 100 has become increasingly higher, with the rate of increase being roughly 0.3 of a point per year. This means that if the new standardization samples were given the old test, the new samples would score roughly 0.3 of a point per year "too high," with the total improvement depending on how many years it had been since the old test had been standardized. As Flynn didn't have access to either the old tests or the new standardization samples, he has cleverly tried several different statistical approaches, working with old and new norm tables and the results of dozens of published studies where students have been tested with two different tests standardized at different times. Although his results are not completely tidy, each approach brought him back to this estimate of 0.3 of a point gained per year.

One immediate implication, of course, is to ask how this forty-year increase in IQ can be reconciled with a widely publicized twenty-year decline in Scholastic Aptitude Test (SAT) scores. Flynn agonizes at some length over this paradox and finally, after proposing some possible, though improbable, explanations, essentially concludes, "I don't understand it myself . . . but just because I don't understand it doesn't mean that my data aren't important."

One possible explanation that he suggests is the following: Assume that IQ is a core attribute of the person; further assume that a high performance on the SAT requires both this core attribute and other personality attributes, such as motivation and self-discipline. Can it be, he muses, that even though the IQ gains were real, these other attributes showed a large enough decrease not only to offset the IQ gains but also to produce the detectable drop in SAT scores? If so, he says with muted emphasis, this "suggests societal trends of the most alarming sort." Can it be, to extend the earlier example, that we are raising better pole-vaulters but giving them poorer poles?

Before we become agitated about this implausible possibility, we had better be certain that we understand the technology of our tests because they are producing the statistics that are creating our concerns. As Flynn has vividly illustrated, psychological test norms are not fixed, solid, secure anchor points; they shift around, which is not to say they are useless. Indeed, for their purposes, they are far better than any other measure that we have been able to develop, but they do have some peculiarities and for this reason they need to be constantly scrutinized.

Why we should have to wait for this detailed scrutiny to come out of New Zealand is a puzzle; maybe it is so quiet down there that norm tables seem more fascinating. Whatever the explanation, I am glad that Flynn has had some time on his hands, because he has helped us understand some flaws in our best psychological measures—IQ tests.

Regrettably, our current measures of the other potentially relevant attributes—motivation, self-discipline, and the like—are still so primitive that we can't even calculate trends for them, even though common sense (which also can't be measured) clearly indicates their importance. Hard work often is more important than intellectual brilliance.

If you don't believe that, just ask your dumb, hard-working parents.

Imagination Is Intelligence at Play

Following are notes taken during a summer afternoon on the beach when I was pondering someone's definition of imagination as "intelligence at play."

1. I would like to see the amount of money spent on one weapons system, say one Trident submarine (something over one billion dollars), used in imaginative ways to lessen the probability of worldwide war. For example, we could take the money and have an international competition asking people to submit ideas as to how ten million dollars might be spent to lessen nuclear tension. With one billion dollars to work with (less than the price of one submarine), we could fund one hundred imaginative projects of ten million dollars each. Surely *something* better would happen.

My candidate for spending ten million dollars to lessen the probability of nuclear war would be to establish a couple of classy summer camps in both the USA and the USSR for the children of the leading politicians and military leaders of the opposing countries. We could bring about five hundred Russian teenagers here for camp each year for ten years, and send an equal number of American children there, making certain that they were the children or grandchildren of prominent leaders. Who's going to nuke a country where their own kids are at camp?

2. I am positive that twenty percent of the things that I do creates eighty percent of my successes. I want somebody to tell me which twenty percent it is so that I could cease doing the useless eighty percent.

3. I would like to go to a party where the one hundred people I have known best in my life have been anonymously invited with no explanation for the event . . . It would just be one hundred people milling around in some resort hotel/swimming pool/restaurant complex, with me circulating among them. I wonder how long it would take them to realize that I was the common element. Would they ever? How good is my network?

4. I would like to see some other legal system evolve that doesn't involve providing good legal talent to absolute scoundrels. I have a lawyer friend who says that he will represent anyone no matter how reprehensible the person or his crime, "and, David, not only is that ethical, in the long run it is necessary to preserve your legal rights also."

Well, maybe, but it really frosts me to see kooks, liars, assassins, and brutal psychopaths getting the same quality of legal advice that I do. How can it be ethical to defend people so unsavory that they constitute the same threat to society that a cancer cell does to our body? No one defends the cancerous cell; why must we defend the cancerous person?

I know, I know . . . it's because the next government might pass a law defining me and my kind as cancerous and I'll need the protection. Still, I wonder . . .

5. On a long airline flight to some interesting city I would like to work my way down the aisle, interviewing everyone on board as to where they are going and why. I spend a lot of time on airplanes, and I am always wondering who these other people are.

On a recent flight to San Francisco the flight attendant, to break the boredom, used the public address system to give away a bottle of champagne to the couple on board who had been married the longest. Thirty-eight years won. Then he offered another bottle to the couple who had been married the shortest time. Three couples identified themselves as having been married the day before, and the contest came down to the specific hour of the ceremony to determine the winner.

There were perhaps two hundred people on board; on any given plane going into San Francisco, are three percent of the passengers newlyweds? (This was a Sunday flight.)

6. I would like someone to tell me, once and for all, with no on-the-other-hand scientific waffles, whether or not vitamin supplements are necessary or beneficial. I read a couple of good health newsletters each month, and I usually follow their recommendations—such as reducing salt and sugar intake, exercising regularly, not smoking, drinking moderately—and in general I can tell the difference physically, and I like the results.

But about vitamins, what should I do? The experts seem to disagree, and during the periods that I take vitamins religiously, I can't tell any difference in my body from the times that I skip them because I am traveling or have run out.

Should I bother?

I suppose I should because the cost and inconvenience is not much, and twenty years from now when medical science finally decides, I'd hate to look an unnecessarily aged body in the eye and say, "Sorry, old boy, the data just weren't clear enough."

7. In the same vein, I wish someone would tell me what I did that was right and what I did that was wrong as a parent. I now have decades of cumulative child-years behind me and I still don't know. The children are turning out well; is it because of the parenting or in spite of it?

8. I wish someone would give me two million dollars to do what I really want to do next in life, which is to establish an Archives of Psychological Tests of Famous People. It would be fascinating to be able to go somewhere and look over Abraham Lincoln's MMPI profile, or Joan of Arc's vocational interest profile, or Einstein's College Board results.

We can't do that, but we can start now to test currently famous people for the benefit of future generations.

I have already tested enough "famous people" to know they are willing, even eager, for this kind of psychometric immortality, and I even have my eye on a twenty-thousand-square-foot mansion with walls two feet thick where the results could be permanently stored.

Such a magnificent idea should not be allowed to wither away for lack of a measly two million dollars.

Actually, there are several interesting extensions of this psychological test archival idea. For example, somewhere there should be a repository of psychological tests from convicted murderers. Anyone who has been sentenced to death or imprisoned for life should be thoroughly assessed to see if there is something to be learned that would help society prevent future heinous crimes. Convicted murderers should be studied, just as hurricanes and earthquakes are, to help prevent future catastrophes.

9. I would like to have lunch with Robert Heinlein, noted author (*The Notebooks of Lazarus Long,* among others), and Nora Ephron, another best-selling author (*Heartburn,* among others). These two writers produce as many memorable sentences per unit of writing as anyone else I am familiar with.

I doubt that they are acquainted, but imagine the luncheon table conversation between two people who have written the following sentences (these are not necessarily their own opinions; some of these quotations come from characters they have created):

> When the need arises—and it does—you must be able to shoot your own dog. Don't farm it out—that doesn't make it any nicer, it makes it worse. (Heinlein)

> My first husband was so neurotic that every time he had an appointment, he erased the record of it from his datebook, so that at the end of the year his calendar was completely blank. (Ephron)

Leave your clothes and weapons where you can find them in the dark. (Heinlein)

It's true that men who cry are sensitive to and in touch with feelings, but the only feelings they tend to be sensitive to and in touch with are their own. (Ephron)

Writing is not necessarily something to be ashamed of—but do it in private and wash your hands afterward. (Heinlein)

The desire to get married—which, I regret to say, I believe is fundamental and primal in women—is followed almost immediately by an equally fundamental and primal urge, which is to be single again. (Ephron)

When the ship lifts, all debts are paid. (Heinlein)

Now what is the point of all of this? The point is that for most of us, new ideas flow better when we are in a nonwork setting, away from the daily demands of telephones, staff meetings, and the other bureaucratic needs of an organization. I should be able to have such thoughts while working at my desk, but I usually don't.

But are they good ideas? I dunno, some of them are pretty screwy, but that's the way most new ideas start out . . . as pretty screwy. And one thing is clear: An idea that is not in existence anywhere can't be a good idea; for the best idea in the world to work, it has to be thought of first, and then expressed.

Lying on the beach, listening to the winds, waves, and seagulls, is a pretty good place to think up imaginative ideas. The next step is application, and if imagination is "intelligence at play," application is "leadership at work."

Now, how are we going to find the necessary leadership to get those camps established for the teenage sons and daughters of the Russian and American decision-makers?

Where Are You, Mike Wallace, When I Need You?

I played Mike Wallace last week. I tried to be an aggressive, hostile, relentlessly pursuing television interviewer.

I was surprised by how difficult it was, and a bit dismayed by how much I enjoyed it. I see myself as a nice guy, a pleasant fellow, one who is warm, charming, and friendly toward others, no matter now distasteful they may be. What I found out was that, given the proper institutional permission, I can really get into nasty. I wanted to make people sweat, squirm, and blurt out unguarded reactions which I then, as a brilliant, incisive commentator, could knit together into a demolishing analysis of the person's rotten inner core.

As it turned out, I wasn't very good at it. I barely laid a glove on the company presidents that I was interviewing.

Still, it was fun. The occasion was a five-day retreat seminar, organized by the Center, for top-level executives. Called "Leadership at the Peak," it was held in Colorado Springs at the foot of Pikes Peak. The use of the word *peak* is a triple wordplay on the geographic location (Pikes Peak), the person's role in his or her organization (at the top), and the career point in the person's life (they averaged about fifty years of age and were mostly early in the prime of their leadership phase).

One of the central ingredients of the program was several hours in a television studio to give them some practice in dealing with the media. Organized and conducted by Linda Moore, a Center associate and a television news reporter at the NBC affiliate in Colorado Springs, the television session provided each person with several media experiences in a low-risk environment: (1) using a teleprompter, (2) being interviewed by a probing reporter in a talk-show format, and (3) dealing with an on-the-street television crew covering a late-breaking potential scandal in their company.

Linda briefed the group on some of the dynamics of television:

Appearance, both physical and psychological, is important.

Try to be open, warm, and responsive. Reporters are human, too, and will usually react positively to a cooperative approach.

When you are being interviewed, you can be in command; for example, the deadline is the interviewer's problem, not yours.

If you don't believe that television can be credible, then your appearance probably won't be.

Liveliness is memorable. An animated reaction from you will probably be chosen for the six o'clock news over a calm, reasoned recitation of the facts.

Brevity is valued. A television news editor seldom runs a news "bite" of more than twenty seconds.

My responsibility, along with Linda and Professor Tom Cronin of Colorado College—a noted author, political scientist, and commentator on the current political scene—was to be an aggressive talk-show host. Linda did about half of the interviews. She was very good; her experience and talent showed. Tom and I did the other half; he wasn't any better at being vicious than I was.

We did try, using a series of "damned if you do—damned if you don't" questions, such as asking, "Who really makes the long-range decisions in your company?" If the answer was some version of "I do," we followed up with questions implying that they didn't know how to delegate or involve others. If their answer was something like "It's a lengthy process, with relevant input from a range of others," we followed up with questions implying a lack of decisive leadership on their part. "Did Thomas Watson build IBM by seeking consensus?"

In the talk-show setting, the interviewer has a substantial edge. The interviewer is familiar with the physical setting, is in control of the flow of the conversation, and has had an opportunity to rehearse. Balanced against these advantages is the fact that the interviewee knows far more about the topic under scrutiny—his or her company, his or her career—and, with practice and presence of mind, can contribute to an interesting, informative, perhaps even sparkling television show.

And therein lies the reason for my opening comment: It is not easy to simulate Mike Wallace, to draw blood publicly. These company presidents were no pushovers. They were fluent, outgoing, well informed, and, for the most part, enjoyed themselves in the interview. They had climbed to the top of their respective pyramids and had learned something along the way about dealing with conflict and various kinds of attacks. Although they were novices in dealing with television, they were neither dumb nor inarticulate. When I asked the president of a large real estate development corporation, "Don't tax considerations play a greater role in commercial real estate development than good design? Aren't we building a lot of suburban office ghettos just to create tax shelters for the wealthy?" he countered with, "Maybe some firms do that, but ours doesn't," and went on to list some specific design awards won by his firm. I did not have a well-researched follow-up question, and in that little tussle, I didn't even mess his hair.

As the Lee Iacoccas of the world have learned, television can be a powerful force. People in power should have some experience with it, especially before some crisis throws them into it headlong as a naive beginner. Practice does help.

We apparently did not fail completely in our attempt to emulate Mike Wallace. In a laudatory end-of-course evaluation one of the participants wrote, "With very little practice, both David Campbell and Tom Cronin will become typical obnoxious interviewers. They both have the genes for it," intending this, in context, to be a compliment. Another one said, "As an interviewer, Campbell resembles a loose cannon on the deck!"

Author's note: The Center has continued Leadership at the Peak. Enrollment is limited to twelve presidents, CEOs, and others at the top of their organizations. A few special slots are held for women, minorities, and foreign leaders who are interested in attending.

Travel Nonsense from *The Wall Street Journal*

The Wall Street Journal recently published an unusual amount of nonsense in a series of articles on "Executive Travel." The four-part series, which ran during the 1984 Christmas travel season, was roughly fifty percent on "This is what it feels like to be a frequent business traveler" and fifty percent on "Here are some helpful tips from these busy folks who live on expense accounts and airplanes."

I travel often, almost weekly, and I am aware of the stress and strain of being on the road. Consequently, I read these articles avidly, looking for tips to make my life easier.

I was appalled at the irrelevancy of most of what was printed.

Here, for example, is one suggestion:

After days on the road on company business, sleeping in look-alike hotels, just keeping track of where you are can be a problem. Lona Jupiter, a vice president of San Francisco-based Wells Fargo & Company, found that out on a recent marathon trip that took her to Cleveland; Birmingham, Michigan; Bronx, New York; Phoenix; and Chicago. "One morning," she says, "I had no idea what city I was in until I went downstairs and bought a newspaper." Now she advises making sure your hotel room has matchbooks with the name of the city on them.

I was reading along, enjoying this, thinking, "Yeah, I've had weeks like that," when I hit the end of the paragraph and saw Ms. Jupiter's tip: Matchbooks? MATCHBOOKS? I read it again, then again, but sure enough, that's what it said, seriously, not in jest, matchbooks.

Now, I'm thinking, can this be the kind of executive talent Wells Fargo is sending out on the road? I can just hear her secretary making the reservation: "Hello . . . the Hilton? I'd like a reservation for Ms. Jupiter for Tuesday night, guaranteed late arrival, and would you please be certain that her room has matchbooks in it with the name of the city on them."

Or does she ask the bellhop carrying her bags up to her room, "Pssst, know where I can get any good matchbooks with the name of this city on them?"

Here's another helpful quote from the series:

Edward Bleier, a senior vice president at Warner Communications, and Jack Valenti, president of the Motion Picture Association of America, stay at the Beverly Hills Hotel on their frequent trips to the West Coast. Both executives leave some spare clothes and a toilet kit with the concierge; they also leave dirty laundry when they check out and find it clean and waiting for them when they return.

You can see why *The Wall Street Journal* is required reading for anyone on their way up the corporate ladder. Think of the status you can gain by casually stopping by the concierge's desk on your way out, tossing some dirty laundry and a toilet kit at him, and saying, "I'll pick it up the next time I'm in town." The logistics of this bother me, however. Even if we skip over the fact that getting a shirt laundered and held for you at the Beverly Hills Hotel is probably as expensive as simply buying a new one each time, what about this toilet kit you're leaving? Where did it come from? Do you bring a new one each time? If you leave one there, what about your trips to other cities? Do you leave one everywhere? Can you remember which cities you have them stashed in? Wouldn't you have to carry a spare one anyway, just in case your memory is faulty? Or do you ask your secretary, "Ms. Jones, will you please keep a list of the cities and hotels where I have shaving kits stored?"

Wouldn't it be simpler to have a single plain old kit (K-Mart, $9.95) like the rest of us? I can't come up with a single scenario where it makes sense to leave a toilet kit at an out-of-town hotel. Same thing with the clothes: If you are really a busy executive, how can you remember what you left where? Bleier and Valenti must have better memories for clothes than I do.

Actually, Valenti was a good source of quotations for this series. To avoid airline food, "Mr. Valenti says he occasionally takes his own sandwiches. That way, he says, 'I eat when I want, not when they feed me.'"

I don't know, I have a little trouble reconciling the image of Mr. Valenti leaving his laundry with the concierge in Beverly Hills and then brown-bagging it on airplanes.

The series would also have us believe that life on the road is a constant aggressive battle to keep "them" from getting there first. Look at these quotes:

[In dealing with airport lines,] "you've got to be aggressive," says John Henry, president of Abar Corporation, a Feasterville, Pennsylvania, manufacturer of industrial furnaces. He says he hasn't any qualms about barging to the front of the line if his plane is about to leave. And he says he chews out clerks and demands to see their bosses if they won't help him. "You can't be a nice guy," Mr. Henry says.

It disturbs me that this quotation fits a stereotype of what a man named John Henry who makes industrial furnaces in Pennsylvania would be like. Is this the kind of guy who screws up the system, shouting at clerks, waving a big, black cigar, and in the end doesn't get one bit better service than the rest of us standing there awaiting our turn? In fact, friends who are service personnel have told me that this is precisely the sort of person whose luggage is deliberately misrouted to Nairobi.

[When checking into hotels,] to be on the safe side, it's a good idea to approach [the situation] as an "adversarial relationship," says Joseph G. Smith, president of Oxtoby-Smith, a New York-based consumer research firm. You should ask to look at the room and then, if it isn't satisfactory, ask for something better. "Don't settle without reaching a bit," he says.

Where are they getting these names? Lona Jupiter, John Henry, Joseph Smith. I began to wonder if this was an April Fool's story, but no, it appeared in December.

If Mr. Smith finds it necessary to be adversarial with hotel personnel, I wonder how he feels about rental car clerks, taxi drivers, waiters and waitresses, ticket agents, shoeshine boys, and indeed, the American consumer, who is apparently his bread and butter. I have checked into hotels well over two hundred times, and in two or three percent of those times I have found something unsatisfactory about the room. I have simply gone to the front desk and asked if something could be done; when they could accommodate me, they did, which was often. Hotel personnel are people like us; they are our brothers and sisters, aunts and uncles, high school classmates. They get up in the morning, brush their teeth, sip their coffee, and go to work, intending to do a good job. If the system works, they succeed. If the system frustrates them, as, for example, when Chicago is hit with a major snowstorm just as you are checking in, they have their hands full, and an adversarially oriented customer simply adds to that complexity.

I have watched the Mr. Smiths of the world check into hotels at such times. They do indeed blow their stacks and throw their weight around. And in the morning they wake up in precisely the same kind of room as the rest of us.

I arrived recently in Chicago along with a snowstorm. My plane was several hours late, and I stepped up to the line at the hotel registration desk a few minutes before midnight. I had a guaranteed reservation, as did the six people ahead of me. There were no more rooms available. One of the six people ranted and raved, invoked his friendship with someone high in the hotel corporate hierarchy, and announced that he was not leaving the counter until a room was found for him. The manager was summoned. The clerk, who had undoubtedly been dealing with weather-frustrated travelers all evening, said wearily, "Please step aside and let me help these others."

She managed to find some solution for everyone in front of me, usually by putting them in conference rooms and, when it was my turn, said to me, "All I have left is the ballroom. Will that be all right?"

So I slept comfortably in a room which, as we used to say in Iowa, would sure hold a lot of hay. When I checked out the next day, there was no charge, and about a week later, I got a nice letter from the hotel manager apologizing for my inconvenience.

The last I saw of the angry man, he was still leaning against the counter, waiting for the manager. I suspect his luggage is still in Kenya.

> [When dealing with airline seatmates who won't quit talking,] fight back. "If all else fails, you have to get nasty," says Eugene W. Cattabiani, executive vice-president of Westinghouse in Pittsburgh.

I began to see what was happening here. The paper had almost certainly called up a bunch of mobile executives, interviewed them at some length, probing for the most extreme travel experience the person had ever had, and then stitched them together in an article implying that these extreme cases were the norm.

I say that here because I happen to know Gene Cattabiani, and he is not a nasty person. Quite the contrary; he is a big, tall, congenial, outgoing man with a lot of charm. It is inconceivable to me that he would get nasty with a seatmate, though I can imagine him, as a fluent, spontaneous

Travel Nonsense from The Wall Street Journal

gesture, throwing off some line to a persistent reporter who is probing for a spicy quote. I can't prove that is what happened, but it would be more in character. Quotations are what the reporter hears, not necessarily what the person says.

That was also the case with the apparently spacy Ms. Jupiter quoted above about the matchbooks. Several weeks after the article ran, I met an associate of hers from Wells Fargo. I asked him if he remembered the article and her quotation. "Oh, yes," he smiled, "that got a lot of circulation around the office—and she was a bit miffed." He continued, "She said she had made a throw-away quip about the matchbooks, and they had reported it as a serious comment."

So now, perhaps, we have the answer. The articles were not about executive travel; they were about what the editors and reporters of *The Wall Street Journal* created as their own "hey-we-are-really-with-it" image of executive travel. (I couldn't find a good place to work in their quote on caviar; it was in the context of trans-Atlantic flights and was to the effect that the first thing you should do on such long flights is eat your caviar and go to sleep. I have flown the Atlantic twenty-six times and have yet to encounter caviar.)

The reason those of us who travel a lot did not recognize the traveling life in these articles is simply that that is not the way it is.

One more travel story, which I am going to use as a lead-in to a subsequent column:

I took my first commercial airline journey in December 1954. I was a senior at Iowa State, and Procter & Gamble had invited me to Cincinnati for a job interview. This was before jet airliners and the trip was made from Des Moines via Chicago by United Airlines on little DC-3s. On the way home from Cincinnati to Chicago, the plane was almost empty, and the stewardess spent most of the trip perched on the arm of the seat across the aisle, chatting with me. In those days, stewardesses still had time to chat with passengers.

I still remember her name and hometown: Sharon Taylor, University City, Missouri.

As we rolled up to the terminal at Midway Airport, I asked her if she wanted to go out for a beer. She did, and we closed up a nearby bar, at which point she went her way and I went mine.

Several months later, for college graduation, a friend gave me a little leather notebook with a travel log in it. I entered the Cincinnati trip in it, and have continued that practice for the subsequent thirty years. I still have that little notebook, and in it is a one-line entry, showing date, place, and purpose for every trip I have ever made.

I did a quick count from the notebook to establish my credentials as a frequent traveler for this column, and I can now tell you that I have been on 1,368 airline flights, which calculates out to roughly one per week for thirty years. In my next column, I will give you some of my impressions of the life of a frequent traveler and some of my survival tips. A warning though: They will be much more prosaic than those in *The Wall Street Journal* because the blunt fact is that after a point, travel becomes just another routine. My traveling life has not intersected with much caviar.

To document that, and to keep you from waiting breathlessly for the next scandalous whiff, I'll tell you now that Sharon Taylor, the United Airlines stewardess that I met thirty years ago on my very first trip, is the *only* airline stewardess I have ever taken out for a beer or ever said more than "hello" to. "Coffee, tea, or me" is also another myth.

But I will give you some sensible ideas about what to pack in your toilet kit that even your mother will approve of.

Campbell's Travel Tips:
Carry a Swiss Army Knife and Put the Rental Car Keys on Top of the Hotel TV

In my previous column, I twitted *The Wall Street Journal* about the considerable nonsense they published in a series of articles on "Executive Travel" (December 20, 21, 27, and 28, 1984). Using a maladroit collection of allegedly verbatim quotes from a variety of ostensible traveling executive experts, the paper apparently sorted out the weirdest, most oddball answers and then knitted them together as if they represented the usual experiences of the typical business traveler. Working from that base, they then generated "useful" tips for future travelers.

Although this approach may have generated good copy, it produced a distorted picture of what life is like as a frequent business traveler, and the subsequent useful tips were nothing short of ludicrous.

Let me tell you what frequent business travel is like. It is boring, repetitive, and tiring. The only thing that makes it worthwhile is that what happens to you at your destination is often exciting, stimulating, and lucrative.

Before making further pronouncements, I feel the need to establish my credentials as a frequent traveler.

Sometime in the 1950s, a college friend gave me a little black looseleaf leather notebook. It had a travel-log section in it, and I began jotting down a one-line record of each airline trip I took, listing date, destination, purpose, and sometimes the people involved. I have continued that practice for thirty years, and consequently have a complete, though tantalizingly skimpy, record of all of my air travel. According to the information in my little black book, I calculate that in the last thirty years I have taken 1,368 flights. That is a lot of travel.

In thinking back over it, the most startling conclusion is how routine it all has been. Note again that I am drawing a distinction between the travel itself and the subsequent activity at the destination. I have had some great times—and some substantial tragedies—at destinations but the travel itself has always been uneventful. And as a consequence, as I warned in the earlier column, the travel tips I have developed are themselves prosaic.

I am impressed by the number of things that have never happened in my travels. For example, I have never irretrievably lost a piece of luggage; I have never, so far as I know, been in any physical danger—no hijackings, no close calls in the air, no emergency landings. There may have been flights where the pilots had white knuckles. If so, I have been blissfully unaware of it. With two exceptions, which were special cases, I have never missed a flight. There are some who argue that this suggests that I am getting to airports too early, wasting time, that I should be cutting it closer. Could be, but I don't enjoy last-minute fretting. There is always something to read, people to watch, phone calls to make, thoughts to think.

This does lead into one of my modest but sensible tips for travel, which is to buffer your departure with some discretionary time, especially when other people control your schedule. Often someone else will drop me at the airport, thereby taking control of my departure away from me, which can be a problem because other people are often more cavalier about getting me to the airport on time than I am.

In anticipation of this, I build in an hour's buffer. When they ask, "When does your flight leave," I finesse the question by replying (for a 5:00 flight), "I have to be at the airport by 4:00." If they press for a specific time and flight, I fumble in my pocket or briefcase and say, "I can't find my ticket, but I know I have to be there no later than 4:00."

I have noted that I am often dropped off ten to fifteen minutes after the time I told them I had to be there, so the buffer is quite necessary.

I am not a talkative traveler, so I don't meet people on airplanes. On only one occasion have I ever seen a seatmate later. I was divorced and searching, she was single and charming; according to my notes, we met over Nebraska. After an exchange of correspondence, we later had a lovely rendezvous at a secluded mountain lake. A spicy occurrence, right? Well, one such event out of 1,368 flights is a pitiful record of adventure.

I have also never been robbed, mugged, or otherwise accosted—possibly because I am quite cautious. This doesn't mean that I haven't been in interesting places; some of the more remote trips have included the high Andes mountains of Peru, the Russian monastery of Zgorsk about fifty miles outside of Moscow, the casbahs of the Sahara Desert in southern Morocco, and the Orkney Islands off the northern tip of Scotland. Perhaps I'm lucky, or perhaps I'm chicken; anyway, nothing violent has ever happened to me or my possessions. I have lost four cameras, one that was stolen out of an unlocked rental car, and two that I did other stupid things with (I dropped one into an ice bucket).

I attribute some of the luck to the fact that I travel with a low profile, using beat-up luggage, plastic bags for my cameras instead of expensive cases, and not wearing expensive watches or jewelry. For a time, I used a classy aluminum case for my cameras. When it was checked as luggage once, a camera disappeared, which means that some baggage handler somewhere had enough time to try all 999 combinations of the lock.

Three classes of objects create much of the frustration of travel: papers, keys, and luggage. Using some simple systems to control these three elements will save you a lot of grief. Here are my suggestions, which are personal and idiosyncratic. You need to develop whatever feels comfortable to you.

Papers. I try to keep the important paper debris of travel in one of four places: Airline tickets and passports live in the breast pocket of my suit, other necessary travel information is in a folder in a designated compartment of my briefcase, the rental car contract stays in the glove compartment, and the credit card receipts go into my wallet. Whenever I deviate from that routine, I create potential problems for myself.

Keys. When they are not in my pocket, the hotel key and rental car keys stay on top of the television set in the hotel room. I have a spare car key in my wallet, and a spare house key hidden outside. When I leave my car at the airport, I leave my key ring in it, so I don't have to fuss with my normal keys while traveling.

Luggage. Don't take more than you can carry by yourself. Don't travel with expensive, matched sets; it marks you as having something worth stealing. Don't try to squeeze "one more trip" out of a worn-out suitcase. I can't seem to live up to this one. Over the years, I have gone through perhaps a dozen suitcases, and in about half of the cases I had to have them fall apart on me in the airport before I bought a new one. The last time was just this spring. After an all-day flight home from Spain, I stood wearily in Kennedy airport watching my open suitcase coming toward me on the carousel, underwear dribbling out, thinking, "Campbell, you are too tired to deal with this now. Will you never learn to think ahead?"

One aspect of luggage is worth some more space here, for it is an area that I really think I have learned something about, and that is how to raise the probability that your luggage will arrive when you do. (There is a school of thought that says the best way to accomplish this is to carry everything on board with you. There is merit in that argument, but I usually reject it because I want to take more along than I can fit in an overhead bin.) Several years ago I noticed that my luggage was delayed about fifteen percent of the time, and on a few occasions I knew exactly why. In thinking about it more, I came to the conclusion that about twenty-five percent of the time it was my fault; twenty-five percent of the time it was the fault of the agent checking me in; and the other fifty percent it was the fault of the system, such as when the flight was late and the baggage missed the connection. These percentages are crude, from memory, but they are in the ballpark.

I set out to cure at least the fifty percent of the time when it was my fault or the agent's. Here are two examples of when it was my fault:

On one occasion I was late getting to the Greensboro airport for a trip to Minneapolis, changing planes in Chicago. I ran up to the counter, said, "Can I still get on the Chicago flight?"

"Yes," said the agent, reaching for the phone, "if you run. I'll tell them you're coming. They will take your ticket at the gate."

"Can I get my luggage on?" "Yes, give it to me, and run." I ran down the concourse and made the flight. Before we left, a luggage trolley came out to the plane. I relaxed, flew to Chicago, idled away an hour's wait between planes, and flew on to Minneapolis. When my bag did not show up on the luggage carousel, I went to baggage services, where they pointed out the obvious to me: my bag had only been checked to Chicago. The agent couldn't have known that I was going on to Minneapolis.

On a second occasion I changed my ticket by phone from the hotel room before leaving for the airport. The reservations agent said to me, "Get to the airport forty-five minutes early and we will rewrite your ticket for your new flight." I took a taxi to the airport, turned my ticket and luggage over to the skycap at the curb, he checked my bag through for me, then I went inside and had my ticket rewritten. When I reached my new destination, I once again found out the obvious: my luggage went to the destination on my old ticket, which is the one that the skycap was working from.

I probably should be ashamed to say it, but in neither case did I tell the baggage service office that I knew what had happened and that it was my fault. I naively said, "I seem to have a problem with my luggage," and they solved it for me.

The other source of error, besides me, is the counter agent. Because they are human, they can make a variety of mistakes. The two most common seem to be that they simply write the wrong flight number on the baggage tag or they don't send my bag to my final destination. Because my wife lives in Colorado Springs, I fly there often, which requires

Greensboro-Atlanta-Denver-Colorado Springs connections. On two occasions my bag has only made it as far as Denver.

The solution to both sets of errors is to watch carefully when the agent or skycap writes out the luggage tag. More often than you might imagine, you can catch the error.

The solution to the other fifty percent of the delays, those due to "the system," is harder, but you can at least learn to expect that your luggage will be delayed, plan for it, and don't be overly distressed when it happens. Have your luggage well marked, with both your name and some kind of colorful identifying tape. Don't put anything in your bags that you absolutely must have at your destination. In particular, think through what you have on. On a trip to the Caribbean, my wife said to me as we were leaving, "You'd better put your swimming suit in your briefcase." Fortunately, I did. My luggage was delayed for three days, during which time I lived in a business suit and swimming suit, which was perfectly fine.

Another bit of travel advice is so primitive that I am almost embarrassed to include it, but I still violate it occasionally, creating problems for myself. The advice is, "When you get on an airplane, know exactly where you are going."

It is not sufficient to know "I am going to a resort hotel somewhere in the Poconos." In that case the moment of truth came at the rental car counter when she asked me what my local address would be.

It is also not sufficient to believe that someone is going to pick you up and deposit you wherever you are supposed to be. Once I was attending a conference at the Washington base of the Aspen Institute, which is somewhere on the eastern shore of the Chesapeake Bay. I didn't bother with precise directions because I was to be met at the airport. When leaving Colorado Springs, I checked my briefcase, which had my travel folder in it; that was not wise. The airplane we were to leave on developed mechanical trouble and we had to be put on another plane, which created enough of a delay so that I missed my Denver-Washington flight, the one that was going to be met. I stood in the Denver airport on a Sunday afternoon, feeling impotent. My trip folder was in my briefcase, which was lost in the system. I didn't know where I was going, I didn't remember who was going to pick me up, I had no phone numbers, there was no one in on Sunday in any offices to inform me. I was lost.

I invoked my support system at the Center, which is magnificent. I phoned Vicki, who has learned to take a copy of my travel folder home with her just in case, and she told me what to do. I arrived several hours late, without my luggage, feeling only mildly disrupted but, once again, stupid.

Finally, I have to tell you about my shaving kit. (I warned you that these tips were going to be prosaic.) Several years ago I realized that the one stable companion in my traveling life was my shaving kit. No matter where I was going, what kind of event I was heading for, or what wardrobe I was packing, the travel kit was a constant. So I decided to make it a depository of the ABSOLUTELY ESSENTIAL THINGS I have to have while traveling.

The list is fairly short. Along with the usual toilet articles, in my kit is a spare pair of glasses, a Swiss Army knife with seven blades—I hardly ever use any of them except the scissors and corkscrew, but having all those blades around gives me a sense of confidence—a sewing kit which I often use, a Bic lighter that I have only used once (to light some candles at a birthday party in my room), a copy of my birth certificate and two passport photos in case I lose my passport, and $100 in travelers checks—I'll give American Express the benefit of the float for the security of the panic money. Those few items, plus Band-aids, aspirin, and vitamin C, have solved most of my travel crises, which have been few.

Curiously, given the genesis of this column, the one other constant in my traveling life has been *The Wall Street Journal*. It is the only newspaper that I read every day, and I normally find it informative and trustworthy, at least when they stick to stocks and bonds. At a minimum, when they publish future travel articles, they should find people with enough travel experience so that they won't have to find their way through the world by reading matchbook covers.

Writing this column has been a pleasant exercise in nostalgia; it has stimulated me to think back, usually with pleasure, seldom with pain, over the many events. As you might suppose, the one-in-1,368 weekend stands out. We planted rhododendrons at the lake that weekend. They are still alive and thriving. Each spring when they bloom, I think of Nebraska.

Fathers, Sons, and Mutual Respect

All men are sons of fathers; most men are fathers of sons. Consequently, the dynamics of the father-son relationship is a topic of universal interest, at least among males.

That thought was careening around in my head recently when I found myself in a peculiar, personal predicament. I was deep in the forest of the Pacific Northwest, standing on the edge of a fifteen-foot-high rock, looking down into a crystal clear trout pool. It was a warm summer afternoon; I was fully unclothed and under insistent social pressure from below to jump in. Fifteen feet high looks higher from above than it sounds here, and my psychological anxiety was rapidly getting translated in psychological indices: my adrenalin was racing, my heart was pounding, my palms were sweating, my toes were curling.

"C'mon, Dad, time to go for it," came from below, from the sole source of the social pressure on me: my muscular, trim, red-bearded, natural outdoorsman, twenty-five-year-old son.

Moments like that activate the mind wonderfully, speeding up the mental process to something like the speed of light. Entire philosophies are created under the pressure of avoiding the plunge.

My kaleidoscope of thoughts, standing naked there above the forest pool being coached by my son, included the dinner party conversation of the night before which, through the miracle of jet travel, had been on the other coast. That conversation had focused briefly on fathers and sons, stimulated by an observation of one of the guests who had just returned from her twentieth high school reunion. She had graduated from one of those high-socioeconomic-level high schools in the outer environs of New York City, and twenty years later reported that most of her classmates were doing well and were interesting, achieving people, "with one dramatic exception," she said.

She continued, "Our class president had been a real sharp kid, outgoing, a good student and a good leader; his name was . . ." and she reported a family name that would be recognized in most educated households of America.

"Today," she said, "twenty years later, he seems sort of pitiful. Hasn't done much with his life, is still working on a master's degree in Medieval European history . . . basically, he's floundering. I don't think he ever got out from under his father's shadow."

That conversation, plus several other related observations of father-son competitions, has led me to the following conclusion: Every son, sometime between the ages of fifteen and thirty, has to believe that he has matched or bettered his father's achievement in some arena that is important to both of them. Otherwise, he is doomed to a perpetual feeling of personal insufficiency. A son who in his own mind never matches his father's performance is vulnerable to a life that feels incomplete, unfulfilled, and unsatisfying, no matter how much he, the son, objectively accomplishes.

Freud attributed this competitive need to a deep-seated fear, based on the son's innate respect for the power of the father. He said, somewhat paraphrased, "The decisiveness of thought, the strength of will, the forcefulness of his deeds belong to the picture of the father; above all other things, however, is the self-reliance and independence of the great man, and his divine conviction of doing the right thing. . . . He must be admired, he may be trusted, but one cannot help being afraid of him."

I wonder what Freud would have said about a scaredy-cat father shivering nude in the forest, chattering aimlessly away, trying to avoid looking foolish in the eyes of his son. To avoid action, I commented on the litterless beauty of the place, on the hydrodynamics of the trout I could see swimming below me in the pool, on the lack of bureaucratic interference with our use of this place . . .

"C'mon, Dad, we're missing the sunlight . . ."

My thoughts raced on. A few days earlier, I had called up my friend, David Bork, a management consultant in the Washington, D.C., area, whose specialty is working with family-owned businesses. He has worked with over one hundred seventy-five families, and has often dealt with the issue of passing power from one generation to the next. I tried out my theory on him—the Freudian notion that the son has to, in some conceptual sense, kill off the father to feel good about himself.

David mused on that a few minutes and then said, "I think that is a bit simple-minded; each situation has its own peculiar dynamics. Sometimes I see that, sometimes I don't."

What's the good of having your own expert if he won't agree with you?

David continued, "For example, in the families that I work with, money is often a complicating issue. Some fathers reject any achievement of their son that doesn't produce money, and some sons are so put off by the father's competitive financial stance that they simply refuse to compete on those grounds."

"Well," I said, "that's my point. The son's achievement has to be in an area valued by both of them. If the father values only money, the son's only avenue to success is to make more of it than did the father. This is particularly relevant to leadership issues, because the father-son relationship may thus completely define the area where the son must focus his leadership energies to achieve a sense of fulfillment."

"Too simple-minded, David; there are too many other things going on, like sibling competition, for example."

Not being able to resolve all of those philosophical problems at once, I jumped. The water was so cold that it erased any other thoughts except that of survival, and I paddled quickly to shore. My son crouched over me. "Great, Dad, terrific!"

I beamed. The roles were reversed, I felt like a kid again being praised by an adult whom I admired, and I was proud of my performance in an arena valued by him. Perhaps Peter Pan was right; maybe one should never grow up. It may be the one way to avoid being killed off by your sons.

"Now," he said, "once more for the camera. I missed the focus . . ."

Risk-taking, or How I Came to Jump Out of a Banquet Cake

By the time you read this, I will have been wheeled into a hotel ballroom, jumped out of a cake, strode to the podium, and delivered a speech on, what else, risk-taking.

Geez, how do I get myself into these situations?

"I'll tell you how," said my friend, wife, and confidante. "You get yourself into these situations because you are always saying yes to crazy ideas."

"Not true. I never said yes—I just couldn't figure out any way to say no."

"I will teach you how. The next time someone says to you, 'Campbell, will you jump out of a cake and give an after-dinner speech?' you say 'No.' Actually, you might say 'Absolutely not, positively not, under no conceivable circumstances would I ever jump out of a cake and give a speech, no, nein, non, nyet.' Sooner or later, I think your point will get across."

"That would not have solved this situation," I said plaintively, "because no one ever came right out and asked me to do it."

"You volunteered?"

"Not exactly. It just sort of happened."

"I'm listening . . ."

This friend called me up and said, "David, we're having our annual management conference at this spiffy beach resort, and I have been asked to see if you will give an after-dinner speech." I told him there are usually two constraints: the Center's fee and the calendar.

"What's the fee?"

I told him, and explained that it helps support our research efforts.

"We'll come back to that," he said. "Are you free on the evening of March 15?"

"Not really—I have to be in the Boston area the next day for a meeting, so I will be traveling."

"No problem," he said. "We'll have the corporate jet pick you up in Greensboro in the afternoon, fly you down to the beach, you give your speech, we'll put you back on the plane and have you in Boston by 10 or 11 p.m., no sweat."

"Sounds good."

"Now about that fee . . ." and we negotiated an agreeable figure.

"Okay," he continued, "here's the situation. Monday night at these meetings is always the let-your-hair-down night, and the agenda is being planned by our Conferences and Meetings Coordinator. She is absolutely adamant that the plans be kept secret. She won't even tell me, but she is going to come on the line in a minute and explain it all to you. I'll talk to you later."

In a moment a young, enthusiastic voice came on the line and said, "Dr. Campbell, we have been told that you are creative and adventurous—and a really good sport, somebody willing to try something new. Is that true?"

What am I going to say? That I am over fifty years old, stodgy and conservative, just trying to keep my nose clean until I retire?

My wife said, "How young and how enthusiastic?"

I asked the Coordinator what she had in mind.

She sketched in a scenario that made a weird sort of creative sense and finished by saying, "and for the grand finale, we'd like to have you jump out of the cake and come up to the front and give your speech. Would you do it?"

My wife repeated, "How young and enthusiastic?"

I said to the Coordinator, "Do I have complete freedom to say whatever I want to?"

"Complete freedom," she said, "as long as it is creative and adventuresome, and, of course, entertaining."

As she was talking, I was thinking. I know two millionaires whom I consider to be Olympic-class risk-takers, and they both tell me the same thing: "The secret to successful risk-taking is to keep trying new things, but don't do anything dumb. Take some chances, yes, but only when you are in control and can handle any negative fallout. Push the limits, but only so far, and only when you can call the shots."

The Coordinator continued, "We're trying to shake these people up a little, get them out of their conventional mold for an evening. We think it would be a lot of fun. What do you think?"

I kept thinking to myself, "You know, I bet I have given over two hundred speeches in the last five years, and in a variety of settings from hotel ballrooms to YMCA camps to high school graduations. I gave an impromptu speech once in a mountain inn in Bavaria because the scheduled speaker had been marooned in a Middle Eastern country by a yellow fever quarantine. I spoke once in a K&W Cafeteria, with people swirling all around me, because my host organization didn't have enough money to eat anywhere else. I gave an after-dinner speech one night to six people because the speech, scheduled months in advance, fell on a World Series night in a city gone crazy over baseball. Still," I thought to myself, "I have never jumped out of a cake, and the odds are pretty good that I will never have another opportunity to do so."

"Further," I'm thinking, "I believe that one should keep taking risks in a variety of areas, to stave off stagnation and to prepare for the inevitable challenges that life eventually throws at you."

There are at least four categories of risks:

Physical: the most obvious one, risking life and limb. For me, this is usually skiing slopes beyond my ability.

Career/Financial: risking your job or pocketbook, not a place where I am very adventurous, though I have accepted a position as Distinguished Visiting Professor at the Air Force Academy next year, which will be a considerable change.

Intellectual/Artistic: trying to look at the world in new and creative ways and then presenting your viewpoint publicly. For me, this column serves that purpose, especially because I do apparently overstep the bounds of propriety on occasion. (A recent column suggesting that academic manners are eroding was vetoed by my peers as "in poor taste.")

Interpersonal: making friends, falling in love, opening yourself up to another person. A place where many of us succeed, at least according to Voltaire, who said, "Marriage is the only adventure open to the cowardly."

"Dr. Campbell?"

I said to her, "Sure, I'll do it."

"Oh, I'm so glad," she said. "They really were right about you."

"How young and how enthusiastic?" persisted my wife, who a few years ago showed up on Easter morning in a head-to-toe fuzzy bunny outfit and hopped all over the house, one step ahead of the children, hiding Easter eggs.

"Look," I said, "where would we be if the Hillarys of the world, the risk-takers, had said to themselves, 'No, I'm not going to do that. It's foolish and impractical and, anyway, I'm too old'?"

"Oh, I get it," she said. "When they ask you, 'Dr. Campbell, why do you jump out of cakes?' you are going to say . . ."

And we both collapsed in hilarity as we recited in sonorous, unison tones, "BECAUSE THEY ARE THERE."

But only once.

One Hundred Punch Lines

Each year the magazine *Better Homes and Gardens* publishes an article entitled, "100 Ideas for Under $100." I usually read that issue, not because I am likely to buy, build, or sew together any of their new projects (Pocket Watch Stand, $2; Table Top HopScotch, $5; Tail Gate Desk, $74) but simply because I like being in the presence of 100 new ideas.

While leafing through one of these listings of new ideas and products recently, I was once again reminded of the similarity between the psychological dynamics of creativity and humor. Some new ideas are so good that they produce an aha! response that is, at its weakest, a chuckle or, at its strongest, a hearty laugh.

The latter was vividly demonstrated last week for me by an ad in *The Wall Street Journal* for a new beverage can. This can has a sleeve around it containing some sort of CO_2 mechanism that, when activated by opening the can, chills the contents within fifteen seconds. I read that and laughed out loud with amazement. A self-chilling can: why didn't I think of that?

Thinking along this vein, I decided to make this column into a listing of 100 Great Ideas, hoping for 100 hearty laughs from each reader. One hundred ideas of the self-cooling-beverage-can class ought to leave an audience in stitches.

Regrettably, I did not get far with that plan; do you know how tough it is to come up with just one Great Idea?

Cowed by my failure, I decided to aim lower, and simply aspired to create one hundred chuckles, using humor instead of raw creativity. However, with brevity being the soul of wit, and editorial restrictions being what they are, all I have room for is punch lines.

Consequently, following are one hundred punch lines. Because many of them have been around long enough to be universally familiar—a really Great New Joke may be as difficult to come up with as a really Great New Idea—you should be quickly entertained simply by reading the punch line and then reminiscing about the entire joke or story.

In this form, this listing also becomes a "Test of Humor Awareness."

One index of how much time you spend in and around joke-telling is the number of these lines that are sufficiently familiar to you to create a chuckle. If you are into self-testing, circle the number of each line that you recognize, count them up and see how you do.

1. "There has got to be a pony in here somewhere."
2. "Oh, that's George. He never could tell a joke."
3. "A drink named Irving?"
4. "He ran over me fifteen minutes ago."
5. "No, but that's the way I made Colonel."
6. "The backstroke, sir."
7. "Shoot me first: I can't stand to hear another lecture on Japanese management."
8. "That's God. He likes to play Doctor every now and then."
9. "Patio furniture."
10. "Poor Spellers of the World—UNTIE."
11. "They're more plentiful, they don't learn from experience, and the students don't get so attached to them."
12. "Pilgrims."
13. "A stick."
14. "Right where you left him."
15. "I am leaving you with Great Reluctance."
16. "Actually, officer, I was looking for my lantern."
17. "He was looking for love in all the wrong places."
18. "Bo Derek aging."
19. "Second grade."
20. "No, but it will make the six months seem like forever."
21. "That's close enough. Let's go."
22. "Wanna buy a toothbrush?"
23. "I am, too. Let's get off and have a drink."
24. "A six-pack and a Polish sausage."
25. "I jish thout she wass English."
26. "You go buy yourself a gun. You're going to kill someone with that two-by-four."
27. "I just won him in a raffle."
28. "I did, boss, and they really enjoyed it. Today we're going to the art museum."
29. "My, what a lovely finish."
30. "They didn't last year."
31. "Redundant."
32. "Trendy."
33. "Stand two shovels up against the wall and tell him to take his pick."

One Hundred Punch Lines 65

34. "We get Popes up here all the time, but that's the first lawyer we've ever seen."
35. "Therish better light over here."
36. "Neither has she."
37. "Okay, but we're almost out of arrows."
38. "A dead school bus."
39. "I don't know. I never looked."
40. "I just don't want to be there when it happens."
41. "It's when the mashed potatoes melt the jello and it runs over and makes the bottom of the hot roll soggy."
42. "Decomposing."
43. "There are some things not even a hog will touch."
44. "A bowling ball for people who like to make decisions."
45. "I don't know his name, but his face rings a bell."
46. "My God, I'm walled in."
47. "No sir, the men ride the camel into the village to meet the local girls."
48. "That's not it. My ear had a pencil behind it."
49. "I'm nearing my clothes."
50. "Where did you get that lousy haircut?"
51. "Rats. That's what I had for lunch."
52. "He sure keeps everybody on the sidelines alert."
53. "You know: January, February, March . . ."
54. "He wouldn't eat his mushrooms."
55. "Well, tell him I can't see him right now."
56. "I can't remember."
57. "Okay, okay, it's your deer. Just let me get my saddle off of it."
58. "You are going through a bad spell."
59. "This is the stone."
60. "I haven't been doing anything and I'm going to quit."
61. "I thought it was supposed to be perpendicular."
62. "Oh my, does that show up on that dial too?"
63. "His clock is in Saint Peter's office, being used for a fan."
64. "I did. She allowed for it."
65. "Oh, they fired her too."
66. "But it sure as hell isn't those biscuits."
67. "What did you say your name was?"

68. "When their lips stop moving, you know it is time to go on to the next slide."
69. "A theological doctrine holding that if California falls into the ocean, it is Saint Andreas' fault."
70. "My God! I'm pregnant. I wonder who did it?"
71. "Sweetheart, your name never came up."
72. "Perverted is when you use the whole chicken."
73. "All the rest are crustaceans."
74. "He couldn't decide if he was simply divine or just gorgeous."
75. "My father would have been amused, and my mother would have believed it."
76. "Wind it up and it takes Ken and Barbie hostage."
77. "I'm at the corner of WALK and DON'T WALK."
78. "A frog with a machine gun."
79. "Well, lemme a talka to Tonto."
80. "If you ever want to see your mother again . . ."
81. "I don't know, either. I was sitting quietly inside this refrigerator, smoking a cigar, when all of a sudden, BAM!"
82. "I always carry a bullet in my breast pocket in case anyone ever throws a Bible at me."
83. "Till his mother hollered 'STOP.'"
84. "The Swiss are in charge of the orgies."
85. "The cheerleaders kept grazing at halftime."
86. ". . . then go home without changing either one."
87. "Why don't they just put him in the slow group?"
88. "Two, but don't ask me how they got in there."
89. "Both of them."
90. "Shredded tweet."
91. ". . . the only state in the Union where there is still a market for gray food coloring."
92. "A pig that good, you don't eat all at once."
93. "NO. Do you know anything about gas stoves?"
94. "I'll name the other one Hose B."
95. "Chicken teriyaki."
96. "Knowledge."
97. "Eight. One to change the bulb and the other seven to sit around and talk about how good the old one was."
98. "What about us grils?"

99. "You've got to keep the worms warm."
100. "Turned green with envy."

One characteristic of humor is that the element of surprise is crucial. If you read one of these lines and don't recognize it, and then ask a friend to explain it to you, the joke will fall flat. In this sense, I may have just killed off up to one hundred unfamiliar jokes for you.

A second characteristic is the frequently experienced difficulty in remembering jokes, which probably comes from the surprise element. Because the punch line is a novelty, there are no familiar connections to hang the rest of the joke on.

This feature of humor has frequently frustrated me because when I hear a new story, I often jot down only the punch line. Over the years, I have accumulated a list of punch lines for which I can no longer remember the joke, such as "And the cricket said 'click, click.'" I remember that that joke was especially funny but, alas, I can no longer remember the body of it.

Another unidentified punch line is simply, "3:30."

Experience: The New Management Fad

As every good consultant knows, management training goes in fads. Over the last thirty years we have had the managerial grid, sensitivity training, situational leadership, brainstorming, management by objectives (MBO), EST, assessment centers, lateral thinking, Outward Bound, theory X/theory Y, the one-minute manager, and any number of other themes that have momentarily caught the attention of people responsible for the classroom training of managers.

Only cynics, of which I am not one, would say that these have all been useless fluff. Although fads do come and go, kernels of useful knowledge are usually winnowed out from each. Sometimes this new knowledge proves so useful that it is adopted widely, essentially becoming part of the management culture itself. Brainstorming, for example, introduced by Alex Osborn in the fifties and a favorite workshop topic of the sixties and seventies, is now a standard part of most individual and organizational problem-solving repertoires. "Let's have lunch next week and brainstorm about the scheduling problem" is a completely normal-sounding sentence in almost any institution today, more than thirty years after Osborn suggested the concept.

One of the most visible current fads in management training is "EXCELLENCE," a movement created single-handedly by Tom Peters, first with his book, then with his follow-on newspaper column, speeches, and a week-long management seminar. From shop floor to board room, his jargon permeates current organizational conversations. Managers now know that they should be out MBWA-ing (Managing By Wandering Around), and many an executive knows the definition of "skunkworks"—a node of unjustified, unfunded, illicit activities that sometimes produces the next technological breakthrough—and feels uncomfortable if there isn't one lurking around somewhere on his turf. (Organizational theorists are now grappling with whether skunkworks can be formalized. If they are recognized and funded, will they still be autonomous and creative?)

Wherever EXCELLENCE goes from here—and Peters' $20,000 speaking fee suggests that the momentum has not yet run out—it will undoubtedly leave behind a residue of concepts that will serve us well, such as listening to customers, sticking to what one does best, and allowing some slack for innovation.

Now, the intriguing question is: what will be the next fad? I have a candidate, but I have not yet quite figured out how to package it in a way that will create satisfyingly large tax problems for me. My candidate is "EXPERIENCE," with some suitable subtitle such as "How to Get It, Use It, Keep It, Give It Away, and Avoid Suffocation." Partially because I am aging, I suppose, but also because I see the value of experience cropping up all over the place—in my personal life, in the media, in anecdotal discussions with executives and other industrial psychologists, and in formal research projects—I have come to believe that EXPERIENCE is a topic worth studying, writing about, and teaching.

Examples of the pervasiveness of the EXPERIENCE concept are easy to cite because anyone with any organizational background can recognize many relevant applications immediately. A common one has to do with the selection of an outsider to come on board to serve some specific purpose:

> We need somebody who knows their way around Washington, especially the Funny Fort on the Potomac. (from a board of directors meeting)

> We need someone who has an in with the unions. (from a community fund committee session)

> We need someone who knows the VAX, SAS, and OMR. (from a social science research panel)

> We need someone who can call CEOs and get through to the Chief himself. (from a group trying to organize CEOs for political clout)

In short, what is needed is someone with EXPERIENCE.

The interesting follow-on question here is, "Exactly what does it mean 'to have experience'?" Or said differently, what are the differences between an experienced person and an inexperienced one? Or, still further, how can you systematically describe experience? Like pornography, everyone can recognize experience when they see it, but coming up with a publicly verifiable definition is difficult.

Without knowing exactly how to define it, I have concluded there are at least four important components of experience. The first is simply learning the business, whatever it is, which frequently means learning the relevant vocabulary, the jargon of the setting. I am in a different institution this year, serving as a visiting professor at the Air Force Academy, and I am constantly grappling with a new vocabulary, especially the strange acronyms and abbreviations. AWOL and ROTC are ones I can handle, but when AOC, OPR, OTF, TDY, PCS, SAMI, and WUBA come at me, several to a sentence, I have trouble following the conversation and definitely appear inexperienced.

Another example occurred recently when I helped my graduate-student son buy a condo. When we went to the bank to see about financing, we were bombarded with abbreviated terms like ARM, GEM, APR, and PTI. None of those things are particularly complicated, but until we learned the lingo, we felt at sea.

The second component of experience involves the collection of contacts; we are talking here about a (to use a word so overworked it makes me nauseous) network. Experienced people know a lot of other people who can make things happen. Inexperienced people are captive to a small set of acquaintances. Examples of the power of personal contacts can be seen daily in the news, from international episodes such as the Camp David accords, which were helped along immensely by the personal warmth and friendship between Carter, Begin, and Sadat, to decisions made by local councils on issues as mundane as garbage collection and stop-sign locations.

A vivid example of the power of personal contact happened this fall at the University of Nebraska. Nebraska, with its powerhouse eighth-ranked football team, was scheduled to open the season against thirteenth-ranked Florida State, but at the last minute the NCAA suspended sixty Nebraska football players for inappropriately using their complimentary tickets. For a few days it appeared that Nebraska would have to forfeit its first game, losing its visibility in the rankings and its chance for a national title. At the last hour the suspension was lifted long enough for the game to be played.

How did that happen?

According to the *Dallas Morning News,* "In what appears to be a compromise, primarily engineered by Nebraska athletic director Bob Devaney and NCAA executive director Walter Byers, the NCAA granted Nebraska a stay until Tuesday. . . . Unusual was the direct involvement of Byers [who] normally does not participate in individual cases. But when

Devaney, a long-time friend, called him Thursday morning, Byers became involved."

Recognize, however, that it is not simply whom you know. It is what whom you know knows about you. Acquaintanceship is not enough: loyalty, respect, trust, and shared values are also important.

The third component of experience has to do with institutional or professional socialization; that is, learning the rules of the game.

Newly elected members of Congress have for years been told, "To get along, go along." Most other institutional settings have their list of rules, explicit and implicit, frequently called "ethics," which the newcomer must absorb before really being considered "experienced."

The fourth component of experience is a catch-all category that I call "Cause and Effect" and includes a grab bag of Murphy's Laws. Every occupation has its own set of axioms, which have to be learned painfully, one at a time. Examples include the computer science guideline, "Manpower added to a late software project will make it later," and one from the financial services arena, "The trouble is not that the stock market is driven by mathematical factors or that it is driven by non-mathematical factors but that it is driven by nearly mathematical factors," and a generic one, "Experience isn't worth what it costs, but I can't seem to get it any cheaper."

Both Ronald Reagan and I Are Growing Older

I have been musing about the impact of aging individuals on organizations, stimulated partially by President Reagan's troubles in reporting when he okayed the decision to sell missiles to Iran ("I simply don't remember . . . period"), partially by some recent discussions I have been privy to about whether there should be a maximum age limit for membership on a board of directors, partially by a visit to my ninety-three-year-old uncle who hasn't recognized me in years, but mostly because I can't seem to win any squash matches lately.

I am spending this year as a Distinguished Visiting Professor at the Air Force Academy, an institution with unparalleled athletic facilities—including eighteen squash courts—and for the first time in fourteen years, I am playing squash a couple of times each week. I have always played in the upper part of the "A" ladder, and I prefer to continue to do so. The trouble is that, even after the rust came off my game, I can't beat anybody.

One explanation is that I am not good enough, but I reject that possibility. For years I have been good enough. Why not now?

Another possible explanation is the altitude. The academy is 7,000 feet above sea level, and oxygen is spare here. My opponents, regular Air Force officers, are like squash opponents everywhere—dogged, driving, fierce competitors on the courts; warm, friendly, diplomatic gentlemen afterwards—and they often use this altitude excuse to protect my ego. After soundly drubbing me on the court—leaving me panting, feeling old, achy, and whipped—on the way back to the locker room they usually say something like, "You were sharper today, sir, at least for the first few games; then I think the altitude got to you."

They are almost sweet in their determination to keep me from feeling inadequate, and the "altitude" explanation does hold water . . . for about two weeks. But I have been here seven months now.

The most likely explanation is simply age. At fifty-three, I am always giving away at least five years, sometimes twenty. Because of the liberal military retirement policies there are no fifty-year-olds around here, and I am an elder—a creaky, short-winded, dull-reflexed, slow-to-recover period piece, not yet quite an antique.

I do not like this role one bit, but it is highly unlikely that anyone is ever going to call my attention to it. Even these aggressive, competitive types are going to allow me to continue the fiction that I am as good as I once used to be. "When you get used to the altitude, sir, you're going to be a tiger."

I see quite a bit of similarity between my self-assessed skill level, the altitude alibi, and the President's memory problems. Some of his apologists have attempted to deflect criticism by suggesting that details such as missile sales to Iran are trivial. "After all," they say, "do you remember what you were doing on a specific day in August 1986?"

To demonstrate the ridiculousness of this explanation, let us develop a more personal scenario. Assume that you live down the block from a wild-eyed, emotionally volatile, dangerous psychopath, someone with a reputation for beating up his kids and for capturing and tormenting the neighborhood pets, sometimes even on TV. He gets into lots of public fist fights. After he kicked your dog around once, you spoke harshly to him, and he now hates you, has in fact thrown garbage on your yard.

Now suppose your spouse comes home one day and says, "Dear, let's sell your hunting rifle to that wacko's kids, just to start a dialogue. They want one, and perhaps if they had a gun in the house, he would be easier to deal with."

The question here is not whether you would agree to sell your rifle to his kids—there might even be a rational reason to believe that, if armed, they could help keep the old man in check—but whether you could remember this dramatic decision five months later, whatever you agreed to do.

I suggest that the decision to sell millions of dollars worth of missiles to one of our most virulent enemies is hardly similar to remembering what you were doing on some randomly selected day several months ago. The "trivial detail" argument holds no more water for explaining the President's memory lapse than the "altitude" explanation does for my miserable won-lost record.

The most likely explanation for the President's confusion is that he is old and his memory is feeble, but just as my squash opponents are not going to batter me with the truth ("Sir, you are simply too old for this league. Have you ever thought of moving down to the "B" ladder?"), neither are the President's staff and associates going to suggest that senility may be the most parsimonious explanation for the Iran scandal and that he should find a slower league to play in ("Mr. President, have you ever thought of, well, resigning and leaving this game to younger people?").

They are not going to say that to him for a variety of reasons. One of the main ones is, and I have learned this fact through long experience, no one is ever willing to confront someone in power with the age issue.

My own belief is that people ought to get out of line positions before they are sixty, and out of staff or policy-making positions before they are sixty-five. Both of those limits may be a couple of years too young, but the problem with the age delusion, such as the one that I am now having with my squash game, is that you never notice the deterioration today, and you probably won't notice it tomorrow either, but when you do catch on the damage will have been done yesterday.

The elderly in power do have four definite strengths: First, they have a personal sense of history, mostly because they have lived through so much of it. When historical context is important, they are indispensable. Second, during long careers, they have created many innovative solutions to a diverse set of problems. When current problems are solvable using solutions they have seen before, senior people can be very effective. Third, they know a lot of people. When contacts are needed, they can make the phone calls. Fourth, their glandular slowdowns keep them calmer under stress, less acrimonious. When calm, reasoned, dispassionate discourse is helpful or indeed essential, a well-aged participant can be a virtue. (Not the least of the reasons for including this paragraph about the strengths of the elderly is that when a copy of this column is thrown into my lap seven years from now with the suggestion that I move down to the "C" ladder, I will have some arguments for holding on.)

But when decisive actions are necessary, along with the energy for putting the decisiveness in place; when new ideas are crucial, especially ideas that break with the past; when facile intellectual work is needed and synapses cannot be loggy with age; when understanding a new order in the relevant universe is demanded and notes on tattered 3-by-5 cards won't substitute for computer data banks, we need to find kind but firm ways to gently ease out the J. Edgar Hoovers, Hyman Rickovers, Claude Peppers, and Ronald Reagans of the world.

It won't be easy. Once we are there, we all love the "A" ladders.

Pink and Blue Test Forms:
The Single Greatest PR Mistake in the History of Psychological Testing

While walking through O'Hare Airport recently, I noticed a young couple with two babies—probably twins—one decked out in blue, the other in pink, presumably color-coded. Although the mother did not wear saddle shoes and the father did not sport a crew cut, in many other respects the whole montage could have stepped right out of the 1950s, especially given the emphasis on sexual identity—boys in blue, girls in pink.

The scene reminded me of a mistake that I made many years ago that led to the biggest single public relations goof in the history of psychological testing, a mistake that centered around pink and blue.

In the fall of 1958, when I entered graduate school at the University of Minnesota, I was hired to do some data-processing work for Professor E. K. Strong, Jr., of Stanford University. Though he had been retired for ten years, he was still actively working on his psychological test, the Strong Vocational Interest Blank, and was in fact revising it for the first time in twenty years. To do this, his archival database was being computerized. Since I was one of the few graduate students in the fifties who had had any computer experience, I found myself with a nice job, supported in part by a National Science Foundation Fellowship.

At that point in history, there were two versions of Strong's inventory, a Form for Men and a Form for Women. Although they were sixty percent identical, where they differed the emphasis was on traditional sex roles: men were queried about their mechanical and outdoor interests, women about children and office work.

Between 1958 and 1965, a lot happened: Strong continued with his research but at a gradually slowing pace as he became ill and then passed away (in 1963); in 1960 I finished my Ph.D. and joined the Minnesota faculty, continuing to work on the revision; in 1962, just before his death, Strong transferred all of his research materials from Stanford to Minnesota, a treasure trove of twenty-two filing cabinets of completed interest inventories (including data from such luminaries as H. L. Mencken, Marjorie Rawlings, Count Basie, and Arthur Fiedler); in 1963 the University of Minnesota awarded me tenure, established the Center for Interest Measurement Research, and appointed me director.

Two years later, in 1965, the revision of the Men's Form was finished, and I flew to California to go over the last details with the publisher, Stanford University Press. I had many questions to be resolved: scoring details, distribution issues, and more mundane topics such as typeface and color of the paper to be used.

At the press, a technical editor and I sat down at a large table in a conference room with the manuscript spread around. We began working through the list of questions. When we came to the issue of paper color, he picked up the phone and asked the supervisor of the printing room to bring in some samples. The supervisor arrived shortly, spread out eight or ten color chips on the table, and said, "These are what we have in stock. We can get others but it will take several weeks."

We were already behind schedule and wanted no more delays. We knew we were going to pick one of those colors lying on the table.

Anyone who has ever worked with psychological tests knows that it is highly desirable to have different forms of the tests color-coded, just to keep them straight. The first thing that we did was to eliminate all of the colors that had been used for earlier versions. That left, as I recall, about four color chips: a pleasant blue, a drab brown, a dull gray, and a pale pink.

The choice was easy. We went with the blue.

The next year, 1966, the revised version of the Men's Form was published, printed on the pleasant blue paper. It was rapidly adopted, and within a year had replaced ninety percent of the earlier (1938, yellow) edition.

Nobody said a word about the color.

Back at Minnesota, we decided that we next needed to tackle the Women's Form, initially published in 1933, slightly revised in 1946, and badly outdated. Because we had already done the men's revision, we knew more about what we were doing and progress came much faster. The computer programs were already written, the analytic problems had been solved, and we pushed the women's revision through in three years. Because we had the benefit of experience, we produced a superior product, compared to the Men's Form. The new questions for the Women's Form were better selected, the scoring scales were longer and thus more reliable, and the separation between occupational samples was larger, producing more accuracy.

I was very proud of the improvements.

Once again, in 1968, preparing for publication, I flew to California, once again with questions in hand. Once again I sat down at the same conference table with the same editor, and once again he called the same print-room supervisor who came in with much the same collection of color chips. When the elimination was over this time, again if memory serves me right, we were left with drab brown, a dull gray, a light green, and a pale pink.

We looked at each other and grinned.

"Do we dare?"

"Why not? After all, the purpose is color-coding."

Today, in conventional, corporate gray 1987, it is hard to remember just how colorful and experimental the 1960s were. Whimsy was possible, or so I thought, and color was in. Indeed, although I don't recall specifically, it is highly likely that I made that decision while wearing a print shirt, a loud tie, and plaid slacks.

Thus, in that relaxed, spontaneous manner, one of the most controversial psychological test issues of all time was spawned, because we chose to print the Women's Form on pink paper.

Before it died, some three hundred thousand pink Women's Forms were distributed, and they really created a ruckus. I was considered, by almost any index you wish, the most chauvinistic psychologist in America. I received angry letters and abusive phone calls. I was chastised in class by students. The Wayne State University Faculty Senate passed a resolution condemning the inventory. I was questioned vigorously by a cluster of women's groups, including the President's Commission on the Equal Status for Women. The American Personnel and Guidance Association sent an official task force of psychologists to investigate me. Doonesbury focused on it when Joanie Causus was handed a pink form on her first day in law school (the men got blue), and dozens of feminist teachers and professors waved the blue and pink booklets in faculty meetings, conventions, and colloquia, insisting, "See what they are doing to us, pigeonholing us in the same old sexual stereotypes—secretaries, nurses, and teachers!" (The profile also included results for women doctors, lawyers, and engineers, but that got lost in the static.)

It took about a year to catch on that we had unknowingly created an unnecessary hassle, and we switched to green paper in a belated attempt to demonstrate some gender empathy.

The change in paper color did not still the clamor for change, however. The Women's Movement demanded that the separate forms for each sex be eliminated, and that a single version of the test be used for both sexes.

So I began the third revision, and, in 1974, the biggest change in the history of the oldest, most widely used career counseling inventory in the world was published. The Men's and Women's Forms were combined into a single test booklet, all sexually suspect questions were removed (e.g., "Do you like to go to stag parties?" "Would you like to be a cheerleader?"), the scoring methodology was substantially changed, the computerized output was expanded, the name was changed to the Strong-Campbell Interest Inventory, and—because we had learned from sitting on one hot stove lid—it was printed in a sociologically neutral color: purple.

This entire pink-and-blue episode, in which many people can see elements of whimsy, taught me a serious lesson. Acts of discrimination can be grouped into two classes: The first is *actual* discrimination, which includes acts that deny some category of people their rights such as full access to high-level jobs, equal pay, or the right to sit at lunch counters simply on the basis of some demographic characteristic. Such discrimination demonstrably produces damage to those affected and today is usually illegal. People who perpetrate such acts, although perhaps arguing strenuously for some philosophic basis supporting their actions, can usually see the impact they are having—e.g., "Yes, there are too few women in the executive suite, but that's because they are too emotional or get pregnant, or whatever." These arguments can often be countered by hard facts and legal action.

The second class of discrimination is *perceived* discrimination and usually includes more abstract, symbolic acts, such as using sexist or racist terms, ill-advised humor, or, as in the pink-and-blue adventure, offensive symbolism. These biased actions, I now understand, are harder to counter and eradicate, partially because the perpetrators of such acts are often woefully unaware that they are doing anyone any harm, as indeed I was. In 1968 it never occurred to me that the selection of colors for a psychological inventory would disturb anyone.

I learned that the perception of discrimination can depend solely on the perception of the recipient and can be totally independent of the motives of the actor. This increased sensitivity was, for me, a valuable personal lesson.

Which brings me back to my initial observation of the children in O'Hare Airport. Because symbolism often reflects social change, and because social change pendulums do swing, we are likely seeing a swing back to more conventional values represented by short hair, close dancing, thank-you notes, and, perhaps, color-coded kids. Surely, however, we are more sophisticated now and will not use those symbols so glibly in a way that results in perceived discrimination. This is real progress.

A Passionate Corrections Officer with Sparkling Eyes

Oh, I love enthusiasts. When their eyes sparkle as they talk, their particular passion hardly matters. I'm interested. Consequently, my attractive luncheon companion easily held my attention with her blend of excitement and knowledgeable observations of what might be viewed as the black hole of leadership—the justice system. "This," I said to myself, "is a corrections officer?"

A little background: In 1973 I left the University of Minnesota and came to work for the Center. In the subsequent years I have had almost daily contact with a wide range of people, most of them sharing the common theme of wanting their organizations to be more imaginative and better led.

Early on, I noticed that the majority of our clients tended to come from organizations that, in a relative sense, need us least. They came from well-managed corporations like GE, IBM, Procter & Gamble, and Richardson-Vicks; from governmental agencies like the GAO, IRS, and the Secret Service; and from the General Officer ranks of the U.S. Army. Whatever your opinion of any one of those organizations, I can tell you that—as large organizations go—collectively they are more sensitive to leadership-development issues than most other organizations. The presence of their employees in our high-priced, intensive seminars attests to that.

I also noticed, back in the 1970s, that there were some obvious gaps in the array of organizations that were working with us. For example, there was no one from either the hospitals or railroads, two categories of organizations that to the outsider looked poorly managed. I took this as one sign that these organizations were stodgy and outmoded, trapped in their earlier cultures, not interested in exploring current offerings in leadership thinking. In those two cases, however, some interesting changes have occurred in the 1980s. As competition and change have caught up with them, some of the more forward-looking representatives from both hospitals and railroads now show up in Greensboro or Colorado Springs at our leadership-training programs.

I also noticed that a third category—the prison systems—was never represented in our programs and, while all I know is what I read in the newspapers, that appears to be another group with management problems. With one exception, among the hundreds of people I meet each year at the

Center there was never a single corrections official. The single exception was an interesting case. Someone from the Federal Bureau of Prisons came to a CCL Visitors' Day once, took me aside, and said, "One of the problems in prisons is that informal leaders emerge among the inmates. They develop their own power base and then challenge our formal authority. Do you have any ideas about how to keep leadership from happening among convict groups?" He was an imaginative thinker, and we briefly discussed the implications of squashing leadership in prison populations, reaching no resolutions.

In this context I was particularly fascinated by what my luncheon friend was telling me. Her name is Cay Shea, she is from Minneapolis, and she is the Director of the Program for Serious Juvenile Offenders in Hennepin County. She is responsible for the rehabilitation of about twenty-four kids at any one time: all male, ages thirteen to eighteen, about fifty percent white, thirty to forty percent black, and ten to twenty percent Indian. Their average stay with her is about six months.

"What does it take," I asked, "to be a 'serious' juvenile offender? Car theft?"

"Oh, no," she laughed. "That's mild. To be sent to our Cottage, you'd have to steal a whole lot of cars, or perhaps lead police on a high-speed chase. Typical infractions would be assault or aggravated burglary, really serious crimes."

"What do you try to do with them?"

"I teach these teenage renegades to think right!"

It was her enthusiastic blend of (1) street-savvy language, (2) a solid educational background (B.A. in political science, M.A. in human development), and (3) comfort in the setting ("My father was a mayor. I grew up around police officers, lawyers, and judges") that made her so credible.

"The basis for our approach," she said, "comes from the research on what causes crime. Although no one cause has been identified, one similar finding running through many studies of criminals is that they are guilty of what we call 'errors in thinking.'"

"Such as?"

"One example is called 'The Victim Stance.' A kid gets into trouble in the classroom, and instead of saying 'I did something wrong,' he says, 'The teacher was outrageous in what she expected' or 'Some other kid started it.' They don't accept any responsibility for the problem. They see themselves as the victim."

"How do you change that?"

"We teach them to think differently, and that takes a lot of work. Basically, each kid in my Cottage is rated every day by every staff member on sixteen errors in thinking. Each offender also keeps a journal where we teach them to write down their thoughts, and then analyze them. Each day they must log at least three incidents, and for each they must list, first, a brief description of the incident and what they were thinking at the time (for example, 'I was in the gym and another guy bumped me and I thought, "you did that on purpose, try it again and I'll cold-cock you."') and, second, their errors in thinking."

Here she paused for emphasis. "We absolutely insist that they think about what they are thinking. Some kid will tell me about breaking into a store to steal a knife or some drugs and I'll ask him why he did it. He'll say, 'I dunno, I just did it,' and I'll pin him right to the wall, 'Hey c'mon, a lot of thinking went into that. Tell me about it.' They all think they're just impulsive, but a lot of thinking goes into what they do, and we want them to begin to realize that.

"Back to their journals. Third, we want them to generalize from each incident, and especially to see some patterns. Most of them are 'now' thinkers, very concrete about what is happening today, and they haven't seen the themes in their behaviors. By logging these behaviors over several weeks, some of them start saying, 'Hey, I've been doing this stuff since junior high.' And, of course we try to get them to see the future implication, which basically is, 'If you don't change the way you are thinking, you're either going to wind up in jail forever, or dead.'"

She hesitated. "Unfortunately, we have plenty of powerful examples to show them. This year," she was very pensive now, "I have gone to funerals for two of my kids who were killed in fights.

"Anyway, back again to their journals: Fourth, they have to suggest some corrective alternatives. 'What could I have done differently?'

"A staff member reads their journals every day and grades them. Their journal grade is combined with the daily ratings from the staff on their 'thinking errors,' and if they do everything well, they 'pass' the day. For every three days they pass, they get one day off their sentence. That's powerful motivation," and she added, with obvious pride in her co-workers, "and of course this whole system works because we have a strong, alert, dedicated staff."

She went on to describe the many other ways she works with her kids, including contact with the parents. "If I can't get the parents on my side, I might as well hang it up." She said the average parent wants to be helpful but almost invariably has little awareness of how much trouble their child is in. "These kids have conned everyone around them . . ." A slight hesitation for effect, "until they met me. I let them know early on that I'm tough but fair, and I expect them to change. Then we show them how."

At another meeting recently I heard a federal executive say, "I don't know why, but all of the interesting stuff seems to start in Minnesota." Add Cay Shea and her Cottage kids to that list. Maybe we are starting to learn how to apply some powerful psychological methods for change in the justice system.

Affirmative Action Poker

During the 1986-87 academic year I was a Distinguished Visiting Professor at the U.S. Air Force Academy in Colorado Springs. It was an invigorating year, filled with new experiences. Because I was given the formal rank of a two-star general, all of the perks were right, including the important ones—an office with a spectacular mountain view, convenient underground parking, and football seats on the 45-yard line.

Contacts with individual faculty members and cadets were by far the best part of the year. I made some quick and close friendships, some of which will surely be enduring.

The cadets in particular were considerably more likable than I had anticipated. I had expected a lot of Top Gun, Rambo types in this military academy. Although there were certainly some of those around, the average cadet is much more ... well, enthusiastically wholesome is one phrase that comes to mind. The cadets are mostly bright, energetic ex-high school achievers; eleven percent of the males and twenty percent of the females graduated in the top one percent of their high school classes. Over half of them held some important high school leadership position, such as student body president, athletic team captain, or newspaper editor.

Because of the constrained military environment of the academy, however, with its strong emphasis on orderliness, discipline, and duty, the average cadet seems more naive and less worldly than his or her counterpart in a comparable civilian university. Cadets are, for example, in a situation where "the system" dictates many of their choices for them, and thus their span of decision-making control is narrower than that of the typical college student. No cadet ever gets up in the morning wondering what to wear, where to have lunch, or whether to cut class. Those decisions are locked in.

The payoffs, however, are substantial: a superb free education, the opportunity to fly, daily access to what may be the best athletic facilities in the world, a guaranteed career, and, not a trivial issue for many of them, the opportunity to serve a protective role for a free society. The cadets sum up both the good and the bad with their conclusion that "you get a million-dollar education at the academy, shoved up your rear end a nickel at a time."

Little Awareness

The lack of experience among the cadets showed up in a specific way in a senior-level course that I taught in industrial psychology. When we reached the section dealing with EEOC issues and affirmative action, I became aware that these kids had essentially no appreciation of the searing, gut-wrenching clashes our society went through in the sixties and seventies over racial and sexual equality. All of them had been born several years after JFK was assassinated. Topics like civil rights marches and bra burnings ranked right up there in their historical awareness with WWII and Daniel Webster.

The class consisted of six white males, two black males, and two white females. Although this demographic mixture assured some variability in viewpoint, their disagreements lacked the passions of the sixties. In particular, they seemed to feel that goodwill and "the system" could cure any inequity without the necessity for personal pain or confrontational anger.

I decided to run a simulation. One day I announced, "Today we are going to play Affirmative Action Poker. Here are the rules: (1) Only white males can play. (2) Each player gets fifty M&Ms for a stake; when these are gone, you are out. (3) There is an up-front ante of five M&Ms per hand. (4) There is a table stakes limit. (5) To save time, only five card stud will be played. (6) The women and minorities can only sit and watch."

We pulled some classroom desks together into the semblance of a poker table. I distributed the M&Ms, and the cards were dealt. The six "good ol' boys" thrived on it and played with gusto. One cadet especially enjoyed it because he was dealt good cards and played them cannily. His nickname was Ace, which was exceedingly appropriate for my purposes. He was captain of the cheerleading squad, a good student, and one of those physical marvels who preceded the football team onto the field with a long series of successive back flips and handsprings.

After a few hands, Ace had accumulated a majority of the M&Ms. A couple of the other players had to drop out because they lost their stake. At this point I said, "Okay, now we're going to change the rules. The women and blacks can join the game." They moved up to the table, and I gave them each twenty-five M&Ms, in contrast to the fifty that I had given each white male.

The women and blacks complained, of course, to which I airily replied, "At least I'm letting you join the game and giving you some stake to start with. I can't change history all at once, you know. Go ahead and deal the cards."

Heavy Bettor

A couple more hands were played, and two things became obvious: First, because of his skill and large winnings, which allowed him to bet heavily, Ace was going to clean everybody out. Second, Sue, who was as close to an outspoken feminist as we had, did not know how to play poker very well; in fact, not at all.

I told her, "Sue, you need a consultant." I turned to one of the white males who was sitting on the sidelines because he had lost his stake and said, "You can't seem to manage your money very well. C'mon over here and we'll make you a consultant to the women." (To make the simulation more potent, I dramatically hammed it up. I suppose I should feel sheepish about how easy it was to be chauvinistic.)

More hands were dealt and the pile in front of Ace grew bigger and bigger, so much so that he was occasionally popping M&Ms into his mouth, chewing with glee. Other players, including some of the blacks and women, dropped out because they lost their stakes.

"Okay," I said, "time to change the rules again. Now we are going to try quotas. What this means is that you 'protected classes' (pointing to the blacks and women) can continue to play whether you have any stakes to bring to the table or not. You don't have to bet, but if you have the best hand, you still win the pot."

Nobody much liked these arrangements and there was some grumbling, but I said forcefully, "Shut up and deal the cards."

Soon, the game began to break down. No one, not even Ace, knew quite how to bet when there were so many sandbaggers at the table, and the sense of reasonable competition disappeared. Tension rose, and I realized, as an instructor, that unless I did something different, they were going to mutiny.

"Okay," I said, "new rules. Now I am going to constitute this entire group as a state legislature, and give you ten minutes to decide on new laws to govern this game of poker. You can adopt any rules you want to concerning the allocation of the stakes, who gets to play, or what defines winning."

This opportunity energized them, and they plunged headlong into rewriting the rules—only to immediately face the fact that Ace had most of the M&Ms.

"First," said someone, "let's redistribute the M&Ms so that everyone has an equal share."

"Wait a minute," Ace jumped in. "These M&Ms are mine. I won them fair and square. You guys had as many opportunities to win as I did. I earned these M&Ms by the sweat of my brow." (Ace was also into a bit of drama.)

"Not true," bristled one of the women. "We had a smaller stake than you did to begin with. Now, it is only fair that you share some of your winnings with us."

Ace persisted, "I didn't have anything to do with what your stakes were. I don't make the rules here."

Taxing Rockefeller

We were running out of class time so I leaned on them for a quick decision. They jointly decided to commandeer some of Ace's M&Ms, "taxing Rockefeller" as they put it, and with some of his stake redistributed, played a few more hands.

I stopped them with five minutes of class time remaining, and said, "Let's talk about it."

The discussion was animated, with lots of familiar phrases:

"The world isn't fair."

"I didn't make the world."

"People who have a head start should have to help those less fortunate."

"Two wrongs don't make a right, and besides, if you subsidize people, it will make them weak."

"After I have worked hard for something, why should I have to give it to someone else?"

"It is grossly unfair to have to enter the game several laps behind the leaders. How can you ever catch up?"

At one point I turned to Sue and asked, "How did it feel to you, not knowing how to play poker?"

She is a poised, attractive, well-spoken young woman with strong feelings about women's issues. Her eyes flashed as she talked, her words gushing out like the release of a pent-up torrent. "Sir, this game is exactly how it is to be a woman at the academy. You show up here and you are expected to be able to do everything that boys do, whether it is useful or not. I don't play poker, I've never played poker, I don't care about poker.

And there's no way that poker is necessary to be a good Air Force officer. Yet because I don't play poker, I am made to feel silly and insignificant. And worse, as someone who has to have a consultant who can't even handle his own money assigned to her to get her through the day. Sir, it is really degrading and disgusting."

She went on for three or four minutes with one of the most persuasive and appealing extemporaneous statements describing the plight of young women in macho settings that I have ever heard. The class became silent, and I am convinced that no one who heard her eloquence could ever quite look at the academy's EEOC issues in the same way in the future.

Coincidentally, I conducted this class on the Friday before Parent's Weekend, a day that the academy encourages parents to show up and attend their cadet's classes. As a result, two sets of parents were in the classroom during the poker game. One set was white, from Staples, Minnesota, named Anderson; the other was black, from Denver, named Butler.

When I walked into the classroom and saw them there, I thought, "Whoops, what if this experiment goes awry in some way: will I have some offended parents on my hands?" But it was too late to develop another lesson.

A few days later, during the next class meeting, I asked Anderson, "What did your parents think?" He smiled a pleasant Scandinavian smile and replied, "Sir, they were real interested and impressed. They were surprised that teaching like that would go on at the academy."

"Rhett," I asked, "what did your parents think?" (Rhett is black, about six-feet-four-inches tall and two-hundred-and-twenty pounds, with an easy, attractive smile.)

"Dr. Campbell," he grinned, "my parents told me, 'Rhett, you pay close attention to what he is teaching you because that's the way the world really works out there.'"

Working through these weird, intense dynamics of the sixties with these youthful, much more placid children of the eighties once again reminded me that the Chinese had it right with their curse, "May you live in interesting times."

Corporate Taboos and Junk Detectors

I had my first exposure to the concept of the "Corporate Taboo Topic" sometime in the fall of 1955. As an eager, new college graduate, I had started work for Procter & Gamble. For my initial assignment, they sent me to one of their hinterland locations—a soap factory in St. Louis—and as a member of first-line management I was being socialized into the P&G culture.

It was not a time of rebelliousness. Quite the contrary. It was the time of "The Man in the Grey Flannel Suit" and "The Organization Man." Hair was short, shirts were white, and orders from on high were followed slavishly.

Corporate travel was not as common as now, and a visit from Cincinnati (Mecca) was a special occasion. When a high-ranking executive visited the plant that fall to participate in the annual management dinner, we hung on his every word.

In the question-and-answer session that followed his briefing, my boss, a wonderful guy named Fred, asked a question like, "What is the company doing about the deleterious impact of phosphate detergents on the environment?"

I was not a particularly perceptive young man. Many powerful psychological dynamics floated over my head in those days. But even I could pick up the sense of charged electricity that hit the room, not only because of the question but also because of the flustered way that this top executive replied. He clearly was bothered by the question. He didn't know how to answer, but he managed to transmit very definitely that he didn't think those of us down in the trenches should be worrying about such things. I had a vivid sense of a parent talking to the kids, and the kids cowering. Basically he said, "Look children, we (parents) know what we are doing. Trust us, and don't raise these issues in public."

The next morning, my office-mate commented, "Geez, can you believe Fred would ask a question like that? No wonder his career hasn't gone anywhere! The company knows what it's doing with phosphates, for Pete's sake! I mean, that's what those top guys are paid for."

Fred was somewhat older than the average second-level manager, and he did indeed seem to be stuck. He had been caught in World War II, never made it through college after the war, and thus was not a good candidate for advancement. He was, however, one of the brightest, best read persons in the company, and he had much broader interests than the rest of us. He also had a strong sense of social concern, which in the fifties was often suspect. I remember thinking to myself, as a docile product of the Eisenhower years, "Boy, I'm never going to screw up like that." I avoided embarrassing questions, I stuck to Ivory soap, and I certainly didn't talk about phosphates.

An Atheist?

A few years earlier, as a high school senior, I was attending an Iowa Regional Methodist Youth Fellowship Conference. During a lull in a discussion on Genesis, I stuck up my hand and asked the presiding minister, "If God created Heaven and Earth, who created God?"

The minister's reaction was much the same as the P&G executive's reaction to phosphates: somehow it was made clear to us that such concerns were outside of the boundaries of useful discussion, that "someone up there" knew best and was not to be challenged. Afterwards, I was teased by my compatriots: "What are you trying to do, Campbell, be an atheist? God doesn't need to be created." In a rural church in Iowa in the fifties, alternative explanations of Genesis were heresy.

It may seem like a huge conceptual leap, but I have often thought about those two episodes whenever I see an example of a taboo topic, a topic that some culture simply cannot tolerate, no matter how intellectually relevant it might be. Now, thirty years and a couple of psychology degrees later, I am still trying to puzzle out the central issue in such taboos.

Following is a list of some taboos that I have run across recently. I should report up front that I can't see any single dynamic that explains all of them. Most are situationally bound. The only common theme that they may share is that, at least to outsiders, many of them look ridiculous.

A few years ago, I participated in a human resources conference within a tobacco company. The company is a progressive one, with many forward-looking policies and programs, including a corporate wellness program. During the conference, this wellness program was enthusiastically described by the people in charge. They listed its components—weight control, exercise programs, sensible use of alcohol, regular physical exams, an emphasis on seat belts, and so forth—but there was a total lack of any mention of smoking. In fact, in the back of the room with the coffee urns was an assortment of free cigarettes. Here, the topic of cancer was taboo.

In the early 1980s I was a member of a National Academy of Science commission formed to study the issue of "comparable worth." According to this concept, people should be paid according to some absolute measure of the worth of their job, instead of by competitive marketplace forces, under the assumption that women are often paid less than men just because they are women, not because their work is worth less. It was a volatile issue. The commission found it impossible to even discuss the possibility that some women are paid less because they become mothers and thus interrupt their career paths. In this setting, pregnancy was taboo.

In a couple of recent sessions with auto manufacturing executives, I have asked, "Why do American cars have two keys, when even the most expensive European cars have only one?" The immediate answer is, "So you can leave your car with a parking attendant and keep the key to your locked trunk with you." My response is, (a) I have never done that in my life, and I'll bet most other people haven't either; (b) my American car is a large suburban station wagon that doesn't have a trunk; and (c) even American pickups have two keys. In this setting, efficiency is taboo.

I spend a fair amount of time these days in military settings. The military is highly concerned with concepts of leadership and our Center is often asked to become involved. A universal feature of today's military culture, no matter which service, is short hair. I often ask, "Why? What is this devotion to haircuts? What evidence is there that hair length has anything to do with combat readiness?" If I am feeling ornery, I refer to two terrorist events: a young man killed on a hijacked TWA flight and two Marines bombed at an outdoor café in Central America. The press reports suggested the victims were identified as U.S. military personnel because of their out-of-place white-sidewall haircuts. Thus, the potential liability is clear. But what are the advantages? No military leader has ever given me a rational answer. Usually they shuffle away from the topic as quickly as possible, treating me as a civilian who couldn't be expected to know any better, and of course in that reaction, I am reminded of phosphates.

Even in that cathedral of open ideas, the university, taboos abound. Recently I had occasion to sit in on a recruitment discussion in a situation where some outside funds were potentially available to fund a new position. The position in question was in the Economics Department, and a knowledgeable inside observer said, "Of course, the candidate will have to be a member of the reigning school of economic thought in that particular department. They simply couldn't tolerate someone who looks at the world through a different prism than the rest of them are using." We quizzed him and others on that point. There was general agreement that the professors in that department were so insular that they would make life very difficult for anyone who brought fresh ideas to their discipline. Academic priests can't tolerate much atheism either.

Junk Detectors

So, after listing this smorgasbord of taboo topics, what unifying conclusions can we draw? Taboos are universal. They are passionately held. Their specific topics vary greatly from setting to setting. To the insider, they appear obvious, certainly not in need of defense. To an outsider, they often appear frivolous, like sacred cows in India, or stupid, like making six million unnecessary car keys each year.

The dilemma is this: Organizations need to be disciplined, predictable, and responsive to their environments, and taboos frequently grow out of those needs. For example, short hair and neat uniforms in the military provide visible evidence of military discipline. Ignoring such requirements can be organizationally destructive.

Yet slavishly adhering to outmoded behavior can be equally destructive to an organization's capacity for innovation and forward progress. Finding the balance between valuable traditions and inventive changes is one of the most important tasks of top leadership.

My boss, Center President and CEO Walt Ulmer, a former three-star general, has a great concept which is relevant. He believes that all large organizations need to have "junk detectors," some way of cleansing themselves of outmoded practices.

Because the taboos I describe are often organizational "junk," this concept is appealing to me. The challenge for the leader is to determine which of the organization's traditions are stabilizing influences to be nurtured and supported and which are meaningless, burdensome, and stupid. The more conservative the organization, the stronger the need for these decisions to be made directly at the top and then forcefully executed.

Fortunately, in this mess of contradictions about taboos and innovations, my own belief systems are acutely accurate, crystal clear, and pristine pure. Others may have to spend energy defending dubious conclusions, but ever since I have learned that space may be curved, with no beginning and no end, thus relieving me from worrying about where it all started, I have dismissed many of the major taboos from my immediate concern by believing that "somebody up there really knows what's going on; let them handle the phosphates."

The CCL Power Eating Plan Diet:
If Nobody Sees You Eat It, It Doesn't Count

One of the joys of my current situation is that people often send me examples of office humor—those dog-eared missives, often of dubious taste, that circulate sub rosa in most work settings.

I have before me, for example, the Performance Appraisal Dimensions for Superman: "SUPERIOR—able to leap tall buildings in a single bound. GOOD—handles small buildings well. AVERAGE—splats into the sides of tall buildings. POOR—trips over picket fences."

Another is a phrase book for traveling in the troubled Middle East, with colorful translations like "Thank you for allowing me to travel with my hands tied in the filthy trunk of your smelly automobile!"

A wonderful new sample came in last week—as usual, undated, unsigned, "source unknown." It is a diet plan, certainly relevant to one of our society's current problems. A recent study has suggested that the United States population is collectively about two billion pounds overweight and that it costs us about a million extra barrels of oil each day to carry this weight around in cars and airplanes, to develop and manufacture the extra cloth needed to tent it, and to grow and process the food needed to maintain the plumpness.

Thus, another diet can be very useful, if it works. The reason most diets are ineffective is that they do not take into account the demanding pace of life that most of us are leading. That is why I am particularly enamored with this new diet, and, with proper modifications for our audience, I am passing it along to you as the "CCL Power Eating Plan Diet" or, for short, the "CCL PEP Diet." This diet is designed to help you cope with the stress that comes from being in charge.

BREAKFAST
1/2 grapefruit
1 slice whole wheat toast, dry
8 oz. skim milk

MID-MORNING SNACK
6 oz. plain yogurt
Decaffeinated coffee

LUNCH
4 oz. lean broiled chicken
1 cup steamed spinach
1 cup herb tea
1 Oreo cookie

MID-AFTERNOON SNACK
Rest of the Oreos in the package
1 pint Rocky Road ice cream
3 tbs. of hot fudge sauce, 3 tbs. of caramel sauce
Nuts, cherries, whipped cream to taste

DINNER
1 loaf garlic bread with cheese
Lg. sausage, mushroom, & cheese pizza
2 lite beers
Choice of 2 med. Snickers bars, or 1 giant Hershey's with Almonds

LATE EVENING NEWS
Entire frozen Sara Lee cheesecake eaten directly from freezer
2 cups hot chocolate (optional)

Rules for the CCL PEP Diet

1. If you eat something and no one sees you eat it, it has no calories.

2. If you drink a diet soda with a candy bar, the calories in the candy bar are cancelled out by the diet soda.

3. Food consumed for ceremonial purposes should not be considered detrimental to the quality of life. Thus, Valentine's candy, office birthday party cakes, and champagne toasts drunk at the weddings of daughters of your clients should be judged in the context of the rhythms of rituals. Leanness in a life barren of the punctuation marks of tradition is a dubious trade-off.

4. Cookie pieces contain no calories. The process of breaking causes calorie leakage.

5. Movie theater foods (such as Milk Duds, buttered popcorn, Junior Mints, and Tootsie Rolls) do not have additional calories because they are part of the entire entertainment package and not part of one's personal fuel.

6. Food binges that occur just before a deadline or just before a project ships don't count because you know that next week after the manuscript is done or the machine is out the door that you will catch up on all of the exercise you have been putting off. That will cancel the pre-deadline calories. The same goes for any calories consumed in celebrations of completions.

7. Food eaten in late-night conferences organized to fight off takeover attempts must not count because the other side must also be stoking up on Pepsis and Frito-Lay Corn Chips, too, and you never see a fat investment banker.

8. When you are upgraded to first-class status from a tourist ticket, the free drinks, peanuts, and filet mignon cannot be counted against your self-discipline. If these foods were harmful to you, God would not have created frequent-flyer programs.

9. It is rumored that the digestion of chocolate creates exactly the same chemical changes in your body as the act of falling in love; therefore, in a world desperately yearning for an increase in warmth and affection among all peoples, eating chocolate is almost an international obligation.

Following this diet has nothing to do with weight reduction but rather with maintaining one's sanity in a world gone increasingly ballistic. If you cannot control your stress, why worry about the obsolescence of a perfectly good wardrobe sized to fit you during your college days? Thinness is a reasonable obsession only for those people who also want too much money.

A final note: There is a point of view that argues that the world is governed by The Law of Constant Fat, which says that, like all other matter, the amount of fat in the universe is constant. This means that if you lose ten pounds, someone somewhere else has to pick them up. Under this theory, losing weight is an act of social aggression.

So, another column finished, another deadline met . . . please pass the Oreos because tomorrow I really *am* going to exercise.

A Collection of Old Watches: "Time Flies, Never to Return"

I collect old wristwatches. Although my taste runs to solid gold, classic LeCoultre watches, my budget runs leaner. In poking through flea markets, pawn shops, bankrupt jewelry stores, and antique galleries, I have acquired an array of Mickey Mouse, Batman and Robin, Cinderella, Alice in Wonderland, Pinocchio, and Charley the Tuna watches, mostly in good working order.

I have also developed an interest in the so-called presentation watches given for some particular occasion or purpose—perhaps service to an organization, the proverbial "gold watch for retirement." Among my most beautiful watches, for example, is a solid gold Howard with the following engraving in spectacular penmanship:

> Presented to W. Bro.
> Stewart Houck Michales
> Master 1916
> Brethren of Bethel
> No. 733 F.S.A.M., N.Y.
> March 17, 1917
> *"Time flies never to return."*

This watch, in mint condition and still in its original box, raises many questions. Whatever happened to Brother Michales? How did this watch ever get out of his hands and into the vintage watch market? Am I dealing with hot merchandise? It had apparently been sitting in some safety deposit box for seventy years, as it now sits in mine. Is this the normal destiny of a beautiful old watch?

In discussing this phenomenon with many people, I have found that a surprising number have an old gold watch with some family history, usually in a safety deposit box. Does squirreling away the gift serve the recognition and motivational ends intended by the givers?

I mentioned this topic over dinner recently with Dick Shepard, President and CEO of Linclay Corporation, a real estate management and development company with headquarters in St. Louis. His eyes lit up. "Let me tell you what we are doing to recognize long-term service among our employees!" he said. He told me such an interesting story that I stopped on a recent trip through St. Louis and spent a half-day talking to recipients of the Linclay Ten-year Awards. Dick and others, especially his assistant Donna Rushing, who oversees the program, gave me some history.

"We are just twenty-five years old, with about two hundred and forty employees," said Dick, "and we pride ourselves in treating them not only well but creatively. And it shows. We have a relatively low turnover in a business—real estate—not known for employee stability."

The idea for an idiosyncratic award was spawned during a series of discussions in Linclay about how to find something memorable to present to people with ten years of service. After going through the usual list of clocks, plaques, and various other ceremonial awards, the company came up with the following policy, unmatched as far as I am aware in corporate creativity. Sometime before the employee's tenth anniversary, a committee of people who know the employee well is given $2,000 and a charge to find a gift especially meaningful.

The results are astonishing. Here, for example, are some recent awards and the reactions of the affected employees:

David Schneider (Tenant Finish Coordinator) was given a hand-crafted Winchester Classic double-barrelled shotgun with stock, comb, and trigger pull adjusted specifically for him. David, a pleasant, thoughtful family man (one son, five daughters) was quietly fluent in telling me about it. "I'm basically a Missouri kid, grew up here, always liked to hunt and fish. My family still has a large farm nearby where I love to roam. I've been hunting there since I was seven or eight, and have been interested in guns ever since. A year or so ago, my family said, 'Dad, you're really hard to shop for. What do you really want for Christmas?' I joked, 'A Winchester Model 21 double-barrelled shotgun.' I knew I would never get one of those. They cost about $15,000. But that comment made its way back to Linclay, and I got the next best thing, a Winchester Classic, specifically designed for me. You have to know about guns to know how wonderful this feels to me."

Millie Eversole (VP, Marketing) was given a complete set of Waterford crystal. Her reaction was: "I just couldn't believe it—not in my wildest dreams would I have predicted this. I had a couple of brandy snifters and a pitcher, and people knew I loved them, but now I have eight snifters, eight water glasses, eight red wine glasses, eight white wine glasses, a decanter, and on and on. We just moved into a nice, new house, and I am going to have to spend another couple of thousand for a case!"

Larry Sanders (VP, General Counsel) received a portion of a limited partnership in a racehorse. Larry said, "I've been interested in racehorses for a long, long time. I spend a lot of time at the track, and I guess people picked up on that. What I actually got was a certificate for $2,000 to apply against a share in a syndicated horse. I haven't bought my share yet (and I get a lot of teasing about which part of the horse I'm actually going to own) because I have been doing research about what is available." He went on, "Actually, my family is so much into this that my son is entering the University of Louisville this year, and he intends to major in their Equine Management program. His eventual aspiration is to manage a racetrack."

He continued, "The really exciting thing about this award program is that it shows that the company is willing to take the time and trouble to treat each employee as a unique individual. This is much more meaningful than a plaque or some other conventional award."

Herb Prince (VP) got the opportunity to play in a major bridge tournament as the partner of Mike Lawrence, a world championship bridge player. Herb said, "I've been a Life Master since 1972, but I have never had the opportunity to play with a partner of this caliber, and I'll probably play bridge another thirty years and it will never happen again either."

I asked, "Are you nervous?" (The tournament was coming up soon.) "No, not really," he laughed. "I take my mind off of it by mentally preparing my victory speech." He went on more seriously, "You know, it means an awful lot to know that the people you work for care enough about you personally to go to the trouble to make something this spectacular happen in your life."

Jan Poling (Administrative Assistant) was given a complete home entertainment center. Jan was the most emotional in describing her feelings, even a little teary. "I was the first of the office support staff to be here ten years, and on my anniversary day they had a little party for me, and I got a bunch of gag gifts and insults, the kind that good friends give you, and I felt really good that someone had remembered. I didn't get the big gift then because (I found out later) Dick was out of town and wanted to make the presentation personally. I didn't expect it because of my status. I mean, I know Larry, my boss, and those other executives got this award, but they make all those decisions (big deals and saving money for the company and all that); I didn't expect it for a support person. I had really wanted a VHF and a CD player and the works, but I could never have gotten them for myself. Believe me, Linclay is a wonderful place to work. They really care about you."

As Mike Lee, Director of Human Resources, pointed out, "What the employees like about this is the individual creativity in each case. The cost is relatively modest spread over ten years (it costs about eighty cents per working day for each ten-year employee), and the motivational return is terrific. Just the visibility is probably worth it. Each of these people tells everyone they know about his or her award!"

Which takes me back to my watch collection. Perhaps my favorite is a gold wristwatch so modest in design it is almost trivial, with the following poignant inscription:

In Memory of Mother
H.P.Q.
21st Birthday, 1936

Again, the questions: Who was H.P.Q.? Who had the watch inscribed, and for whom? A daughter, a son, a husband, a parent? There in the depths of the Great Depression, what was the financial story behind the gift? And how did the watch fifty years later make its way into a pawn shop in Denver?

One conclusion seems certain: If H.P.Q. was able to scrape together the wherewithal to honor "Mother" in the lean times of the thirties, more organizations ought to be able to find that extra eighty cents per day and creative ways to recognize loyalty today.

Who Gets the New Truck?

So you want to be in charge, you want to make decisions, you want to be a leader, right? The question is, do you have to be born a leader or can you be trained? Many of us believe the latter, and, further, we believe that some of the findings of psychological research can help. Here, for example, is a training case paraphrased from one professor's research.

You are in charge of a small group of repair people. Each of them has his or her own truck and territory. They spend most of their time in the field, responding to customer requests. Within normal limits, they are all experienced, loyal, and motivated to do good work. Because of the nature of their work—skilled technicians who plan their own days and spend little time in the office—they are also independent. Their work is intricate, unpredictable, and geographically dispersed; therefore, they are difficult to manage in the usual sense. You must trust them to be productive without much direct guidance. In short, they have to be led, not managed.

Yesterday, corporate headquarters informed you that your team has been allocated a new truck. As you came to work this morning, you saw it in the parking lot, gleaming white, more spacious than your older trucks, with the company logo shining in the sun.

Now you have a problem: Who is going to get the new truck?

You have five drivers: Smith, Jones, Brown, Davis, and Murphy.

Smith is your classic "company man." He has been with the company eighteen years and is steady and dependable. He believes in giving "a fair day's work for a day's pay" and always adheres to the company line. A few weeks ago he did express a wish for a better truck, one with more space and a smoother transmission. As the most senior of your drivers, he probably will expect to get the new one.

Jones is young and assertive. In some circles he would be called "an agitator." He is capable, highly trained in the new technology of your company, and prone to question your judgment. On a few occasions he has not-so-subtly reminded you that his skills are portable and that he can easily find comparable employment elsewhere. Because he is young and energetic, he has been assigned the longest, most isolated route. As a result, his truck has high mileage and has taken a beating. Because of his intellect and intensive training, your customers value him. He is clearly the best you have in diagnosing and correcting complicated problems. In fact, the other drivers often consult with Jones about their toughest dilemmas. He enjoys this role and likes to feel important.

Brown is another solid citizen. He is quiet, unassuming, a good team player. He did call your attention a few days ago to a problem with his truck door. Someone apparently backed into it, and it won't close properly. Winter is coming, and he gently complained about the draft created by the ill-fitting door. Otherwise, his truck is among the newer models.

Davis is a modern phenomenon, an older woman driving a repair truck. Although she is the most junior of your crew, she has more than twenty years service. She worked in a clerical position for years and was respected in the office because of her natural affinity for machines. She could always fix jammed copiers or help untangle the mysteries of new machines with complicated manuals. After some persistent politicking on her part, the company, in what was clearly an EEOC-motivated action, transferred her to the repair crew, where she has been happy and highly regarded, even though she has had to endure a certain amount of heavy-duty hazing as a result of being both the new kid on the block and a woman. She has the oldest truck. You don't quite know how that happened—the trucks were in place when you came in—but because she has been assigned the easiest, shortest route, her truck has the lowest mileage, and because she is so proud of it she has kept it in immaculate shape. She is aware that the company has not had a sterling record when it comes to treatment of women in nontraditional jobs and that the CEO has publicly stated that that must change.

Murphy is a character. He is a large, expansive fellow, and everyone who meets him is immediately his friend. Although you don't like to deal in ethnic stereotypes, Murphy is undeniably Irish and never lets anyone forget it, especially with his rich store of Pat and Mike jokes. ("How do you confuse an Irishman? Stand two shovels up against the wall and tell him to take his pick!") He is your most popular driver, both with customers and the other drivers, and on a couple of occasions he has stepped in and smoothed out hurt feelings of one kind or another. He seems to have a natural sense of tact, particularly in understanding other people's feelings. His problem is that he doesn't much care for truck maintenance, and his truck usually looks grungy. Furthermore, you have reason to believe that Brown's truck door is caved in because Murphy backed into it, but because Murphy is so popular, no one will admit to that. You have the sense

Murphy doesn't really care which truck he drives, as long as everyone is happy.

Your name is Rodriguez. You recently joined the company after finishing an MBA at a prominent Ivy League business school where you were a visible member of a demographic minority. Although your academic record has been superb, you never have managed anything, and this assignment is clearly designed to acquaint you with the nuts-and-bolts of the company, while at the same time giving you some managerial experience. You are also aware through the grapevine that the allocation of a new truck has frequently created problems for team leaders. Too often, the drivers who don't get the new truck create subtle sabotage.

Such episodes have occupied the research efforts of Professor Victor Vroom from Yale University for more than twenty years, and, with Professor Arthur Jago of the University of Houston, he recently published his second major book on this type of managerial dilemma (*The New Leadership: Managing Participation in Organizations,* Prentice-Hall, 1988).

In studying such situations, Vroom has described five different approaches that you, as the person in charge, could use to arrive at a decision, ranging from the most autocratic to the most democratic. They are:

1. The leader decides alone. Working with information you already have, or can easily look up in various files, you decide alone, in private, how to handle the new-truck assignment.

2. The leader seeks information, then decides alone. You might call Brown and ask him how hard it would be to fix his door, and then use that information to arrive at a decision.

3. The leader privately seeks information, opinions, and suggestions and then decides alone. You might call Davis in, explain the situation to her, and ask her if she would be happy with Smith's truck, if he were given the new one. If not, you might ask her what else she would suggest.

4. The leader calls the entire group together, outlines the situation, asks for suggestions, listens to the discussion, and then decides alone. This is a substantial change from the earlier styles because it means that the drivers can hear each other's concerns and can also offer compromise solutions. As long as you make it clear that you are going to make the final decision, however, their persuasive efforts will be directed at you. In

particular, they will probably put the worst possible face on their own trucks so that they will be more likely to get the new one.

5. The same as number 4, but the leader makes it clear that the group is going to decide together. "We have an opportunity here, and let's all decide together how to allocate the new truck. I will agree to any solution that the entire group is happy with": participative management at its best. In this situation, the drivers will quickly perceive it is in their best interest to praise their own trucks so that someone else will agree to take it and they can get the new one.

Vroom argues that the decision style chosen should be based on the following considerations:

Quality. Some decisions may be better than others in a technical sense—that is, there is a "right" answer. With one caveat, that is not true in this case. You don't really care who drives which truck, as long as the drivers are happy. The one caveat is that the decision must result in the discarding of the worst truck, which may be a fact that you do not know. Unless you are intimately familiar with all the trucks, if you make this decision using the style in number 1, you risk making a poor-quality decision.

Acceptance. Even if you make a "correct" decision, it may not be accepted by the drivers, and several of them are in positions to thwart any action that they do not approve of. Listening to their suggestions or, better yet, letting them help develop the eventual solution increases the probability of their acceptance and enthusiastic implementation.

Conservation of time. Participatory decision-making generally takes more time than autocratic decisions, and because time is valuable, you should make decisions autocratically when possible. If you have all the facts and are certain that your decision will be accepted, or at least not opposed, you should make the decision unilaterally. Group decisions should not be routinely adopted but used only when the circumstances dictate them.

Development of subordinates. Other things being equal, the opportunity to participate in important decisions is a developmental plus. It usually gives subordinates a clearer picture of the overall situation and allows them to grapple with some of the dilemmas faced by their superiors, which will stand them in good stead when they are themselves promoted into policy-making positions.

Vroom and Jago present sensible rules for analyzing each situation where a decision affecting subordinates is involved and then choosing one of the five styles in a manner to optimize the four criteria. As with anything learned "by the numbers," the individual has to learn the basic sequence first and then practice, practice, practice, until it comes smoothly and naturally. My own observation is that most "born leaders" have spent years instinctively practicing the kind of systematic approach advocated by Vroom and others in leadership training programs. In this sense, having the rules clearly laid out speeds up the experiential process and allows us to create leaders faster than is possible through natural selection.

Incidentally, in the above new-truck dilemma, the best leaders often stress the "good news" aspect: "Hey, gang, the front office sprang for a new truck!" The mediocre ones use a heavy, leaden presentation: "We got the same problem we had last year—one new truck—four of you are going to be disappointed."

I sometimes think that, at the most primitive level, leadership training programs should at least teach optimism and confidence. In the swarm of ambiguous forces that most leaders have to deal with, having some well-established rules available may well lead to success simply because the person has some confidence in a contemplated action. Leaders can be made, or at least developed from good stock, by teaching them the analytic techniques developed by good research. Vroom and Jago's book is a good addition to the leadership training literature and will surely spawn even more research on their practical, applied approach.

My Life with Industrial/Organizational Psychologists

"The average CEO could care less about management development. They may give it lip service in public forums, but when push comes to shove, when it's time for them to commit corporate funds or, heaven forbid, their own time, they find a lot of other immediate issues that are more important."

That comment, from one of the country's leading industrial/organizational psychologists, came during a recent meeting at a pleasant seaside conference center. The attendees, who collectively represented a vast array of organizational and professional experience, nodded in agreement. Several added confirming comments.

This august group of psychologists, mostly in their mid-forties and fifties, has been meeting once a year for more than twenty years, both for professional stimulation and personal socializing. (The entire group contains about twenty-five members, though for any given meeting, only about forty percent solve the time and budget constraints, or are attracted to the location.) In *Future Shock* (1970), Alvin Toffler predicted that new social groupings would emerge to combat contemporary rootlessness, and this group is one example of that phenomenon. Many professionals in mobile America now have closer friends among their professional colleagues living hundreds of miles away than they do among the people living down the block.

This particular group, though historically durable, has been administratively casual. There are no rules, no bylaws, no dues or budget, no officers, and only the vaguest of policies. The membership is roughly half corporate, half academic.

An agenda is produced for each meeting, partially because the group is sensitive to wasted effort, partially to justify the value of the meeting to those who approve travel budgets. The topic this year was "High Level Executive Development." Since many of them have explicit responsibilities for corporate training programs, and others serve as faculty members at leading business schools, there was a high level of experience present.

The conversation was free-flowing and wide-ranging. To capture the flavor of what such specialists in executive development are doing and thinking these days, here are some selected, edited quotes from the meeting:

"What constitutes a 'top executive'? In the food-service industry, for every 100,000 workers there are roughly 280 group managers, generally at the vice-president level. Approximately 70 above them are covered by an executive compensation bonus plan, which is one practical definition of a 'top executive.' In one of the steel companies, there are 30,000 employees, including 300 Hi-po's [High potentials], another 125 high-level managers who are included in the company's succession planning, and about 25 top execs, again defined as someone covered by the executive bonus plan. Given these statistics, we seem to be talking about roughly one-tenth of one percent of the workforce."

"What's happening with Hi-po's these days?" "Companies differ widely but one constant seems to be that almost every corporation is about to begin a new succession-planning process. It's hard to keep a plan in place, partially because one thing that we have learned is that identifying Hi-po's also creates Po-po's." "What's a Po-po?" "Passed over and pissed off."

"Let me tell you one thing I learned from being on the inside of an LBO (leveraged buyout). In the chaos, all of the top-level training courses were killed off. A related major casualty was the morale of the younger managers. They didn't get rich, and they no longer saw any way to the top. Corporations need to keep executive development programs alive, if for no other reason than to keep hope flourishing in the trenches. As it is, you still see many middle managers whose only apparent goal is to reach senility with dignity."

"Succession planning for the CEO in our corporation is determined by LS's." "LS's?" "Yeah, Lucky Sperms." (Everyone knew that this corporation, a Midwestern service firm, was a paternalistic, family dominated business.)

"'The secondhandedness of the learned world is the secret of its mediocrity'—Alfred North Whitehead. Whitehead's concept is alive and well in the business schools. The faculty there know nothing about executive development; they just teach what they want to teach. The good executive development programs are going on outside of the universities."

"Anyone who manages to a cost-effectiveness criterion will do all the wrong things."

"Our study [on the effectiveness of executive development programs] produced some strange statistics. But as you all know, there is no set of data so random that you can't explain the relationships. The most important outcome seemed to be an increased sense of self-confidence, which translates into both a broader perspective about what might be done and a willingness to put one's neck on the line to make it happen."

"Twenty-five years ago, I started with this company, just doing highly analytic test-validation studies. Now I'm writing a global human-resources strategy because our CEO thinks that's where the competitive edge is. I have had to work hard to change my own mentality from a narrow, analytic focus to a broad, systems approach."

"I'm starting to work on a study of people in jobs where a small mistake can have catastrophic consequences, like pilots or nuclear-power operators. It is easy to demonstrate that pilots, at least in small planes, don't use checklists. We have deliberately disabled systems that the pilots are supposed to check before take-off, and they often don't." In such informal settings, comments like these invariably produce black humor and dubious anecdotes: "Did you hear about the pilot who left the mike on . . . ?"

"I have stopped doing market-research surveys, and now use video-taped focus groups almost exclusively." "Why?" "They are much easier to sell to top management. I'd do some great survey, with sampling precision and elegant statistics, take the results into the marketing VP, and get the response, 'I can't buy those numbers.' 'Why not?' ' 'Cause I was talking to my hairstylist and a couple of other customers last week and that's not the way they see it.' So now I get the stylist into our observation room along with some other people off the street and everyone believes that what they say is pure science."

The group meandered its way to the end of the agenda. In the closing hour, it argued about whether the next meeting should be on the beach or in the mountains, assigned the responsibility for organizing it to someone who wasn't in attendance, agreed that to be in human resources these days is to be relevant, compared notes about competing job offers, exchanged the latest lawyer jokes, and flew home.

How Can I Stay Out of Their Way Today?

For several years I have been trying to figure out how to measure the psychological impact that "leaders" have on organizations. Because of the nature of my job, I spend a lot of time hanging around various kinds of organizations—corporations, universities, government agencies, military units, family businesses, schools, hospitals, and the like. In some there is a feeling of vibrancy, of forward motion, of innovation and excitement. In others the atmosphere feels heavy, leaden, and oppressive. Morale is low; suspicion is high. There is a furtive sense that everyone is continually updating their résumés.

What are the relevant dynamics? What are the forces creating these different climates?

Sometimes the answer is obvious. In a dying industry, or in a company where market share is plunging, no further explanation is necessary. Economic gloom creates its own audible death rattle. Conversely, if the company has a hot product, or if inflation is papering over all sorts of silly mistakes, it doesn't take much brilliance to understand the crest of the wave.

In most organizations, however, the forces are not so apparent. Often they seem tied to the perceived quality of top leadership. Optimism, and a collective sense of direction and self-confidence, seem to emanate from the top—but how? What do the good leaders do to create such an environment?

Poignant quotations about how to lead abound: "Most men ask, 'Why?' Leaders ask, 'Why not?'" "Leadership begins with the ability to inflict pain." "Of the best leaders, when their work is done, the people will say, 'We did this ourselves.'"

One military leader told me, "As a young officer, I was taught that leadership consists of telling people what to do, then punishing them if they don't do it."

In my quest to better understand the impact of leaders on organizations, I have collected forty-four statements that reflect an employee's feelings about his or her working environment. These statements are particularly oriented toward leadership and creativity. Some examples are:

New ideas are welcomed and nurtured here.

I am proud of the people who hold the top leadership positions here.

Along with these, there are several others that tap the individual's feelings about other aspects of work, such as:

I enjoy my work.

I am satisfied with my pay.

(In the actual survey, for procedural balance, some of these items are stated in the reverse, "I am NOT satisfied...," but for this column I am stating them all in the positive form.)

These statements have been gathered together into a questionnaire, the Campbell Organizational Survey, and a scoring algorithm has been developed to assess the major themes. Such a technique permits an analytic, quantitative approach to testing out some of these emotional, will-o'-the-wisp opinions.

Over two thousand people have responded to this survey, in clusters of roughly fifteen to fifty each. They have ranged from the CEO and his direct reports at a major publishing house, to military academy cadets; from R&D directors in a chemical lab, to first-line managers in an electronics firm.

In looking over the summary data, three themes caught my eye. They were the highest non-obvious correlates with "Innovation" and "Top Leadership." By non-obvious, I mean statements other than the obvious, such as "I am proud of top leadership." The non-obvious statements that correlated highest with "Creative Leadership" statements concerned planning, feedback, and individual control.

Examples of the first were: "A visible, clearly stated planning process is used to guide our future actions," and "New projects here are usually well planned." The second cluster of non-obvious statements included items such as: "Our organization does a good job of keeping us informed about current developments," and "Feedback on performance for people at my level is timely, accurate, and constructive." The third cluster included statements such as: "On decisions affecting me, my opinion is listened to here," and "I have a lot of freedom to decide how to do my work."

A quick and dirty summary seems to be that in order for people to feel creative and well led, they want the following: "Tell me where we are going, figure out some way to let me know when we get there, and then stand out of my light."

Some factors that do not seem to be particularly important for innovation and pride in top management include pay, fringe benefits, working conditions, job security, and satisfaction with co-workers. All of these are indeed correlated with overall job satisfaction. And they are probably related to other outcomes, such as turnover and productivity. But they are not directly connected with innovation and pride in leadership.

Summarizing these trends, the implication for people at the top is that in organizations where people feel both innovative and proud of their leaders, the following three features characterize the environment:

Planning—a purposeful sense of direction.

Feedback—appraisal and communication systems that tell people how they are doing.

Elbow room—a feeling of control over one's own work space, both physical and psychological.

No particular surprises here. But I wonder how many leaders sit down every morning and think about achieving these ends for their followers, especially the last one. Perhaps the atmosphere would improve in those organizations where morale is low if more leaders thought, over breakfast, "How can I stay out of their way today?"

Money Can't Buy Happiness,
But It Helps If You Look for It in Interesting Places

Every now and then a travel experience comes along that is so wonderful, so memorable that I am convinced heaven is out there, waiting, just at the far edge of an American Express credit card. I spent a month this summer wandering around Europe, working a day or two every now and then, but mostly just hanging out, knocking on the doors of old friends. It was a delicious experience. I wonder why I don't do something like this more often.

My reactions fall into three categories: First, as a tourist. Second, as a returning resident—I had lived there almost twenty years ago, and it was fun to revisit the old haunts and find that the food is still good, the scenery is still spectacular, ice cubes are more prevalent, the bathrooms are much improved, but the traffic is daunting and prices are sky high. And third, as a professional interested in what is going to happen in the European Community in 1992.

To the last point first: Twelve of the major European countries, with a combined population of three hundred twenty million, have begun the process of removing trade and travel barriers. The exact changeover date is, I believe, January 1, 1993. I found it difficult, as a casual traveler, to get good information on just what is going to happen when. Every European executive I talked with was uncertain about the changes. The goal is to permit unimpeded access for "goods, personnel, and services." But exactly what that means is still being debated. During a press interview, a veterinarian who is stationed at one of the borders asked, "Are animals going to be considered as goods or personnel? What will happen to my job?"

The simplifications will only be relative. Many of the European complexities will still exist. They will still have multiple languages, although English will be the common choice. They will still have multiple currencies. They will still have different postal systems so that the cards you wrote in London, but forgot to mail, will have to be re-stamped in Paris. They will still have different electrical outlets, complicating life for the hair dryer or personal computer. They will still have different phone systems; to call home on your credit card, you will need a different access code for each country. And the English will continue to drive on the left-hand side of the road.

Because they are often based on comments from loquacious taxi drivers, or whomever you joined at dinner, sociological conclusions from travelers are suspect. But I did detect some country trends in the anticipation of "1992." The English, in their aloof and reserved style, seem fairly optimistic, more so than one would think from reading Margaret Thatcher's statements. The Dutch and the Germans seem eager. The Swiss, who are not among the twelve countries in the EC and are retaining both their national sovereignty and their personal distance, don't seem to think that anything much would change.

The most interesting reaction came from an enthusiastic Frenchman in a small village in southern France. As he finished sipping his coffee, his eyes gleamed and his hands waved. "It is going to be terrific," he said, his English tumbling forth. "Europe in 1993 will become the world's dominant economic and social force. That is because we will build on synergy. We will take the best each country has, and the combination will be fantastic."

He rushed on, "The Dutch and the English and the Germans will teach us—that is, those of us in Southern Europe—about business and efficiency and the bottom line, and we—the French and the Italians and the Spaniards—will teach them about life and love and how to live." When he finished, we all toasted that potential outcome.

Some features may remain stable and universal. In the same café, I was seated for dinner with three interesting people: a Spanish administrator, a French sculptor, and an American Air Force officer. They were all women, all successful in their careers. At one point I asked, "How has life changed for professional women in Europe?" After a brief but poignant pause, the Spaniard said, "On the surface, many things are different. Underneath, nothing has changed." They all nodded in unison. In Europe, as in America, the glass ceiling persists.

I suggested that the elimination of immigration restrictions, both for studying and working, might lead to the same professional mobility we have in the U.S., with its attendant disruption of the extended family. I told them I hardly know anyone who lives in the same city as their parents or their grown children. But I don't think any of my European acquaintances understood the implications of this change.

By the year 2000, I predict family life for European professionals will be well on its way to becoming as geographically fragmented as it is for most educated people in North America today.

A second, lighter sociological trend that caught my attention was the ubiquitous T-shirt. One cannot wander around Europe in the summer without noting that it has become the universal symbol of individuality. A couple of quick tallies, from the vantage point of sidewalk cafés, suggests that T-shirts can be classified as follows:

Scenic, displaying a beautiful landscape, logo, or other artistic creation: about twenty percent.

Geographic, advertising Maui, Dayton, Camp Miniwanca or other exotic sites: about thirty percent.

Public statements, propounding viewpoints such as "I © my attitude problem": about fifty percent.

The most commonly seen T-shirt, outstripping anything remotely in second place by at least twenty to one, was the Hard Rock Café logo. The only other repetitious pattern was some variation of, "My Mom Went to the Oregon State Women's Correctional Institution and All I Got Was This Lousy T-Shirt."

The majority of the European T-shirts were in English, probably because European youth view them as supremely cool. Many times, however, I was certain that the wearers didn't really understand the messages behind their displayed statements. For example, the Scandinavian girl wearing "If God Is Not A Tar Heel, Why Is The Sky Carolina Blue?" probably couldn't tell the difference between Dean Smith and Mahatma Gandhi. The swarthy, muscular Mediterranean type wearing "The Body That Plays Hard Stays Hard" probably did not completely understand the subtlety of that sentiment.

Curiously, I did not see a single auto bumper sticker in Europe.

For the tourist, the delights of Europe are still frequent and powerful. The trains are clean, convenient, on time, and they speed to an awesome array of scintillating experiences: watching Shakespeare performed at Stratford-on-Avon; eating dinner by candlelight on a canal boat tour of Amsterdam; swaying back and forth, arms linked with Korean executives, to oompah music in a Bavarian beer hall; feigning bored indifference in the subdued elegance of the after-hours casinos in Salzberg or Nice; feigning a different, voyeuristic indifference while sunning on the topless beaches of the Riviera; gaping open-mouthed at the beauties of Rome and the riches of the Vatican; haggling with the craftspeople of Florence over their beautiful leather garments. (My bargaining skills were obvious when I said firmly, "I will not pay more than one hundred U.S. dollars for this vest." The sales clerk replied wearily, "Mister, it is already marked down to ninety.") And, finally, at the end, the long, satiated plane ride home to the first glass of really cold, low-fat milk in weeks.

It takes only a few days back home for the in-basket stress to drum out most of the immediate memories. But even now I can lean back in my chair and see the countryside rushing by the train windows—the streams, the fields of flowers, and the mountain villages. There is a lot of beauty out there, if we take the time to go looking.

"ABC—Always Buy Colorado," and Other Nonsense

In Colorado, where I live now, the governor has been pushing a local purchasing program: "ABC—Always Buy Colorado," and this admonition to support our local merchants takes me back to my Midwestern childhood. I spent the first sixteen years of my life in Bridgewater, Iowa (population 197), where my parents ran the general store. We sold groceries, meat, clothes, cattle feed, and assorted other rural supplies. In that restricted market we constituted a substantial share of the local economy, and my father was very aware of that. I can still remember his displeasure whenever he saw a local farmer walking up the street in a new pair of OshKosh B'Gosh overalls that he had not purchased from us. "These folks who drive over to Greenfield [the county seat, thirteen miles away] to do their shopping don't understand what they are doing to our business. They want us here for the penny-ante stuff, but they spend their big money over there [Greenfield] or in the city [Des Moines]."

He would rather see people shopping down the street at the rival store (where the non-Methodists generally went) than have the money leave town. And whenever our family spent money, he made it clear that we should spend it locally. I remember once when I was thirteen or fourteen years old buying a toiletry set in Des Moines for my mother's birthday; it had perfume and face powder and various creams in beautiful little crafted blue bottles embedded in a brushed velvet-type cardboard box, and there was certainly nothing like that in Bridgewater. Yet when I walked out of the store carrying it, I felt like a smuggler with illegal contraband, and I dreaded running into my father before I had it safely hidden at home. (I cannot remember, at this distant date, how I expected him to ignore the source after I had given it to her.)

Bridgewater was founded in the 1880s, largely as a result of a spur of the railroad coming up thirty miles from Creston, which was on the main line from Chicago to Denver. My grandfather was the depot agent, and we were doubly aware of the local economy because he personally presided over every single article of freight coming into or leaving town by rail.

Distances between population centers in those days were based on the "day's buggy ride" principle; that is, you harnessed up the team, left the farm in the morning with your produce, drove to town, sold your milk and eggs, replenished your supplies, and drove home before nightfall. Consequently, many small towns grew up in Iowa roughly eight to ten miles apart. As automobiles proliferated and main roads were paved, these towns began dying in the 1930s, but nobody noticed the early death rattles because of the Depression. World War II brought a brief respite with its gasoline rationing and diversion of automobile manufacturers to jeeps, tanks, planes, and military trucks, but this lull simply heightened the speed of change in the late 1940s when business after business went under in the farm belt. In Bridgewater the blacksmith shop went first, followed by the lumberyard, the stockyards, and the farm implement store. In the 1950s the high school left town to be consolidated with the neighboring town, and the CB&Q depot closed, thus ending the once-a-day train service and throwing my grandfather out of work. In retrospect the handwriting on the wall was always clear, but most of the locals ignored it and fought to survive. At every step, the conventional wisdom was "Buy Locally."

My parents closed down their store in 1950, selling the big brick building, all fixtures, and the remaining stock for $2,500, and moved to Greenfield to open a supermarket. (The old cash register, huge coffee grinder, round metal thread cabinet, and big hardwood-and-glass candy display case would probably bring $10,000 on today's antique market.)

The new store flourished and my parents reached a financial level that they had never known before. The store was uptown on the square, an active trading area, and business was good. When I was home a few years later on a visit from college, my father, never very talkative or enthusiastic, said to me, "David, this store is a gold mine—some weeks we take in $10,000!" At the margins they were working on, probably two or three percent, my parents were clearing $200 to $300 per week, maybe $15,000 per year. In the late 1950s and early 1960s, in a small county seat town in Iowa (Greenfield's population was 2,200), life seemed luxurious. A new round of death rattles had begun, but the incipient clattering was muted by the new rush of national prosperity.

My father passed away in 1956, and my mother sold the business but, as a landlord, retained the store building, prominently located on the town square. (In 1969 Dick Van Dyke and a movie company, looking for the prototypical small town, selected Greenfield as the site for filming their movie *Cold Turkey,* a happy spoof on religion and smoking in small-town America. In their publicity releases they reported they had scouted over seven hundred Midwestern towns to find the most classic small-town architecture in America, which turned out to be the square in Greenfield.)

During the next thirty years, until 1986, the rent from the store building provided my mother with a livable income. Indeed, after my youngest sister graduated from college my mother began to travel and see the world, journeying to exotic places such as Ireland, Spain, Turkey, and Peru, usually with a group of Iowa Methodists, led by an off-duty minister, visiting foreign Methodist missions.

Yet, as a product of the Great Depression, she worried constantly about her money and her future financial security. I had to continually reassure her, "Mother, you have your investments, your Social Security, and the rent from the store—that's a guaranteed lifetime income."

On one trip home, while going over her figures, I estimated, working from her real estate tax statement, that the store building alone was worth at least $80,000. "Look," I told her, "with your lifestyle, with your house paid for, you could easily live on the $10,000 per year rent alone if you had to."

She was not convinced. "David, the new SuperValue store out on the highway east of town keeps expanding and my tenant doesn't go to church. He doesn't understand that if you want to sell groceries to Methodists, you have to go to church with them."

I tried to reassure her that her building on the square was one of the prime commercial locations in town, but she was still uneasy. "Folks can park easily at the SuperValue, and his meat and produce counters look real good, and not only does the SuperValue owner go to church, he sings in the choir."

My mother's premonitions proved to be more accurate than my reassurances, for her tenant went belly-up in 1986, held a "FINAL CLOSING SALE," closed his doors, and left town.

The building stood empty for two years while we alternately tried to rent or sell it. Finally, in the face of relentless tax, insurance, and utility bills, she deeded it over to the town for a community center with the understanding that "an appropriate plaque be displayed designating it as the Campbell Community Center." Perhaps we should have added the line, "SUPPORT YOUR LOCAL MERCHANTS."

Much of this history riffs through my mind each time I hear the governor's "Always Buy Colorado" urging. Is this, I wonder, a new set of death rattles?

I am conscious of, and amused by, the continuing impact that this early conditioning has had on me. I am constantly aware of the local economy and, other things being equal, I do try to spend my money locally. Still, though I try, it is not always clear what "local" is. I spend as much of my time in the Denver airport as in any other single business location. Does that make it "my neighborhood"? If I spend $20 on a book in the airport, will that expenditure improve my life more or less than $20 spent in a "local" chain bookstore, where the profits might flow to London or Tokyo? Perhaps in this time of international expansion, it may be sufficient for the "Buy Locally" cause simply to keep one's purchases within the United States. (In this regard, I am glad that my father is not around to see that I drive a foreign automobile. He certainly would not approve of that.)

One thing is certain: If the economy of Bridgewater, surrounded and supported by some of the richest farmland in the world, can be demolished in my grandparents' generation, and if the economy of Greenfield, supported by the same farmland *and* by a local county government, can be demolished in my parents' generation, maybe not even the Denver airport, currently the sixth busiest in the world, is safe for me. Given the increasing rate of change, my grandchildren may be urging "BUY LOCALLY— SUPPORT YOUR LOCAL GALAXY."

LDP: History's Most Influential Psychological Training Program

The occasion of the Center's twentieth anniversary started me thinking about the Leadership Development Program. LDP is undoubtedly our most important achievement thus far. More than that, it has become the most influential, most impactful training program in the history of psychology.

That is a pretty flamboyant statement, and after I wrote it I leaned back in my chair, read the sentence again, and thought, "Whoa, can that really be true?"

The statistics are persuasive. First offered in the spring of 1974, LDP will be offered one-hundred-and-fifty-one times in 1990 in eleven locations in four countries—Australia, England, Mexico, and the United States. With approximately twenty participants in each course, that means that roughly three thousand people will have this experience and, with a tuition of $3,500, LDP will generate a cash flow of nearly $10,000,000, all in one year. I know of no other program in psychology that comes anywhere near to equaling these numbers.

In addition to these direct activities, the LDP experience has been taken in-house under licensing arrangements with corporations, government agencies, and, in one of the more imaginative applications, the Blandin Foundation in Grand Rapids, Minnesota (which I will have more to say about below).

The participants who go through the LDP course are the kind of people who make a difference. They are, on average, about forty-two years old, mostly college-educated, mostly in positions where they directly influence the lives of other people. Whether they should be called leaders, managers, executives, commanders, coordinators, facilitators, empowerers, or administrators is a conversation I don't enjoy very much anymore—the basic point is that most of them are in positions where they control resources, set goals, direct the work of others, monitor results, and acknowledge accomplishments. As a society, we are remarkably lucky to have so many people so engaged in trying to improve their performance in these activities.

Unlike some events in history, the birth of this program can be precisely pinpointed: February 14, 1974. I took over the Center's programs on February 1, 1974, leaving the University of Minnesota where I had been a professor of psychology. As a brand-new institution, the Center had recently been granted a nonprofit educational status, and to maintain it we needed to have four things: a building (which we had), a faculty (which we had), a curriculum, and students. Neither of the last two were well established and, collectively, they became my first priorities. My half of the correspondence has been lost, but in reply, Bob Dorn, director of the Center's training activities, sent me a memo that began, "In reply to your request of February 14, . . ." and in five pages he sketched out the program that would become LDP.

In re-reading Bob's memo recently, I noted that his most important points were: *the training philosophy* (effective leadership development begins with psychological assessment and constructive feedback); *the specific program objectives* (interactive experiences where participants can learn from each other); and *the intended outcomes* (to help the individual become more productive and happier and, as a leader, to help others achieve these same goals). These guidelines have remained constant over the subsequent sixteen years, and as a consequence of this durable accomplishment I am willing to attribute such descriptors as "brilliant, creative, inspired, and visionary" to Bob and those on his staff who made it happen. (For the historical record, the others were Bob Bailey, Bobbin Franklin, Jenny Godwin, Stan Gryskiewicz, Al Scarborough, and Bill Sternbergh.)

LDP is a week-long mix of assessment exercises, tests, surveys, lectures, simulations, and structured events—all leading to intense psychological feedback for each participant as to how his or her leadership style is perceived by others and what might be done to improve it. Trying to describe the program in any more detail is like trying to describe a piece of music: I can tell you how long it is, what key it is written in, and at what tempo it is usually played, but until you hear it yourself, you can't really appreciate it.

Does the program work? What impact does it have? Like all training programs, we are under constant pressure to document our effectiveness, especially with "hard data, David, not testimonials," and like all other training programs, we are frustrated in our attempts to do that. We have follow-up surveys that have produced positive results, but explaining them takes more tortuous scene-setting than I can do here, so I will fall back once again on persuasive anecdotes from earlier attendees.

One of the more vivid examples of the value attributed to this program by the attendees is provided by the Blandin Foundation. Its board of directors, a powerful collection of community leaders, lawyers, bankers, and corporate executives, was trying to decide how best to use its resources to improve community leadership in rural areas. Its executive director, an LDP alumnus named Paul Olson, persuaded the board that the decision was important enough that members should experience "the best leadership training available" for themselves. In a remarkably gutsy decision for a board of directors, the members decided to do just that. In 1985 the entire board came to Greensboro for the week-long program. The direct outcome was that it then funded, and has sponsored ever since, an appropriate modification of LDP for the Blandin Foundation Community Leadership Program. For their testimonial, board members voted with their budget, and each year approximately one hundred fifty community leaders from out-state Minnesota have access to the same kind of training that the Center and our licensees provide corporate and public service leaders. (For more on the Blandin program, see the article by Bernie Ghiselin in the Winter 1989 *Issues & Observations*, volume 9, number 1, pages 8-10.)

For me, the most dramatic and persuasive testimonial came from a man by the name of Jim Dozier. Remember him? Brigadier General James L. Dozier, U.S. Army, became world-famous in November 1981 when he was kidnapped by Italian terrorists. At the Center we took more-than-normal notice of the news because Jim Dozier had been a participant in the LDP course a few months earlier. (The Army sends all newly promoted brigadier generals through LDP.) He is a fine man, a thoroughly straight-arrow kind of guy, and we feared for his life. Consequently, we were considerably relieved the following February when he was located and freed.

Shortly thereafter I received a letter from him, on one-star letterhead, which read:

> Dear Dave,
> Just a quick note to let you know that the week that I spent with you and your staff in Greensboro this past summer stood me in good stead during the 6 weeks that I spent as an unwelcome guest of the Red Brigades here in Italy. When I return to the States in a month or so, I will contact you and we can talk about it.
> Sincerely,
> /s/ Jim

Let me tell you, receiving a letter like that can make your day. And can send your curiosity soaring: what in the world was there in the LDP course that helped him while he was in the custody of terrorists?

When he returned to the States he was swept up by the media, and it was several months before I ran into him at an evening reception and was able to ask him, "Tell me, Jim, what was in the course that helped you?"

"Well," he said, "as a psychologist, you are going to think this is pretty primitive, but it was those videotapes where we reviewed our group problem-solving skills, where we watched ourselves trying to work in groups. Until that experience it had never occurred to me that the way we treat other people is going to influence the way they treat us in return. A simple observation, I know, but I had never put that together before."

"So," I followed up in my best facilitator's style, "how was that relevant in Italy?"

"The guys that kidnapped me were very volatile and they had guns and they were perfectly capable of shooting somebody, especially me. When they saw what a media furor they had created, they were bouncing off the walls with anxiety. I realized I had to get them calmed down, and I couldn't do that by issuing orders. I remembered what I had learned in those videotapes at the Center—that I could model some behavior for them. So, over a several-day period, I deliberately set out to be very calm and very quiet, and to reassure them continually by my actions that I was not going to do anything drastic, and it worked. They quieted down. I really think that if I had tried some kind of John Wayne stuff, they would have shot me just from excitement. The course may have saved my life."

You can be as cynical as you want about testimonials, but that one, in the form of his framed letter, still hangs today on my wall, and I have a file full of similar, though less dramatic, sentiments from others. LDP works, and today, sixteen years after its conception, it is robust and thriving.

Sad, Poignant Memories

You never know when life is going to double back on you and create a situation that vividly awakens old memories. A recent news article did that to me—it sent me back to the past, and for about twenty-four hours I let waves of nostalgia wash over me.

This story begins almost forty years ago, in 1951, when I entered Iowa State University as a freshman and joined a fraternity. Although my fraternity choice was essentially random, it turned out to be a happy one, and my college years were among the best in my life. Our chapter had a firm rule that we would not admit anyone without a high school grade-point average of B or better, and I know now, as a selection psychologist, that such a policy was quite beneficial, not only because it insured that we had a stable membership—hardly anyone ever flunked out—but also because it subtly elevated our collegiate activities to a slightly higher plane. Good scholarship was valued, and I spent my fraternity years rubbing shoulders with pretty good students.

In fact, I was the only jock in the house, and I took a fair amount of ribbing for associating with the fieldhouse riff-raff.

One of our upperclassmen was a particularly brilliant fellow who had a major impact on me. He was always involved in creative endeavors—playing the piano, listening to classical music, decorating his room with style and flair, attending Broadway shows, reading avant-garde poetry. He was a journalism major, and his fascination with words was contagious. Through him in late-night bull sessions, I was introduced to e.e. cummings ("anyone lived in a pretty how town") and T. S. Eliot ("This is the way the world ends").

Dick was in charge of our Campus Carnival float one year, and under his direction we renounced the usual pattern of building a huge replica of some cute animal by stuffing paper napkins in a large chicken-wire skeleton mounted on a hayrack. Instead, we built a nineteen-foot-high reproduction of a thirty-seven-inch stabile, "Spiny," of Alexander Calder's. After solving some tricky construction challenges, we mounted it on a flatbed trailer, decorated the entire structure in stark, dramatic silver-and-black colors, and it won the grand prize, nosing out the Betas—who did a huge white elephant on a hayrack, followed by six or seven little ones on smaller grain wagons.

In a postmortem session, Dick said, "When we were planning this I looked up the panel of judges and found that they were all either artists, architects, or professors of art history, and I figured they'd be more impressed with modern art than with Dumbo."

That early lesson of the value of beginning a project by evaluating the evaluators has stood me in good stead over the years.

After Iowa State, Dick went to work for Eastman Kodak in some kind of "creative activities" job, a perfect match.

A few years later, after I had joined the faculty of the University of Minnesota, I stopped in Rochester, New York, and had dinner with him. After dinner he said, "Dave, let's go to the office. I've got a really great film to show you."

When we arrived there, he explained, "This is a short film that was sent to us, unsolicited, by a young photographer who is looking for work. He wants to demonstrate how creative he is in hopes that we will give him some contract work—and he really is good."

We watched the film, which consisted of about ten minutes of outrageously clever visual jokes, puns, parodies, and other assorted cinematic tricks, all done with class and strung together in a charming, low-key style.

After it was over I said, "Dick, I've got to have that film—I've got a good use for it."

"Sure," he said, and sent me a copy along with the photographer's name and phone number.

That fall I had agreed to participate in the annual conference of the Minnesota Statewide Testing Program, which was mainly a group of high school counselors who used psychological tests to help students make better informed career choices. They wanted me to speak about my expertise, which was vocational-interest testing, a topic that can be as dry as a dust storm and twice as stifling.

I was looking around for something to spice up my presentation, and this film offered a perfect opportunity. I called up the photographer, told him who I was (probably shamelessly exaggerating my connection with Kodak), and said, "I work with high school counselors and vocational tests, and what I want to do is this: I want you to fill in an interest inventory for me, and then I want to project your test results on one screen and run your movie right beside them on another screen. I want to say something like this to these counselors: 'We should always remember that there is a person behind each of these test scores; to make that point dramatically, here is one person's test scores and here is a product of his considerable imagination.' Would you agree to that?"

"Sure," he said, "it sounds like fun." He was only twenty-five or twenty-six years old, and I think he was a bit flattered to be singled out for this attention.

I sent him the test, he filled it in and returned it to me, I had it scored, and I made an overhead transparency with his results. At the conference I projected his test scores up on a big screen and, with appropriate preamble, showed the movie, making the obvious point that here was a psychological test profile for a truly creative person.

The movie went over well and people commented on it to me for years.

I showed the movie to several classes and at a few parties; then, worried about the effect of the Minnesota heat, cold, and humidity on the film, I took it over to the University Film Library and put it on deposit in their controlled environment. I forgot about it and, as far as I know, it is still there.

The reason this story is currently relevant is that the young photographer's name was Jim Henson, and all of this happened twenty-five years ago before his Muppets burst onto center stage, worldwide. Because of this early exposure, I have followed his career from the beginning.

My personal reaction to the news story reporting his sudden, untimely death—at age fifty-three—was intense. It threw me off my stride for several days.

He was one of my gods, but my worship was all mixed up with the fact that he was three or four years younger than me; thus, my adoration was tinged with a wistful envy. It is easier to admire the achievements of someone older than yourself because you can always think, "There is still time; I'll be able to do that someday." But when your hero is younger than you, there is no way around the unsettling conclusion, "He's playing full-time in a league where I will never even get to pinch-hit."

All deaths are sad. Untimely, early deaths are even worse, and the untimely, early death of a genius with the talent of Jim Henson deprives the world of countless hours of joy, gentle humor, and—through Sesame Street—a model of creative learning that we will not soon see again.

All of this has been churning around in my memory, along with Iowa State, Tau Kappa Epsilon, Dick Reisem, Eastman Kodak, the film *Time*

Piece, the University of Minnesota Film Library, and Kermit the Frog. Death is sad but it does produce rich inner experiences for the living, along with the constant, disquieting realization that whatever you are going to do, you had better do it now, in whatever league you happen to be in. The future may be short.

The Normal Memo Is Normally Dull

One of the more distasteful parts of my working life now is the quality of prose that I am subjected to daily. The world of leadership, management, and organizational life is filled with jargon and obtuse writing. There is no appreciation in the organizational environment for the value of good writing, and the normal memo is normally dull.

In contrast, following are some examples of writing that I have clipped out over the last year or two, simply because I liked them. I wish more examples like these crossed my desk routinely.

"As opposed to Stills, a better guitarist, Young, a better songwriter, and Nash, a better human being, Crosby is a glorified sidekick whose basic job was singing middle harmony, sporting capes and a Cossack moustache, and not demanding that the group put too many of his songs on any one album. In exchange he got enough money to stay light-miles high for two decades. He is no relation to Bing." (Joe Queenan, *The Wall Street Journal,* November 30, 1988)

"We were much in love then but didn't think much about the widely circulated fact that when love is deposited in the institution of marriage, it faces nearly a 45% chance of meeting a shredder of divorce." (Mary Kay Blakely, *MS. Magazine,* December 1988)

"Becoming better at something is called self-improvement, a term with two meanings. It means improving oneself, one's character, one's core identity. It also means an unavoidable loneliness, getting better by oneself, in submission to severe self-judgments, in the aloneness of private determination, under the lash of the necessity to satisfy one's demanding self." (George Will, in his column, April 4, 1989)

"The best rule for dealing with *who* vs. *whom* is this: Whenever *whom* is required, recast the sentence. This keeps a huge section of the hard disk of your mind available for baseball averages." (William Safire, *New York Times Magazine,* October 7, 1990)

"She was fair, brilliant, slender, with a kind of effortless majesty. Her beauty had an air of perfection; it astonished and lifted one up." (Henry James, *The Princess Casamassima,* 1886)

"Who has not had the fantasy, after clearing passport control, of dispensing with his actual identity, inventing a new one, and going forth to live it on the streets of a foreign capital. If only it worked." (Thomas Mallon, *A Book of One's Own: People and Other Diaries,* 1986)

"It is no exaggeration to say that the 'undecideds' could go one way or the other." (George Bush, 1988)

"To appreciate the strength and speed of this pesky invertebrate [the ant], consider that a leaf cutter the size of a man could run repeated four-minute miles while carrying 750 pounds of potato salad." (R. Z. Sheppard, *Time Magazine,* September 3, 1990)

"If you are single and a woman and you spend too much time picking out fabrics and buying nice plates, it adds a certain permanence to your situation. Every purchase is an investment in a life you may still hope to jettison." (Lisa Grunwald, *Esquire Magazine,* December 1988)

"You could be shot, mined, grenaded, rocketed, mortared, sniped at, blown up and away so that your leavings had to be dropped into a sagging poncho and carried to Graves Registration, that's all she wrote." (Michael Herr, *Dispatches,* 1978)

"The client has responded to the MMPI-2 items by claiming to be unrealistically virtuous." (The Minnesota Report: MMPI-2, Adult Clinical System Interpretive Report)

"The school was patient, but not inexhaustibly so. In my last year, I broke the bank and was asked to leave. . . . I wore myself out with raging then I went into the Army. I did so with a sense of relief and homecoming. It was good to find myself in a clear life of uniforms and ranks and weapons. It seemed to me when I got there that this is where I had been going all along, and where I might still redeem myself. All I needed was a war.
"Careful what you pray for." (Tobias Wolff, *This Boy's Life,* 1989)

"An exciting piece of evidence about inhibition in the taste system came via the chicken pox virus." (Dr. Linda Bartoshuk, Science Agenda, American Psychological Association, August/September 1990)

"Shortly after 1 a.m. on January 18, senior linebacker Kevin Salisbury, sophomore offensive tackle Mike Mooney and junior guard Jim Lavin became embroiled in a confrontation with Lisa Steffee, a 5'8", 120-pound senior who was at a nearby table with several friends. According to witnesses and published reports, the three players had drunk lots of beer when the 6'7", 321-pound Mooney began spewing lewd remarks toward another woman at Steffee's table. Mooney approached the table and, after a few more trashy remarks, dared the now-agitated Steffee to douse him with her brew. She did.

"Salisbury, who's 6'4" and weighs 245 pounds, came to his teammate's aid by punching Steffee, cracking her nose in two places, an injury that will require plastic surgery. The ensuing fracas involved the three players, an off-duty police officer who was in the restaurant, and Steffee's date, who was pummeled by Mooney and Salisbury. 'I pretty much figured they were going to kill him,' said Steffee." (Roy S. Johnson, *Sports Illustrated,* April 24, 1989)

"It was one of the cases of no news being good news, and that was not nearly good enough." (Karen Elizabeth Gordon, *The Well-tempered Sentence,* 1983)

"She led a complicated and secret quotidian existence of matinees and intrigues and regrets." (Gordon, *Sentence*)

"Pain stood in the way like a sheet of glass: you could walk through it, but not without a certain noise." (Gordon, *Sentence*)

"A correspondence is a kind of love affair. It takes place in a small, closed, private space—a sheet of paper within an envelope is its vehicle and emblem—and it is tinged by a subtle but palpable eroticism. When we write to someone regularly, we begin to look forward to his letters and to feel increasing emotion at the sight of the familiar envelope. But if we are honest with ourselves we will acknowledge that the chief pleasure of the correspondence lies in its responsive aspect rather than in its receptive one. It is with our own epistolary persona that we fall in love, rather than with that of our pen pal; what makes the arrival of a letter a momentous event is the occasion it affords for writing rather than reading." (Janet Malcolm, *The New Yorker,* March 20, 1989)

"I was suddenly aware, watching her on the ladder, that she had mastered with seeming ease something I had felt to be among the most difficult of feats: at once to be a Navy officer and remain a woman." (William Brinkley, *The Last Ship,* 1988)

"Psychology is a house divided. One group of psychologists sees the field in terms of scientific values and accepts the concepts of objectivism, elementism, and nomothetic lawfulness. The group opposed sees psychology in terms of humanistic values and accepts the concepts of intuitionism, holism, and idiographic lawfulness. The positions seem irreconcilable, and the war goes on." (Gregory A. Kimble, *American Psychologist,* March 1989)

"When ballplayers must be pressed into service as agents of redemption . . . we have evidence of a certain poverty in our religious symbolism. That should probably come as no great surprise. At a time when religious icons are a fashion accessory—for Madonna, a crucifix is a way to lend a touch of mystery to a body in heat—it is perhaps to be expected that the search for redemptive symbols should turn up the 1919 White Sox." (Charles Krauthammer, *The Washington Post,* May 14, 1989)

"The next morning, Susan and David took nice, healthy morning walks, Dianne ate a bowl of nice, healthy Nutri-Grain cereal, and Mary had a nice, healthy extra hour-and-a-half of sleep." (Mary Bloodworth, CWO Research Staff Retreat Minutes, September 1990)

"Writing means revealing oneself to excess. . . . That is why one can never be alone enough when one writes, why there can never be enough silence around when one writes, why even night is not night enough." (Franz Kafka, *Letters to Felice,* 1973)

"Holland must still trap thousands of muskrats a year lest they undermine the dikes with their burrowing. Left to its own devices, nature would possibly work through such problems with normal boom-and-bust population dynamics. On the other hand, people tend to become impatient when forced to live for long periods of time on their rooftops." (Richard Conniff, *Audubon Society Magazine,* November 1990)

"Good writing is on the one hand a beautiful, lyrical sweep; on the other it is the nuts and bolts of punctuation and syntax. It's crucial to make writing correct, so that there is no distraction for the story. I find it helpful to have to think about the nuts and bolts." (Robert Dunn, Copy Editor, *Sports Illustrated,* April 24, 1989)

The Leader As Extravert

I am an introvert and, consequently, have always had great trouble with small talk. When I was in college I once read in *Coronet Magazine* that one way to overcome shyness was to have available a prepared list of conversational topics; so I went out on dates with slips of paper in my pocket listing "current events." When conversation lagged I would peek at my list and then offer up some scintillating contribution like, "What do you think of the situation on Quemoy and Matsu?"

Eventually my selection of topics improved somewhat, and I was confident enough to stop writing out the slips. A quick scan of the front page of the *Des Moines Register* could get me through an entire evening. I was ever aware, however, that at any moment my memory registers could be electrostatically blanked, and I would be as mute as a clod the rest of the evening. The danger was particularly acute if the electricity flowing from my companion was intense. The higher her voltage, the harder I tried to be witty and spontaneous, and the greater the probability that I would be zapped by uncontrollable muteness.

Later, in my thirties, after a graduate education in psychology had made more information available to me, I mused, "Yes, Campbell, the tests definitely show that you are an introvert, but look around: extraverts clearly have more fun. If you would learn to act like an extravert, your life would be richer." So once again I, figuratively at least, carried around little slips of paper with interesting things to say on them.

Even later, when I became involved in the study of leaders and their psychological characteristics, I speculated that not only do extraverts have more fun, they also make better leaders. So much of leadership is enhanced by an easy, natural communication style that people for whom such activities come naturally must have an edge on the rest of us instinctive recluses.

Partially to validate my beliefs, I set out to learn more about leadership, extraversion, and related topics. To achieve this I began working on a descriptive, standardized system designed to capture the differences between effective and ineffective leaders. The system, which is now termed the Campbell Leadership Index (CLI), includes a list of one hundred descriptive adjectives to be used by the person being described and also by three to five observers of that person's choice. It has twenty-two scoring scales. One of them has been labeled "ENTERTAINING" and includes adjectives such as "Entertaining," "Extraverted," "Humorous," and "Witty." The theory is that effective leaders will more often be described with these adjectives than will ineffective leaders and thus will score higher on the ENTERTAINING scale. If that is so, then my earlier instincts will have been validated: good leaders are more extraverted than poorer leaders, at least in the eyes of their observers.

The CLI has been used to date with over thirty samples of leaders and nonleaders, including roughly two thousand people and eight thousand observers. Most samples included people in a wide range of leadership positions such as corporate executives, military officers, government administrators, industrial managers, community leaders, R&D project directors, and university student leaders. Some of the samples were selected because they had outstanding track records and were well regarded by their organizations. Others were selected for exactly the opposite reason; they were plateaued or burned out. Many of the samples were opportunistic—such as attendees at conferences, seminars, or training sessions that I was responsible for. When studying real people in real organizations, one takes advantage of whatever data-gathering opportunities present themselves.

A lengthier report on all of the scores for all of the samples will be published later this year. In the present column I am focusing only on the ENTERTAINING scale.

All of the scales have been standardized so that a "typical" sample of normal individuals averages 50, with a standard deviation of 10, which means that scores of 55 and above can be considered high and scores of 45 and below can be considered low. Considerable experience has shown that a 5-point difference between samples constitutes a notable difference.

The five highest scoring samples on the ENTERTAINING scale, again in the eyes of observers selected by them, were as follows, with average scores given in parentheses:

- Fraternity leaders (59): chapter presidents selected to attend a national leadership conference.
- Financial service managers (57): corporate "fast-trackers" selected to attend a prestigious company training program.
- Marketing managers (57): formally, but secretly, classified as up-and-coming in their companies.
- Military officers (56): "fast track" types selected for an elite advanced training course.

- State leaders (56): a group of outstanding citizens invited to a prestigious state conference.

All of the individuals in these samples had been selected by some competitive process for attendance at a prestigious event.

The five lowest scoring samples, again in the eyes of their observers, were:

- Municipal fire chiefs (50): surveyed during a leadership course made available to all fire service administrators who wished to attend.
- First-time supervisors (50): recently promoted, surveyed during an initial company management-training course.
- Award-winning managers (49): from an electronics firm.
- R&D project directors (49): scientist/managers attending a company session to improve what was viewed as stagnant management.
- Marketing managers (47): formally, but secretly, classified as plateaued.

The conclusion to be drawn from these data is not completely clear. Although the highest scoring samples included people selected for their outstanding performance, and the lowest scoring samples included people with more mundane records, one of the lowest scoring samples did include managers highly regarded in a manufacturing environment, and many other managers in the lowest scoring samples are certainly valued by their organizations. Further, none of the lowest scoring sample groups scored particularly low; "mid-range" would be a better description. The separation between the two groups of samples was substantial but not dramatic.

Still, even with this bit of ambiguity, I feel vindicated. Although many other characteristics are involved in successful leadership, in general, samples of outstanding leaders appear to be more extraverted than samples of average or mediocre managers. Successful leaders like people and are seen as entertaining to be around. Overall the data are persuasive enough to lead me to encourage aspiring leaders to carry around little bits of paper with interesting things to say on them.

The Average Self-rating on "Ethical Behavior" Is Way Above Average

One of the surprising temporary setbacks encountered in developing the Campbell Leadership Index (CLI) came during the attempt to create an ethics scale. That episode makes an interesting story.

In preliminary work on the CLI, when I was trying to decide which psychological characteristics to include, I consulted many sources. I read a wide range of articles and books, including autobiographies, about leaders. I interviewed people in leadership positions. I sat through countless academic seminars on the topic. I worked often in the Center's leadership programs, which are attended by managers, leaders, commanders, executives, and administrators from many types of organizations and from many different cultures. And I had numerous freewheeling discussions with my Center colleagues, a group of professionals who probably have more day-to-day contacts with leaders from a variety of settings than any other group in the world. I also talked with many "followers."

Virtually all of these sources agreed that the concept of "ethics" was central to the practice of good leadership.

Consequently, in the early versions of the survey I included adjectives such as *ethical, honest, trustworthy,* and *candid,* and negative adjectives such as *deceptive* and *scheming.* Eventually, these adjectives, weighted appropriately, were clustered together into a scale labeled "ETHICAL." Like the other CLI scales, this one was normed so that the "normal, effectively functioning person" scores 50.

Early on, when returning the scored profile forms to individuals in the initial studies, I knew from their reactions that we had a problem. The scale was simply too potent, especially for people with low scores.

The problem was partly psychological, partly statistical. Psychologically, almost no one believes that he or she is merely average in ethical behavior, and no one believes that he or she is below average. Yet—and this is a statistical problem—when a psychological measuring scale is standardized on a normal population, by definition fifty percent of the population is going to score below average.

Some low-scoring individuals became so fixated on—almost obsessed with—their low ETHICAL scores that they completely ignored all of the other information in the briefing.

So, a dilemma—the impact of the scale was too great. It impeded the use of the other scales on the index.

It was, and is, my firm belief that people who are rated low on ethics by their observers can be well served by being confronted with that information, but this should be done in a way that makes it possible for them to understand, accept, and do something about what they are told—and it should not distract them from the other scores on the profile. Thus, I wanted to keep the concept in the survey but I also wanted to find some way to defuse its excessive power.

To soften the impact, in the next phase the name of the scale was changed to "TRUSTWORTHY" in the hope that this would retain the meaning but lessen the reaction. This was only a marginal improvement, however. The reactions were still intense.

During the early tryouts I had learned from informal discussions with observers who had rated individuals low on this scale that they seldom saw the low-scorers as dishonest, corrupt rascals; rather, they tended to describe them as not candid or straightforward. Typical comments were, "He makes important, impulsive decisions that directly affect me but he never explains why" and, "When she continually comes at me unexpectedly from left field with no explanation, is it any wonder that I no longer trust her?"

These discussions convinced me that the concept of "credibility" was closer in flavor to the characteristic being described here than either "ethical" or "trustworthy." Consequently, the final version of the CLI names this scale "CREDIBLE." The scale is still potent, but the explanation for low scores is, "You are probably seen as someone who makes important decisions about others without explaining the reasons." This seems more accurate and more palatable than, "You are seen as unethical."

My interviews with people who had scored low confirm this. For example, one executive with a high self score and a low observer score on the CREDIBLE scale said, "How can this be? I am always honest with people, even when the truth is painful for them."

I replied, "My experience has been that those who score low on this scale are seen as people who make important decisions about others without explaining their rationale."

"Like what kind of decisions?"

"Job assignments, allocation of resources, compensation plans, perhaps geographic transfers . . . "

His reply was immediate, gruff, and suggestive of the problem: "Those topics are none of their business. Those are management decisions."

I merely shrugged and gently suggested that he might have some control issues that were getting in the way of his credibility image.

I might have also told him that the other CLI adjectives most strongly correlated positively with the CREDIBLE scale are *considerate, cooperative, helpful, optimistic, resilient, sensitive, trusting,* and *well-adjusted* and that the adjectives most strongly correlated negatively are *cynical, depressed, insensitive, moody, resentful, sarcastic, self-centered, suspicious,* and *temperamental.* If he wishes to be seen as more credible, he should behave in ways that maximize the possibility that he will be described by the first list and minimize the possibility that he will be described by the second.

The average self and observer scores for thirty samples of leaders strongly support the conclusion that a characteristic variously defined as ethical, trustworthy, or credible is crucial to leadership. The fact that it took three attempts to find a palatable means of measuring this is, in a peculiar way, further evidence of its power and importance.

Men and Boys and Their Toys

There was a swimming hole in the Nodaway River about a mile east of my hometown in Iowa, and I spent many pleasant summer afternoons swimming or fishing in that river. In my memory at least, the scenes were right out of Norman Rockwell, though the realities were probably a bit grubbier. Those were also the years that I was reading about Tom Sawyer and Huckleberry Finn, and my sense of river adventure was well honed. I could see myself lying on their raft, watching their homemade skull-and-crossbones flag fluttering in the breeze, a fishing line tied to my big toe, sneaking a smoke now and then from a hand-bored corncob pipe, watching the vast Mississippi slip by, wondering what Becky Thatcher was up to . . . Ah, bliss.

Well, to paraphrase Benjamin Franklin, the only difference between men and boys is the price of their toys.

This past summer I had the opportunity to float down the Mississippi for ten days, from St. Paul to Dubuque—not on a raft but on a fifty-foot houseboat with air-conditioning, color television, a microwave, and hot showers. We flew the flag of King's Cove Yacht Club, and, in the fiercely antismoking group I traveled with, martinis were the drug of choice. Like Tom and Huck, we spent hours watching the Mississippi, but then, along with musing about the Becky Thatchers of our youth, we also dwelt on other delicious topics such as 401(k) plans, employed children, and riverboat gambling in Iowa.

Seldom has life seemed so serene. The only crises were a clogged generator filter, which Captain Bob handily cleared; the absence of *The New York Times* in the small riverbank cafés where we typically had breakfast; and poor TV reception for one of the NBA final games.

The upper Mississippi, from the head of its navigational waters in Minneapolis, down through the middle of Iowa, is arguably one of the prettiest, most secluded parts of America. In this stretch the river flows through limestone bluffs and undeveloped wilderness sloughs; for miles, the only man-made objects in sight are occasional navigational buoys. Although the series of locks and dams built in the 1930s to foster river commercial traffic have tamed—and indeed destroyed—the various falls and rapids on this once-rugged waterway, the visual beauty of the banks, bluffs, timber, and marshes is still mostly primeval.

Each day, one of our group read aloud to us from a historically oriented guidebook of the upper Mississippi, and as we passed by the landscapes being described, we marveled at the sights and lamented the losses. The dams have wiped out the environment for some species of fish outright, and the buildup of silt and the consequent dredging they have caused have gradually destroyed the beds of shellfish that once supported a sizable clamming industry, complete with button factories and pearl shops.

And we cringed at the probable future of this magnificent waterway: billboards, gaudy marinas, more commercial silos, tank fields, and coal piles. Yet, with our excessively comfortable affluent cruising, we were probably part of the problem.

The small towns on the upper Mississippi grew up between the 1850s and the early 1900s in response to commercial opportunities—mostly in the grain and logging industries. Our guidebook described some of the early activity, noting that the biggest Mississippi log raft in history covered some ten acres.

The upper Midwest was logged off during those years, essentially to build the downriver and eastern cities. Places like Winona, La Crosse, Wabasha, Prairie du Chien, and McGregor owe their early histories to the commercial activities generated by the river. Because these activities have changed so much, and now consist mainly of pleasure boating and long-range St. Paul-to-New Orleans barge traffic, many of the smaller river towns are struggling.

Tourism is coming in, and one can spend many pleasant hours in these scenic towns, experiencing something of the past. To the alert eye, some of these towns are almost archaeological sites, where one has access to the various strata of history. For example, on a walk down the main street of these former logging villages, one can see the wave of early history reflected in the crests set in the tops of buildings, proclaiming the "Masonic Lodge, 1873," or the "Anderson Building, 1888," with the number of signature buildings reflecting the economic activity of the time. The architecture of the next several decades is not particularly noteworthy to the untrained eye, probably because the building designs were relatively stable. Then in the 1950s, when the advent of the paved road and autos put economic pressure on these small towns, and local merchants were struggling to find some way to hold onto their clientele, the ghastly aluminum-storefront-and-awning movement came through and some of the more energetic merchants dressed up their properties. A few of these dubious attempts survive. In the 1960s the beads-and-sandals crowd opened candle shops and storefront cafés, and in some cases their murals of peace and flowers can still be seen on the walls. The 1980s brought the conservationist phase, and many small towns now have at least a few lovely restored early buildings, often containing antique shops, muffin bakeries, and quaint cafés. As modern electronics allow cottage industries to be established wherever the workers want, these scenic small towns with calm and healthy lifestyles may yet flourish once more.

One of the recent economic breakthroughs on the river has been the establishment of riverboat gambling in 1991. We spent one evening on the *Casino Belle,* out of Dubuque, enjoyed it, and collectively left about $500 in the local economy.

Riverboat gambling in Iowa is a cross between a second-tier Las Vegas casino, an Elks Club talent show, and a potluck supper at the Methodist Church on Sunday night; the crowd is mostly in polyester and baseball caps and arrives in RVs—basically my relatives.

The gambling is controlled so you can lose no more than $200 each trip, and the maximum bet is $5. According to the newspaper reports when the gambling started, and to a more recent summary report, if you divide the number of gamblers into the house-take, you find that there is about a $30-per-person-per-trip loss. Thus, assuming a $40 admissions fee (which buys an unlimited Iowa prime-rib buffet), a $30 loss, and $30 in drinks and tips, I figure this is a $100-outing for most participants, which is probably about as much as the Midwest can bear.

The river is a decidedly masculine place, both as a playground and as a working environment, a characteristic that stands out in the EEOC-aware world that most of us live in. Of the dozens, perhaps hundreds, of pleasure craft that we saw over the ten days, only one was "manned" by women, and it was two mothers out with their broods for an afternoon's playing and swimming on a sandbar. Otherwise, about two-thirds of the pleasure craft were occupied by couples with the male driving; the other third, by parties of men.

It was likewise in the commercial world. The tugboat operators, whom we listened to on the marine radio band, all seemed to be out of Louisiana, sired by C. W. McCoy. We became almost accustomed to their laconic, Creole machoisms. Although the employees of the U.S. Corps of Engineers who operated the locks had a different Midwestern twang, they were also, with one exception over the ten days, male, and the usual social exchanges between staff and crew in the locks while we were waiting for the water level to change were the normal, easy, trivial masculine bromides: "Nice day." "Kinda warm." "Nice boat." "Been busy?" "River's high." "Where're ya heading?" "Ain't Michael Jordan something else?"

If one of the women on board happened to be sunbathing, the exchange might be: "Nice crew, Cap'n." "Oh, they work out well enough." "Don't happen to have an extra hand you'd like to leave behind and pick up on your way back?" "Don't see how we could make Dubuque without 'em." "No harm in asking." And then, depending on who was within earshot, the conversation would make its politically correct way through contemporary minefields, with everyone safe in the knowledge that no explosions would be detonated.

One of the more entertaining activities in boating is to read the name painted on the stern of each craft; these names are the bumper stickers of the river where owners assert their creative individuality. (We were on the "Il Shea," named with a play on words of the owner's name.) With my propensity for categorization, I tried to find patterns. Probably the most frequent category had to do with someone's name: "Sue N Dave," "Ted 'n' Sally"; with occasional alliteration, "DanNJanNFranNStan."

Family dynamics were often reflected: "Father's Folly III," "John's Temptation," "Mom's Revenge," "Our Significant Other," "The Kids' Inheritance."

Wordplay was common: "Gail Wins," "C-Breeze," "Tide 'N' Knots" and "Tied 'N' Nauts," "I'm Fine II," "Sea-Esta," "Knotty Lady."

For centuries, men on water have been thirsty, and the well-recognized tie between boating and drinking was often expressed: "Suds Set," "I NEEDA DRINK," "Wine Yacht," "Cutty's Ark," "INITRAM III." (Try reading the last one backwards.)

The other factor intricately intertwined with boats is cash flow, and some boat names were blunt about it: "Current Receivables," "Capital Gains," "Pressing Business," "One More Mortgage," "Loan A Ranger" (probably a banker), "Costly II."

Humor in boating is also reflected in the signs posted within. Our bridge, for example, had the following plaque: "OUR CAPTAIN IS ALWAYS RIGHT, misinformed perhaps, sloppy, crude, bull-headed, fickle, even stupid, but NEVER, EVER WRONG"—a sign that might well be posted in many corporate suites. And of course about every other pleasure boat in America has displayed the plaque: "Marriages performed by the Captain are good for the duration of the voyage only."

So that was our adventure for the summer. Although its major purpose was relaxation, and that was achieved, the experience reminded me once again that as a society we need to put a lot of energy into both environmental and community leadership, else we are going to leave behind a bleak country. And personally, I was able to make another check mark on my "To do" list. Although I am not rabid about it, I have had a few things stored up that I have wanted to check off—"Walk the Great Wall of China," "Climb the Eiffel Tower"—and this trip allowed me to cross off the "Float down the Mississippi." Now, what's next? Maybe that motorcycle . . .

Problem-Makers, Problem-Solvers, and Problem-Finders

I had an occasion recently to work with a pessimist, someone who made a problem out of every suggestion offered: a real *problem-maker*. It was a wearying episode, especially as my tolerance for naysayers has been completely exhausted since about 1975. And it depressed me, for I know that my involvement on this project is not over and we have not yet faced the end of his dreary roadblocks.

On the flight home, fuming about the experience, I thought to myself, "At least this was a rare event in your life. You hardly ever have to work with anyone with this mentality." And I mused further, "How in the world can someone with this outlook survive in the go-go atmosphere of the Coast? . . . Well, maybe marrying money helps, but does that always make one cautious, pessimistic, and skeptical of the motives of others?"

As the miles rolled by below and I came closer to the Colorado mountains that provide me with such pleasure and serenity, I contemplated my good fortune at greater length. One of the reasons that I love my work is that I am completely surrounded by *problem-solvers*. I routinely take on too much, too many challenges of increasing complexity, confident that the talent around me will bail me out. At every level, our Center is blessed with bright, motivated people whose attitude is oriented toward accepting increasingly complex challenges and then solving the inevitable attendant problems.

Let me give you a case in point: Several years ago we contracted to run a week-long course on leadership principles for a group of European executives in London. It was our first big overseas production and we had to learn as we went. One challenge came early on when we had to prepare the course materials. We used a wide range of paper handouts, and organizing them for overseas shipping was a lot of work. One of our administrative staff, a problem-solver, said, "Look, it is stupid to ship empty three-ring notebooks air freight to London. Let's just ship the contents, and buy the notebooks when we get there."

Great idea. We did it.

Except that when we got to London, we learned that English notebooks have only two rings, and the holes are spaced differently from ours.

We had a problem, and not much time to solve it.

Not to worry. Our group simply bought a two-hole punch, and we spent one entire afternoon and evening, when people might have been out seeing the sights, re-punching five boxes of handouts and, despite jet lag, there was no complaining. There was some teasing of the person who suggested buying the notebooks in London, but no complaining.

Anyone who has worked at the Center for the last eighteen years could come up with dozens of similar stories. In this sense alone, the Center is a joyous place to work. Problem-solvers abound.

But that is not the best news. Along with problem-solvers, we also have *problem-finders*, and they are even more fun to work with. Problem-finders are people who go beyond problem solving: they find new non-obvious problems and then offer creative solutions for them. A significant body of research and study in the area of innovation suggests that it is the problem-finders who create the breakthroughs—people like Steve Jobs and his buddies, who realized that not everyone could afford a mainframe computer, so they created the Apple personal computer; or like Edwin Land, who noted that people did not want to wait a week for their photographs to be developed, so he created the Polaroid camera.

Closer to home, here at the Center, Bob Dorn and his staff realized in the seventies that an unrecognized problem with most leadership development programs was that they were too academic, superficial, and impractical; their solution was to create an intensely applied, psychologically sophisticated offering, the Leadership Development Program (LDP), which has since become one of the world's most popular leadership training programs. In another vein, Morgan McCall realized that a latent problem in many organizations was what he called "derailed" executives—that is, people with outstanding early track records who failed to live up to their youthful potential; he and his colleagues set out to find out why. A quick-and-dirty summary of their findings is that derailment is almost always caused by interpersonal flaws. The usual technical or business school training has little to offer in such situations. The solution has to be found at the personal level. Another intriguing problem identified, and a possible explanation offered.

At the nuts-and-bolts level, in my own area, Susan Hyne is a genius with the new expanded Microsoft® Excel software for the Macintosh computer, and she is forever finding new problems that can be adroitly solved with this new technology, problems that were not even recognized as problems until she found the solutions.

These "problem found, problem solved" contributions of the Dorns, McCalls, and Hynes of the Center lead not merely to joy but to heartier rapture: their solutions provide a sense of forward progress when we did not even know we were stalled.

Which is why my session with the pessimist was so frustrating. His gloomy approach not only did not solve any problems, it also prevented any useful new ones from being found. Further, his worst feature was that he had an unerring instinct for treating problem-finders as problem-makers. Whether the suggestions dealt with financial, accounting, compensation, marketing, or legal issues, he belittled every attempt at progress, and especially the wild, far-out, "what if we try this . . ." gropings. By the end of the session, faced with this negativism, no one wanted to do anything but slit some wrists.

As I am wont to do on airplanes while contemplating such human foibles, I lapsed into psychological classifications. Hmmm, I thought, problem-makers, problem-solvers, and problem-finders: how many of each do I know?

By this time I was well into the two-hour flight, feeling the relaxation that comes with a glass of wine at high altitude, and names streamed quickly through my memory. Reassuringly, even after stretching for them, I could only think of four "pure" problem-makers in my career—that is, people for whom I could be dead certain that they would react negatively to any new idea. Four is not many, though unfortunately some of them cut a pretty wide swath. Mild depression.

But I could think of dozens of "pure" problem-solvers—that is, people with whom I have worked whose initial stance toward new suggestions has been, "Okay, how do we work this out?" Joy, lots of it.

And I could come up with at least a dozen colleagues, problem-finders, who have the ability to come up with unique solutions to problems as yet unidentified, solutions capable of bringing excitement into my world. Rapture indeed.

Which is how I left these musings, driving home from the airport with the sun's rays setting behind Pikes Peak like a halo, rapturous with my colleagues, and also with the fact that I was miles and miles and miles away from the pessimist.

Seven Ways to Make a Living

How many ways are there to make a living?

Over the last decade, while working on a new career-assessment survey, I have been pondering this question. As it turns out, there are many different ways to answer it.

For example, the *Dictionary of Occupational Titles* (DOT), published by the U.S. Department of Labor, aspires to list every occupation in America, along with a title and brief description. It has over ten thousand entries, including such intriguing ones as:

> *Balloon dipper* (alternative title: soaper) Dips balloons in vats of dye and soap solutions to color and polish them. Pours specified dyes into dye box receptacles. Immerses dye spreader in dye box and passes it over tank of running water to form crisscross colored pattern of swirls on water. Lifts form pan from curing oven and places it on tank rack with molds immersed in dye water to form varicolored swirling pattern on balloons.

> *Defective-cigarette slitter* (alternative titles: ripper operator, slitting machine feeder) Tends machine that cuts paper from defective cigarettes to reclaim tobacco. Attaches hoisting bar to tub of cigarettes. Starts machine and pulls rope to hoist tub and dump cigarettes into hopper that feeds cigarettes under cutting knives and onto vibrating screen separator that separates paper from tobacco.

These vivid descriptions to the contrary, many of the DOT listings are repetitive or overlapping, and the actual number of different occupations is considerably smaller.

The search for elegant simplicity in job classifications has taken me to the other extreme, and I have concluded that the answer to the question, "How many ways are there to make a living?" is, essentially, seven, or combinations thereof.

The following procedures led me to this answer.

First, a vocational interest inventory was constructed by searching through hundreds of job titles and occupational activities to develop a list that covered the entire working domain. Eventually two hundred items were retained, most of them generally familiar—for instance, *be an engineer, organize a political campaign.*

Second, a parallel list of job skills was also developed and one hundred twenty skill items were included, again reasonably familiar activities such as *explain scientific terms to lay people, set up an efficient office filing system.*

Third, these two lists were compiled into one booklet and distributed to several dozen happily employed people in each of sixty diverse occupations. These individuals were asked to report how much they would enjoy the items on the first list and how good they would be at performing the activities on the second list.

Ultimately, some five thousand workers responded.

By means of both sophisticated statistical methods and some down-and-dirty common sense, their responses were analyzed for major underlying themes. Without belaboring the twists and turns in the statistical maze that we followed, I can tell you that there are seven basic underlying themes in these data—thus implying that there are seven different ways, or combinations of seven ways, to make a living.

Influencing: taking charge and being responsible for results (the general area of leading others). Influencers are motivated to make things happen. They are confident of their ability to persuade others to their viewpoints and they enjoy the give-and-take of verbal jousting. They typically work in organizations, not necessarily at the top, but they tend to find their way into leadership positions in charge of the specific functions that interest them. They enjoy public speaking and like to be visible in public. Typical occupations include company presidents, corporate managers, and school superintendents.

Organizing: bringing orderliness to the working environment. Organizers are good at planning procedures, managing projects, and directly supervising the work of others. They emphasize efficiency and productivity, are good with details, and usually enjoy solving the day-to-day problems that inevitably appear in organizations. They understand budgets and cash flow and are often good with investments. Typical occupations include project managers, financial vice-presidents, accountants, office managers, and administrative assistants.

Helping: providing personal services. Helpers are compassionate people who are deeply concerned with the well-being of others. They enjoy having close, personal contact with the people they are working with and are genuinely concerned with helping their students, clients, or patients live full, satisfying lives. They readily understand the feelings of others and can provide emotional support. Typical occupations include teachers, counselors, and religious leaders.

Creating: producing artistic, literary, musical, and design works through writing, painting, performing, and inventing products and environments. Creators see the world through innovative eyes and are confident of their ability to create new products and concepts. They see themselves as free spirits, are often fluent and expressive, and are uncomfortable with the restraints imposed by traditional organizational structures. They spend a fair amount of time in the throes of emotional change. Typical occupations include artists, musicians, designers in various media, and writers.

Analyzing: evaluating data, conducting scientific experiments, and working with mathematics. Analyzers are comfortable with numbers and intellectual concepts and they have a strong need to understand the world in a scientific sense. They usually prefer to work alone or in small groups in laboratory or academic settings. They are mentally agile, need autonomy, and like to work through problems for themselves. They often are disdainful of both leaders and managers. Typical occupations include scientists, medical researchers, and computer analysts.

Producing: engaging in practical, hands-on, "productive" activities. Producers like to work with their hands. They generally enjoy being outdoors and they like to be able to see visible results of their labors. They are good with tools and enjoy taking on new construction projects or repairing mechanical breakdowns. They approach the world with a healthy, straightforward, what-you-see-is-what-you-get kind of common sense. Typical occupations include farmers, carpenters, mechanics, veterinarians, and landscape architects.

Adventuring: risk-taking involving the need for endurance, competing with others, and a degree of physical danger. Adventurers enjoy situations that stimulate the production of adrenaline and a sense of competition. They are confident of their physical abilities and frequently seek out excitement. They like to win but are also resilient in defeat. They often like working in teams. Typical occupations include military officers, police officers, and athletic coaches.

These seven dimensions are helpful for many purposes, especially in career-guidance settings where students and other interested parties are shown around the occupational world.

Consider this example: "Think about the descriptions of these seven career types. Then answer the question: If you attended a large social gathering where people from these seven types gathered in seven different areas, which group would you join first? After leaving the first group, which would you join next? If you could combine two groups, which ones would they be? Which of the seven would you especially avoid?"

Faced with this question, virtually everyone expresses some favorite choices and some strong aversions.

An occupation is, in a sense, an extended social gathering. When one enters an occupation, the people found there will usually be in general agreement about the types of activities that they like to engage in and feel comfortable doing, and these modal preferences will have a strong effect on the flavor of that working environment.

For this reason, the seven major themes provide an excellent place to start searching for a career focus. You had better like the kind of people that you work with because they are going to influence many aspects of the rest of your life.

These seven themes are expanded in the Campbell Interest and Skill Survey (CISS), which will be published this fall. This survey is designed to lead the next generation of career-assessment inventories, pressing on beyond more traditional interest inventories in that it also includes the concept of skills. The issue is not only "What do you like to do?" but "Where do you feel confident?"

Curiously, although the CISS is intended to benefit young people facing their first career decisions, I have found that virtually everyone, no matter what his or her age, is still trying to decide what they want to be when they grow up. As well as seeking this help for your children, your students, your young staff members, and yourself, you also might want to seek advice for your parents. They may still be searching.

Some Nuggets of Bureaucratic Gold

Many years ago, as a young lieutenant in the U.S. Army, I was assigned an office in a deserted barracks building that had been vacated months earlier by unknown parties. In the bottom of a dusty desk drawer I found a wrinkled sheet of mimeographed paper. It was headed merely, "Actual Sentences from Officer Efficiency Reports," and it was obviously one of those examples of subterranean office humor that circulate widely and anonymously. It had no author, no date, no source of origin. It amused me and I tucked it away in my files.

While organizing my office recently, in preparation for moving into the new building for the Center's branch in Colorado Springs, I came across it again and I am reprinting it here, with thanks to the unknown prospector who mined these nuggets of bureaucratic gold.

Actual Sentences from Officer Efficiency Reports

"This officer has talents but has kept them well hidden."

"Combs his hair to one side and appears rustic."

"Does not drink but is a good mixer."

"Can express a sentence in two paragraphs any time."

"A quiet, reticent, neat-appearing officer. Industrious, tenacious, diffident, careful, and neat. I do not wish to have this officer as a member of my command at any time."

"He has failed despite the opportunity to do so."

"His leadership is outstanding except for his lack of ability to get along with his subordinates."

"He hasn't any mental traits."

"Needs careful watching since he borders on the brilliant."

"Makes a particularly fine appearance when astride a horse."

"Believes sincerely in the power of prayer and it is astonishing to note how many times his prayers are answered."

"Open to suggestions but never follows same."

"Has begun to fraternize without realizing it."

"Never makes the same mistake twice but it seems to me he has made them all once."

"In any change in policy or procedure, he can be relied upon to produce the improbable hypothetical situation in which the new policy will not work."

"Gives the appearance of being fat due to the tight clothes he wears."

"Is stable under pressure and is not influenced by superiors."

"Is keenly analytical and his highly developed mentality could best be utilized in the research-and-development field. He lacks common sense."

"Has developed into a good, round staff officer."

"Tends to overestimate himself and underestimate his problems, being surprised and confused by the resulting situations."

"This officer's physical condition is good (broken leg)."

"An independent thinker with a mediocre mentality."

"Maintains good relations unilaterally."

"Recently married and devotes more time to this activity than to his current assignment."

"An exceptionally well-qualified officer with a broad base."

"Tends to create the impression of unpositive personality through needless and undiscerning gentility and soft-spokenness."

"Of average intelligence except for lack of judgment on one occasion in attempting to capture a rattlesnake, for which he was hospitalized."

The only dismaying feature of this list is, in rereading it, I can see six or eight entries that might well have been penned about me by various of my supervisors, both military and civilian, over the years. I mean, brilliant though apparently irrational research and development does have to be done, some superiors are better ignored, and there are rattlesnakes that occasionally have to be captured. And no one from Iowa ever completely escapes "rustic." Once again, humor mirrors reality . . . or is it the other way around?

A Sucker for Enthusiasm

As regular readers of this column know, I am a sucker for enthusiasm. Show me anyone with coiled-spring intensity, whose eyes are sparkling, whose body language is quivering, whose thoughts tumble out faster than routine grammar can serve, and I am mesmerized. Consequently, I was quite taken by the story pouring out of the slender, athletic, young man riding next to me on the ski lift. Even better, his enthusiasm was focused on a new gadget or, more precisely, on an entirely new skiing-oriented application of electronic gadgetry. There may be topics in the world that excite me more but none I can talk about in a business-oriented publication.

Further, all of this was happening high over the ski slopes of the High Sierra near the California-Nevada line, on a day with bright sunshine, new snow, and Lake Tahoe glistening crystal-blue in the distance.

He was explaining to me a new skier-option program. Basically, it is a "frequent-skier" program, with features analogous to airline frequent-flyer programs, with benefits accruing to anyone who skis often, but it is much more than that. It is also a skier-control system, a messaging system, a way to feed the macho skier's ego, and a superb producer of a skiing-marketing-managing database. My instincts tell me that it is one of those new ideas that a thousand people will soon say, "Why didn't I think of that?"

In brief, this is what he told me: You purchase a nylon-web bracelet with a large postage-stamp-sized plastic rectangle fastened to it. At point of purchase, near the ski-lift ticket window, a one-inch-square Polaroid picture of you is mounted on the rectangle; inside the rectangle is a small silicon chip with a unique ID number burned into it. This chip is connected to two bronze prongs that protrude slightly above the frame of the rectangle. If you wish, this ID number can be associated with your credit card number, which frees you for the rest of the season from standing in line to buy a lift ticket; each time you ski, the credit card is directly debited. The pricing is arranged roughly so that if you ski five or six days, the system is free. Any more days and you save about five dollars a day.

Wearing the bracelet, as you approach the ski lift, you find the first big advantage: there is a separate entry gate for program members with a line that is inevitably shorter than that at the regular lift. Then, when you swipe the bronze prongs of your bracelet across the face of a space-age reader that can identify your number no matter what the orientation of your wrist, a variety of things happen. First, there is validation and recording. Your right to be at that lift at that hour of the day is confirmed. (This immediately opens up innovative marketing possibilities: for instance, tickets can be sold for an infinite number of patterns, such as from 9:00 to 11:00 a.m. on alternate Thursdays; or, intriguingly, you might buy a lift ticket good for, say, ten thousand vertical feet of skiing.) For statistical purposes, your presence at that lift at that time is added to the area's database.

Second, a tally of vertical feet is made. Your personal record is incremented for one run on that lift, thereby permitting a permanent tally of the total number of vertical feet that you have skied to date. At the end of the season, for bragging purposes, you will receive a summary of vertical feet skied.

Third, daily performance is registered. A counter resembling a large digital-clock dial immediately shows you how many runs you have had that day from that lift.

Fourth, there is a messaging potential. If someone has called the program number with a message for the skier, a little telephone sign pops up, telling you to use the courtesy phone located near the top of the lift. Thus, you might find a voice message such as, "Dad, meet us for lunch at 1:15 on the ski-lodge deck."

And, fifth, you receive quick access. Almost instantaneously, the gate opens and you can get on the lift.

I had noticed earlier that the designers had done a first-rate job with everything. The nylon-web bracelets and plastic rectangles are in designer colors; the lift gates are formed from breakaway, semihard, rubber bars; the entry wickets are machined from sturdy-looking stainless-steel bars; everything appears sleek, safe, and modern.

I found out later that, in a marketing-research project, seventy percent of earlier users felt the bracelet system was more convenient than the conventional lift-ticket system.

Furthermore, there were many clever marketing touches. For example, when my Polaroid picture was taken for my bracelet, the staff member took two and let me choose which one to use. That was a nice gesture because we all think we are better looking than our pictures and usually think that, "If you would just take one more, I'm sure it would come out better." (I think that every time I get my driver's license renewed.) Having two pictures provides a choice—along with disquieting evidence that further pictures are not likely to show improvements.

This clearly was a class operation.

My companion waved his arm around him, "Look at all of the marketing energy—signs and banners up all over, attractive brochures, no ticket-window lines to stand in, obvious and quick entry to the lift lines, monthly newsletters, annual awards, plus the manager of the ski area will have a database of all the frequent skiers, especially the macho, competitive, serious ones. The manager will also know when each of the lifts is busiest and that will help in assigning personnel. What ski area manager wouldn't die to have information like that?"

I was intrigued by his sensitivity to the marketing and management issues. This was my son, Jim, whom I was skiing with, and I had known him all of his life as a "numbers, not a people" person. In high school he won mathematical, not leadership, awards. He entered MIT as a nerd and emerged as an entrepreneur; since graduation, with his propensity for creative gadgets, he has been involved in four or five imaginative but unstable start-ups. A few years ago, upon entering his thirties with a wife, a mortgage, and family plans, he opted for a more stable corporate environment. With his brashness and irreverence for authority, I had doubted that he would last.

Now, with his own reputation and equity at stake, he turns out to be an exceedingly engaging fellow. During the day I had noted how he schmoozed with the panorama of personnel that it takes to run a ski area: the parking-lot attendants, the ticket-sales personnel, the lift operators, the people in charge of grooming the slopes, the ski patrol, the chief electrician on whom he was dependent for power, the cashiers in the ski-lodge cafeteria, and the back-office accounting people. He has an open, hearty way about him and it serves him well. A lot of people have to be energetically on board to make a new complicated system like this work.

After fifteen runs, counted and tallied by Jim's computers, we knocked off early. I had a nap while he went back to deal with a subtle software bug that he had detected during the day.

For the evening, after dinner we found a bar with a big screen to watch number three Duke knock off number one Michigan, and later wandered into a casino for some action.

"I want to gamble a bit at the blackjack table," I said.

"Ha," he snorted, "playing in a casino is not gambling. It's a sure thing—you always lose."

I was most amused. Here he was, with a two-year-old, a mortgage, and a pregnant spouse, having just walked away from corporate security to risk his career on an unproven technology, and he was decrying gambling. But, as he later added, "In real life, your personal odds are what you make them."

"Come on," I urged, handing him a five-dollar bill. "Pump this through the slot machines while I try a few hands."

Thirty minutes later, just as two face cards on a split pair of aces drew me back even, he came back, dumped five dollars in quarters in the pocket of my ski jacket, and said, "Smoke gotten to you yet?"

"Yeah, let's get out of here."

We were up and out of the condo the next morning at 7:00 a.m., me for the four-hour drive to the San Francisco airport, him to go up on the mountain to check out his connections, recycle his counters, and generally stroke his semiconductor chips.

"Dad," he grinned as he wrapped his six-foot-four-inch frame around me for a good-bye bear hug, "I can't believe how much I love this work. And, you know, I'll never pay for another day of skiing in my life."

As I drove westward in a heavy snowstorm over the Donner Pass (at seventy-two-hundred feet), I mused: few outcomes in life are more exhilarating than to see your adult children happy, innovative, and employed.

Only Art Endures

The economic chaos in Eastern Europe is almost beyond comprehension. In business operations, nothing is logical; economic planning is impossible; what will happen next is unfathomable. The person on the street is being buffeted by external forces that they do not understand, and there is an increasing sense of despair. For outside observers who are immune to this chaos, the specifics of daily life at the personal level can be fascinating, though unsettling.

My wife Rita, a Latvian immigrant, and I spent the 1992 Christmas holidays in Riga, Latvia, with her large array of aunts, uncles, and cousins. It was a warm, joyous family time, their first Christmas free of the communistic yoke, though considerably tempered by the bleak situation in which they are imbedded. They are people of modest means—truck drivers, factory workers, mechanics, and service personnel—living mostly in sleazy, undistinguished apartments built during the Russian occupation. Eerily, virtually all of their apartments have identical floor plans: a small kitchen, a bath, and three rooms, with each of the rooms usually serving at least two functions. Each room is someone's bedroom and also a living room, or dining room, or nursery.

While we saw firsthand many instances of the impact of their current economic dislocations, one specific example, involving the purchase of a work of art, made a particularly poignant impression on me.

For the past twenty-five years or so I have had a personal strategy of buying a significant piece of art on every nonroutine foreign trip. This strategy arose when I noticed that, in my early youthful travels, I was spending a fair amount of money on what might charitably be called "mementos" but was actually tourist junk. I would buy some seemingly important local icon, cart it home, cluttering up my luggage, display it on the coffee table for a few weeks, then relegate it to a closet where it would sit, not paying rent, until some "white elephant" party justified dumping it on an undeserving friend. Examples of this genre included a small wood carving of William Tell from Switzerland, an inlaid enameled brass plate from Spain, an onyx chess set from Mexico, a Campbell tartan plaid tie from Scotland, a string of goulamine beads from Morocco, a pewter rosebud vase from Norway, and a set of wooden shoes from Holland.

Finally realizing the foolishness of these actions, I resolved to spend enough each trip on just one local work of art to ensure that it would retain some unique, durable value, maybe even prove to be a good investment.

During my first trip to Latvia in 1990, I had this strategy in mind. It was purely a tourist visit for me, and I had some time to get to know the country and the Latvian society. As you may know, Latvia was free and independent before the Second World War. After the war the country was ceded to Soviet occupation by the Allied agreements. Its loss of independence and the perceived lack of support by the Western world are sore points with the Latvian population—though, like occupied people everywhere, they look to the West for hope.

One afternoon we were wandering around Riga, the capital of Latvia. It is a seaport city of considerable old-world charm, even though it had been papered over by the gray dullness of the communist society. Remember, this was 1990, a year before the dramatic end of the communist hold on the Baltic countries. The shops were essentially barren, with a mere trickle of consumer goods. There was only one hard-currency store where Westerners with dollars could find a reasonable selection of local products, such as amber jewelry, wood carvings, or embroidered lace tablecloths.

There were occasional pockets of economic-artistic energy. For example, we stumbled across a subterranean artistic co-op in a cellar just down the main street from the Parliament building. They had a reasonable offering of current Latvian artists, and one painting in particular caught my fancy.

It was a large (approximately four feet by six feet), colorful oil painting with a realistic, but slightly surrealistic, flavor—sort of a cross between Norman Rockwell and Picasso. It portrayed a woman standing in a dressing gown in front of a wardrobe that had an assortment of brightly colored dresses bulging out of it. She was clearly trying to make a clothing decision for the day. Her expression was quixotic, and the title was, "A Difficult Choice."

The vibrant colors and the psychological whimsy stood out in the bleakness of the setting, and I was quite taken with it.

It was priced at 1,800 rubles: about 300 dollars, which, for a large, detailed oil painting, is close to a steal. At that time the exchange rate was roughly 6 rubles to the dollar. On the street it was about 20 rubles to the dollar, which would have made the price about 90 dollars. Penalties for black-market exchanges, however, were severe, including imprisonment, and I was not about to take any chances. The 300 dollars was bargain enough.

I said, "Rita, that's it. There is our artistic purchase for the trip."

She said, "You're crazy. You will never be able to get it home. In the first place, you will have to have the Ministry of Art certify that it has no 'significant historical value' before we can take it out of the country, and in the second place, there is no way we can roll it up to carry it on the plane. It is painted on particle board, not canvas."

Two good points.

I persisted. "Look," I said, "the price is so reasonable we can afford to take a chance. Let's buy it and leave it with one of your relatives. The way things are going, Latvia is going to be free soon and we can come back and ship it home in the usual manner."

She looked at me with that particular gaze reserved for spouses who are stepping on the sensitivities of in-laws, sniffed, and said, "Their apartments are tiny, and there is *no way* I am going to ask them to store that painting for us."

She was right. Their apartments are small and the decor runs to conventional, conservative Latvian knickknacks. A large painting of a lightly clad woman would be a bit overpowering in their homes.

"Okay," I gave in.

But later that night, back at the hotel while I was packing to leave the next day, I started again.

"Look, I've got an idea. Let's buy the painting and give it back to the artist. He certainly has room for it—he had to paint it somewhere—and tell him we will be back in a few years for it. Artists are usually responsible about such things, and what the heck, it is only a 300-dollar risk. For that painting, I am willing to take the chance."

Rita was doubtful. (She was staying on another two days, and she was aware that she would have to handle the logistical details.) "I don't know. What if I can't find him?"

"Here," I said. "Here is the 300 dollars. Go over to the co-op; have them contact the artist and give him the cash. If for some reason you cannot find him, give it to one of your relatives and have them take it to him later."

"Well," she said, "I am not going to give them dollars. They could get in a lot of trouble changing money. Go get it changed into rubles."

I went down to the currency exchange in the hotel and changed the dollars into 1,800 rubles.

Big mistake.

The next morning I flew home. When Rita arrived home a few days later, I asked, "What happened with the painting?"

She told me, "I went to the co-op the next day, but it was closed, and then I ran out of time, so I gave the money to my cousin and told her to go make the purchase—but I also implied that if things got really rough for her and her family that she could go ahead and spend it on family essentials."

I thought that was quite acceptable.

Two years passed, during which the communistic regime was overthrown and Latvia became free once again. It was a thrilling, intoxicating time for Latvians everywhere. For Christmas 1992 we went back to help them celebrate.

What we found was an economic disaster. Although they were free of the dread of the secret police and other occupational burdens had been lifted, they were grappling daily, and not very successfully, with the transition from a centralized and stable economy to a free market characterized by unpredictable volatility. The shops were now filled with goods, mostly Western, but the people were penniless. In 1990 they had money but nothing to buy; now there was plenty to buy but no one had any cash. Inflation was roaring. For example, a typical monthly phone bill had gone from about 50 cents to three dollars during a time when their salaries only roughly doubled.

I was quite curious as to what had happened to the painting.

The cousin who had been given the money met us at the airport. Within the hour she took me aside and surreptitiously handed me a roll of bills—1,800 rubles. Because she spoke no English and I speak no Latvian, I could not ask what had happened, but her satisfied smile told me that she was pleased that she had discharged her duty, whatever she conceived it to be. The money was now mine again. However—and it was a large *however*—the exchange rate had soared to approximately 170 to 1, and the 300 dollars was now worth about 15 dollars. The 1,800-ruble painting would now cost about 45,000 rubles.

That basically is the end of the story. I was not able to relocate the painting. It was only a minor nuisance for me; 285 dollars had evaporated in two years. But for the Latvian population it was part of their economic nightmare. Essentially all of their personal resources, no matter how thrifty they had been, had been wiped out. They have nothing. One Western-educated woman, a technical writer and translator, said to me, "We have been pauperized."

Two final anecdotes: The cousin who had held the money was determined that I was going to find a replacement purchase, so she spent an afternoon escorting me around to a variety of art galleries. (On the way in from the airport I had seen a billboard, in English, advertising the new Riga office of DHL Express, so I knew that I could now easily ship things back to the States.) I did find another terrific oil painting that I would have been most happy with, and again it was reasonably priced: 90,000 rubles, or 600 dollars. I could not bring myself to buy it, however, as I stood there with my in-law, a nurse whose salary was about 5,000 rubles a month. I could not spend a year-and-a-half of her salary on what appeared to be such a frivolous purchase. So, again, I returned empty-handed.

Second, in March *The New York Times* reported the ruble-dollar exchange rate was at 660 to the dollar, which would have boosted the original painting cost to 200,000 rubles, and in April a *Times* article on the former Soviet economy included the sentence, "The ruble is essentially worthless."

Should one conclude from this lengthy vignette that economically, in the long run, only art endures?

The Genesis of Weirdo Test Items

A recent lawsuit (Sibi Soroka et al. versus Dayton-Hudson Corporation) in the California courts provides an interesting window on the internal workings of psychological tests, and reminds me once again of some of the quirkier features of my chosen profession, that of psychological-test author.

The genesis of this case was the plaintiff's application for a job as a security officer at a Target store, a division of Dayton-Hudson. As part of the application process he was required to complete a psychological screening battery that included two well-known personality inventories: the Minnesota Multiphasic Personality Inventory (MMPI) and the California Psychological Inventory (CPI). Because security officers may have to interact with the public in potentially controversial ways, such as in the apprehension and arrest of shoplifters, Target wished to screen out applicants who were emotionally unstable.

The plaintiff alleged that some of the test questions constituted an invasion of his privacy. He particularly objected to items dealing with religion and sexual behavior—for instance, "I believe there is a Devil and a Hell in afterlife" and "Many of my dreams are about sex matters."

The legal issues raised by this case are fascinating, profound, and much too complex to be dealt with in this space. For example, the simple question of exactly what constitutes "invasion of privacy" and when, if ever, society is justified in being invasive can lead to heated philosophic discussions. One could argue that virtually any question can be invasive. Even the basic query "How are you feeling this morning?" could be so construed under some circumstances. The potential dialogue, "'I'm feeling fine.' 'Good, then we will drop the charges,'" demonstrates one possible example. (A more extreme example might be even more illustrative: "'I'm feeling fine.' 'Good, then we will proceed with the execution.'")

Even if questions are invasive, the rights of society might arguably take precedence over the individual's right to privacy, especially in the selection of people applying for sensitive positions. An applicant for the position of airline pilot may well be expected to answer truthfully a question such as "Have you ever fainted under stress?" or an applicant for the position of nuclear-power-station attendant might well be asked "Have you ever fantasized about blowing up the world?" Indeed, potential members of the Supreme Court are even now being asked if they have ever smoked dope and if they have ever failed to file Social Security taxes for a household employee.

These questions are clearly invasive and, given the implications of negative responses, they had damn well better be. (True or false: "I am offended by the use of profanity in public.")

Laying aside the legal issues, I have been pondering the historical developments that have created this impasse, and especially how oddball test items—which many people find whimsical at best, obscene in the extreme—first came into existence.

Two early strategies drove the development of weirdo items. First, the authors of the MMPI—two innovative scientists from the University of Minnesota, Starke Hathaway, Ph.D., and Charnley McKinley, M.D.—were interested in developing an analytic method to diagnose mental illness more accurately; they wanted some approach that would be more reliable than a simple interview. At the time, in the late 1930s and early 1940s, this was truly innovative, and its success over the years marks this as a once-in-a-generation breakthrough. To develop their screening items, they interviewed patients in psychiatric wards and then sculpted their test items from the patients' responses. The result was a 566-item inventory with items such as: "It makes me angry to have people hurry me," "There are certain people whom I dislike so much that I am inwardly pleased when they are catching it for something they have done," and "My neck spots with red often."

In addition, Hathaway and McKinley, recognizing that honesty of response might be an issue, developed a set of "validity" items to check on the respondent's apparent truthfulness or lack thereof. To serve this purpose, items such as the following were prepared: "Once in a while I put off until tomorrow what I ought to do today" and "My table manners are not quite as good at home as when I am out in company." The test results of anyone who answers "False" to these and other so-called validity items now come under skeptical scrutiny.

The MMPI, the grandparent of all personality tests, spawned many imitators and, on the lighter side, many parodies. Its technology has been widely adopted, and other weird, whimsical, and disturbing items have been written, some serious, some designed as clever though devious validity items, and some only fodder for in-house jokes among psychologists.

I have long felt that the term "MMPI parody" is redundant. Because of the nature of its content, the MMPI is essentially a parody of itself. To demonstrate that point, and to entertain you with some of the more creative outputs of psychological humor, here are twelve items. Four of them are actual MMPI test items, four of them are artificial validity items, and four of them are parodies made up to spoof the system. How many can you accurately classify?

1. At times I have kept a pet monkey in my room.
2. As long as I can remember, I have had amnesia.
3. I can sleep during the day but not at night.
4. I cannot count past fifty.
5. As a child I used to fantasize about life as an accountant.
6. I like tall women.
7. I have never seen an apple.
8. I never seem to finish anything that I
9. My memory seems to be all right.
10. To improve the accuracy of your test processing, please leave this item blank.
11. I used to be indecisive but now I am not so sure.
12. I have never seen a vision.

The answers are printed at the end of the column. If you were able to identify all of the actual items, you may have a mind devious enough to consider authoring psychological tests. If you were also able to correctly identify all of the validity items, you might additionally consider law school. If you were able to correctly identify all of the parody items, you are weird, man, like really rad-ly weird.

In summary, I offer up these additional items: please respond "True," "False," or "Not Yet Committed."

1. Products of a psychologically trained mind may suggest new meanings for the word *normal*.
2. A combination of lawyers and psychologists working together on legal cases constitutes a substantial threat to our national security.
3. I can now understand the dynamics underlying Campbell's plaintive plea that as a psychologist he often gets no respect.

Update: Since this column was written the case referred to here has been settled. In July 1993, Target stores agreed to award 1.3 million dollars to prospective security guards who were assessed between 1987 and 1991. An additional sixty thousand dollars will be paid to four plaintiffs named in the lawsuit.

Target admitted no legal wrongdoing in the case. A Target spokesperson said, "We just felt it was in our best interests to go on and move forward" (from the AP wire, July 11, 1993).

Answers: actual items (3, 6, 9, 12), validity items (1, 4, 7, 10), parody items (2, 5, 8, 11).

Simulated Foxholes on a New Jersey Beach

Psychologists use a concept called the *critical incident technique* (CIT) to describe significant, tangible, specific events in the life of an individual or organization. The theory is that a study of critical incidents can help us understand the deeper, underlying dynamics in the world of work.

For example, a study of critical incidents in the life of a bank teller might focus on how that person would handle a situation where a customer is trying to cash a third-party check drawn on an account that has insufficient funds to cover it. The teller would be faced with the challenge of explaining to the customer that the bank could not honor the check, obviously a frustrating experience for the customer. Presumably, some tellers could handle the situation smoothly in a way that would not alienate the customer; others might be blunter and leave the customer angry with the bank in a situation in which it was merely an innocent bystander. A study of the ways in which "successful" versus "unsuccessful" tellers handle a specific bad-check incident might help in training future tellers. Thus, we see the value of studying critical incidents.

Recently, while engaged in discussion with a group of brilliant and unrestrained extraverts on how young managers might be trained to empower their people, a critical incident from my early leadership experience flashed through my mind. Although it happened almost four decades ago, it made an enormous impact on me, and I am certain that this event is connected with my current propensity to turn over a substantial amount of decision-making power to my subordinates.

I am standing on a beach in New Jersey with thirty soldiers and a sergeant. It is August 1956. I had entered the Army a month earlier as a brand-new second lieutenant. I was eager and naive—to say I was green would be a vast understatement—and I had been assigned to "The Officer's Basic Course" at Fort Monmouth, New Jersey, conducted by the Signal Corps. In ten weeks, the Army attempted to give me and about thirty-five other equally green lieutenants enough background on a wide array of communication equipment—walkie-talkies, telephone switchboards, radio relay transmitters—that we could go out and supervise the enlisted soldiers who were the technical experts actually operating the installations.

It was excellent but highly technical training. In the classroom, every day from 8 a.m. until 5 p.m., we focused on watts, ohms, carrier waves, and antennae reception patterns. There was little about how to manage people who knew more about what they were doing than you did.

Some of you will remember that 1956 was the year that the Cold War heated up. Russian soldiers invaded Czechoslovakia, and international tensions were high. As young officers, we were taught that the Red Menace was just over the horizon and at any moment we could expect to see Russian uniforms on our beaches.

One afternoon our class was informed, in that peculiarly tense and slightly spicy manner that military officers use when grave secrecy is involved, that the following morning we were going to take part in a large-scale simulated invasion defense of the East Coast.

The Russians were indeed coming—at least in concept.

We were ordered to report "tomorrow at oh-dark-thirty" in full battle dress, including backpacks, sleeping bags, carbines, entrenching tools, shelter halves: the works. There was a certain amount of amusement—"Come on; this is New Jersey"—including the raw ribaldry that young men under stress fall back on. "We'll just let them breathe the air off U.S. 1 and they will frigging suffocate." Then there was a certain tension as we realized this was our first "real" assignment. This was not a classroom exercise.

The next morning, in highly starched battle fatigues, we were loaded into large six-by-six trucks and moved out. Each of us was given a platoon of roughly thirty enlisted soldiers, a platoon sergeant, and a stretch of New Jersey beach to defend.

In the interests of national security, we were told nothing else. The captain who dropped me off swept his arm in an arc and said, "Lt. Campbell, these are your men. Your sector runs from that sand dune up there to that scrub pine down yonder. Get your troops in place. I'll be back later to see how you are doing."

And that's how I found myself standing, in full battle dress, before sunup, on a beach in New Jersey, in front of thirty sleepy soldiers, wondering what in hell I was going to do next.

What to do?

Well, first, look assured. You're an officer now. Don't show fear, uncertainty, or confusion.

Yeah, right.

I had had a few lectures on military tactics and vaguely remembered that in a defensive position I should spread my soldiers out around the perimeter, make certain they had overlapping fields of fire, and have them dig foxholes.

But the more I thought about it, the less certain I was that foxholes were a good idea. Even in those pre-environmental-concern days, digging six-foot-deep holes in a public beach seemed to have some troubling aspects. Still, each man did have an entrenching tool . . .

The sun was coming over the horizon, the truck that had dropped us off was long gone, there was no superior officer to consult, I had no radio, and the troops were shuffling around waiting for instructions.

After just the proper amount of uncomfortable delay, the sergeant stepped forward. "Sir, may I make a suggestion?"

"Sure, Sarge," I said, looking at him more closely. He was an old man of thirty-something; he wore a Combat Infantryman's Badge on his fatigues, undoubtedly from Korea, and a look of calm competence.

"Sir," he said, leading me over to a small knoll, ostensibly for better visibility but really, as I realized later, to get us out of earshot of the troops, "Why don't I spread the men out along the beach about every fifty yards in groups of three and have them draw a circle around themselves in the sand with their entrenching tools to serve as a simulated foxhole."

He paused briefly and gave a slight grin.

"This is a simulated invasion, sir, so a simulated foxhole should be just fine."

Now that was a great idea, but . . .

"Okay, Sarge, but why groups of three? Couldn't we get more coverage if we spread them out singly so there would be better interlocking fields of fire?"

"Yes, sir, we could do that, but my instincts tell me that we are going to be sitting out here on our thumbs for several hours without much to do, and time passes faster when you have someone to talk to. If there are three of them together, the men can shoot the bull with each other and . . ." — there was a brief, almost infinitesimal pause—"smoke."

Smoke?

I turned to look at him. Maybe I hadn't had much training in battlefield deployment but, as a brand-new officer, I had been thoroughly indoctrinated about smoking: soldiers don't smoke while on duty, especially guard duty, which this appeared to be.

Our eyes locked together. His gaze was firm, unwavering. After a few seconds, I looked away. With that, we both knew that communication had occurred. He had made a suggestion and I had not overruled him. The men could smoke.

"Okay, Sarge, spread them out."

He marched them down the beach, dropping off clusters of three every fifty yards or so, and I watched each trio draw its circle in the sand and then take out cigarettes.

I found the highest point on the beach and established what I considered to be a command post, took off my pack, and sat down. When the sergeant finished he came up, sat down beside me, and offered me a cigarette.

"No thanks." He smoked anyway.

The hours dragged by. No hammers and sickles appeared. After a certain amount of chitchat between us, I asked, "Sarge, where did you get that idea for the simulated foxholes?"

"Lieutenant," he replied, "I've been on dozens of maneuvers. I've learned that officers really love simulations . . . Makes everything look more realistic, I guess."

Shortly after that he stood up and said, "Here comes the brass." A jeep was coming up the road with a captain and a major in it. When it stopped beside us, I saluted, smartly I hoped.

The major said, "What's your situation here, lieutenant?"

"Sir, the troops are spread out, covering the beach from that sand dune up there to that scrub pine down yonder. Each group has drawn a circle in the sand around themselves to simulate a foxhole. We haven't seen any enemy activity."

I paused.

"The simulated foxhole was the sergeant's idea."

I wondered at that instant, as I must have wondered a hundred times in the succeeding thirty-seven years, whether I uttered that last sentence to acknowledge the sergeant's contribution or to shift the blame to him if it turned out to be a bad idea. I'll never know what my true motivation was.

"Good idea, sergeant," said the major.

He went on. "The exercise is over. Get your troops back on the road. A truck will be by in a few minutes to pick you up."

There my specific memories end. I don't recall how and when we got home, or whether there were any debriefing sessions, or whether I ever acknowledged to the sergeant that I was vividly aware that he had saved my tail. Left to my own devices, I am certain that I would have done something pretty dumb.

His actions made an indelible impression on me. It was definitely a critical incident in my leadership training, and it was certainly related to empowerment. Although he was my subordinate, he demonstrated clearly but diplomatically that he knew far more than I did about the challenge at hand and his suggestions were superior to anything that I might have dreamed up. The benefits of empowering that sergeant, or turning over authority and responsibility to him, were obvious.

The reason that specific event has had an important permanent influence on me is that it made me aware that the people reporting to me often know more than I do and are worth listening to.

Perhaps it has also made me a more outspoken subordinate. I remember how much the sergeant helped me, and I am prone to thinking that my superiors must also want to be helped. The few occasions where that strategy has backfired have also been critical incidents, but that's another story.

If my calculations are correct and if fate has willed it, the sergeant is now coming into his seventies. I hope he is healthy and happy, and I wish there was some way he could know about his beneficial impact on a naive young officer. In this case, the empowerment was upwards, and I never see a simulated foxhole without thinking of him.

Some of My Best Friends Manage Hotels, But . . .

I'm a fan of Andy Rooney. I like his folksy cynicism and his capacity for lyrical outrage at the trivial vexations of life. In admiration, I thought I would try an Andy Rooney-type column. Here goes.

You know what irritates me, what really torques me off? It's checking into some fancy hotel, where the atrium is filled with enough greenery to look like an endangered rain forest and the bellmen are dressed like Prussian officers visiting Disneyland, and paying more for an overnight stay than my father made in a week—and then being charged every time I use the telephone.

You know what I mean. Just pick up the phone and call some restaurant for reservations, or call the airline to check your outgoing flight, and it costs you 75 cents—96 cents if you happen to be in Manhattan.

It just doesn't figure. They don't charge you for taking a shower; they don't charge you for turning on the air-conditioning; they don't charge you for using two of those big, luxurious towels after a shower when one would do; they don't charge you for turning on the television—unless you happen to punch the pay-TV channels. (My father would have been appalled by the idea of paying $7.95 for sitting alone in a room at night watching a movie. I can hear him say, "Buy a book. At least you will be getting educated, and when it's finished, you still have the book.") They don't even charge you for the ice, which, to be honest, I consider a very good deal. I mean, even the pharaohs didn't get free ice.

Incidentally, did you ever notice how often you hear your father's voice in your ear, even if he has been gone for many years, especially when you are spending money?

Anyway, you know how these fancy hotels really lavish a lot of attention on you. Sometimes when you check in, you find enough free stuff in the bathroom to stock the sundries section of a small drugstore: soap, shampoo, conditioner, body lotion, emery boards, shoe cloths, shower caps, suntan lotion, mouthwash—although, for some reason, there is never any toothpaste. I don't use body lotion (I do fantasize about it a bit), and I seldom use shoe cloths or shower caps, but I use a lot of toothpaste. Why do you suppose there is never any toothpaste in hotel rooms?

And another thing—you get a free newspaper. I have to admit, I really appreciate that. It's usually *USA Today*—except on Saturdays, when you get the local *Daily Bugle* or whatever. When I am in Minneapolis, which I am a lot, and it's Saturday, I get to read Jim Klobuchar and Barbara Flanagan in the *Minneapolis Star-Tribune*; those are very interesting people to start the day with.

But, I mean, if you get a free paper, why not a free telephone call?

On one occasion I complained about telephone charges on the comment card they left in my room. I tried to be funny about it, because humor is usually more effective than anger. I made some little quip about being charged for the telephone but not the shampoo.

In retrospect, I think that may have been a little too cute.

The letter I received back from the customer service department was not cute; it acknowledged that I have an interesting point but that "economic conditions" and the "cost of installation" dictate that the hotel has to charge extra for telephone service.

I don't know. I would think that running the pipes for hot and cold water to my room would be a lot more expensive than simply running a telephone wire.

Maybe I reached a better perspective on this recently when I visited a big city, checked into a fancy hotel, and had dinner with a friend. She lived in our home several years ago when she was a foreign exchange student; she has since finished her BA and MBA and, with superb language skills, has taken a job in the sales office of a "premium" property of one of the major hotel chains.

She took me to a sports bar for dinner, where the decor reeked of testosterone, but it was a Tuesday night and it was quiet. At one point I told her about my irritation with telephone charges in expensive hotels.

She laughed. "I tell you, David," she said in her now-faint, but still exotic, foreign accent, "I sat in on a budget meeting recently and I was astonished at how much the phone charges contribute to our monthly performance. The costs are nothing, so the profits are high. How do you say it? 'They drop right to the bottom line.'"

Well, that's my point. The costs are almost nothing, so why should I have to pay?

I told her about sending in the guest-comment card and she said, "That's the way to do it. Those cards are really important."

Which started me thinking. I am not the kind of guy to start a revolution. (My father would say, "Now don't start trouble that you're not prepared to finish.") So I will try to be moderate.

But what would happen if ten percent of the readers of this column—or even just one percent—sent in guest-comment cards asking gently why they are being charged for telephone service when they are not charged for cable TV or for hot showers or for ice? You might begin by thanking them for the newspaper.

Maybe while you were at it you could mention the toothpaste.

As Andy Rooney might say, I have nothing against the fine people in the hotel business. It is just that some things are rational and other things are not, and, in my opinion, hotel telephone charges fall into the latter, irrational category. I would even rather pay for the ice.

A Cadre of Colorless Leaders

I spend a lot of time at the computer reviewing the results of the psychological surveys of corporate executives. This gives me an intriguing, if somewhat artificial, window on the world. Recently I passed an afternoon browsing through the current collective corporate psyche as reflected in one survey and I ran across some important data.

We have responses from hundreds of people to the Campbell Leadership Index (CLI): an instrument that asks a person to describe himself or herself using a list of adjectives, and which asks knowledgeable observers to describe this person using the same list of adjectives. In reviewing the rank-ordering of these adjectives for several samples of corporate types, I was gratified to see that the data suggested that these were good people. Specifically, the most frequently selected adjectives, by both self and observer, were: *responsible, dependable, ethical,* and *credible.*

Good enough. At that point I should have put on my coat and gone home.

I did not, however, and when I looked at the least frequently selected adjectives, I was dismayed to see that they were: *colorful, dramatic, eccentric,* and *flamboyant.* They were not just average in endorsement level; they were not slightly below average; they were at the absolute bottom. I had put these particular adjectives on the list because of my belief that it is good for a leader to be colorful—to stand out, to be visible, to convey a sense of vibrancy, of uniqueness, of visible energy and imagination, to be different in a notable way; I was thinking of leaders such as Lee Iacocca, Martin Luther King Jr., Golda Meir, Gloria Steinem, and Ted Turner.

Obviously, people do not share my belief. The bottom line, the disturbing news, is that we are apparently being managed by a cadre of colorless leaders, and we are satisfied with this.

I find that distressing and, as an aside, I am beginning to understand why over the years I have been involved in a sizable collection of organizational episodes in which someone in a position of power has reacted to something I did with, "He did what?" My little bursts of, as I saw it, amusing creativity have often not been appreciated. We do not seem comfortable with a person in a leadership position who, as *eccentricity* is described in the CLI, "marches to a different trombone."

You may be saying to yourself now, "So what? Why shouldn't we be happy with this demonstrated high level of dependability, responsibility, and credibility, even if it is tinged with a gray monotony?"

There is a legitimate argument, I believe, that true organizational creativity requires some pizzazz. Left to their own devices, brilliant but colorless men in power suits can steer even the most talented organization onto the rocks. Closer to home, I am concerned with the graying of my own world as I roam through it, and with how little color and creativity I routinely encounter.

To illustrate my point, let me give you one specific example of some colorful behavior and its beneficial impact on the people around me. I dearly wish I had more.

Over the past thirty years I have been on at least 2,500 airline flights. With the single following exception, I have never seen any of my fellow passengers do anything exceptional, creative, or colorful. I have seen a few people throw up; I have seen plenty of selfish acts—hogging the overhead luggage compartment—and unselfish acts—giving up a window seat so that a couple can sit together—but I had never seen anything "colorful" until just before Christmas 1993.

I was returning to Colorado Springs from the West Coast. Much of the eastern United States was shut down that day because of heavy snow and, because of the ripple effect, flights all over the country were running late.

After some preliminary diversions out of Portland, I sat for three unanticipated hours in the Sacramento airport, our pilot waiting for permission from Denver air-traffic control to take off. I finally arrived in Denver long after the scheduled connection to Colorado Springs but, not surprisingly, that flight was even later, so I still had another hour—at 11:00 p.m.—to kill in the Denver airport.

Among my fellow travelers there was a sense of irritation and despair. Almost all flights were late or canceled; luggage was lost; people were tired and hungry and looking for someone to blame. No one smiled or made eye contact. Everyone had long ago read their traveling cache of newspapers, magazines, or books. Long lines of people were at the phones, trying to reach someone to tell them of the delay.

Into this miasmic fog inhabited by travel-weary zombies walked Wolfgang. Portly, fiftyish, well dressed, speaking perfect English with a detectable European accent, he moved among the people waiting at the gate for the Colorado Springs flight. He had a large bundle of expensive silk red roses—fifty of them, as it turned out—and he talked with each passenger.

He asked, with a charming smile, "Are you going on the flight to Colorado Springs?"

It was by then almost midnight, and bone-weary passengers looked up with the glazed eyes of the abandoned, wondering what this guy was up to. He did not look like a pony-tailed Hare Krishna, but they are usually the only people who approach strangers in airports.

In a patient, engaging manner, he explained: "I am Wolfgang and I am flying with you to Colorado Springs. My fiancé, Brunhilde, is meeting me at the plane. [I have changed the names here but the ones that I am using are faithful to the characters.] Today is her fiftieth birthday. I have here fifty red roses. I would like each of the first fifty passengers off the plane to hand a rose to Brunhilde and say 'Happy Birthday' to her. Would you mind doing that?"

Who could refuse? And who could help smiling? Wolfgang passed from one traveler to another, leaving a trail of humor and anticipation; this was different, this was creative, this was fun.

We all trooped on board, clutching Brunhilde's roses.

After the standard preflight briefing ("In case of emergency, an oxygen mask will drop down from above . . ."), the flight attendant added, "I think you have all met Wolfgang, and we are happy to help him greet Brunhilde. He has asked me to tell you that she is easily recognizable: he describes her as a beautiful, buxom blonde with a gleaming smile."

I cringed. "For Pete's sake, Wolfgang, we don't use words like 'buxom' in this country anymore." The other passengers merely grinned, and we took off into the night.

Nineteen minutes out of Denver, we touched down in Colorado Springs. No one napped on the flight. We were all too curious about Brunhilde. A few wrote whimsical birthday greetings on the little tag attached to each rose.

When we rolled up to the terminal there was an air of eagerness among the zombies. We were going to meet Brunhilde! By general agreement, Wolfgang was the first off the plane. By the time I exited, about twentieth in the line of roses, a small queue had built up in front of Wolfgang and Brunhilde; everyone felt the need to offer birthday greetings and shake Wolfgang's hand—and strangely it just felt right for everyone to give Brunhilde a small, warm hug.

She lived up to her billing: fiftyish, blond, buxom, with a gleaming smile, and she was also giggly and flustered. She kept saying, "I can't believe this, I can't believe this, I can't believe this." She looked like a woman well loved.

From her comments, I deduced that Wolfgang had not told her how many roses were coming and, out of curiosity, I hung around to see the fun. The roses kept rolling out of the plane, the birthday greetings, handshakes, and hugs kept coming, Brunhilde kept giggling and not believing, and Wolfgang kept beaming and being debonair.

It was a marvelous event: colorful, dramatic, eccentric, with no downside.

We picked up our luggage—those of us lucky enough to have it—and at 1:00 a.m., I set out for the drive home. I grinned all the way, humming the theme from "The Ride of the Valkyries" in honor of Wolfgang.

So there it is, a colorful incident with a positive glow. Why does something like this happen in my life only once in thirty years, and then only when created by someone from another country? Where has the drama gone? Okay, so we are responsible, ethical, and dependable. Do we also have to be bland?

Perhaps we in the United States should listen more to our colorful ancestors, such as Emerson, who said, "Men grind and grind in the mill of truism, and nothing comes out but what was put in. But the moment they desert the tradition for a spontaneous thought, then poetry, wit, hope, virtue, learning, anecdote, all flock to their aid."

In a personal sense, if you were in a leadership position, and if you were ever brought to trial in the future for being creative, what evidence would the prosecution be able to find?

An Internationally Sized Laboratory for Creative Leadership

I am presently in Riga, Latvia, where my wife Rita—an Air Force officer, Latvian immigrant, Ph.D., and tenured faculty member at the U.S. Air Force Academy—is part of a U.S. mission to advise the Latvian government on how to set up a modern military defense force, professionally trained and responsive to civilian control. During the next five months, I will be observing, thinking, and writing.

There may be no better way to describe our life here than to begin with two street-corner encounters the day after my arrival.

Rita's daughter Erika, aged eleven, and I arrived in Riga on Sunday. Monday morning we all set out from our apartment compound, which was built as vacation homes for Soviet executives from the newspaper *Pravda*, to do some errands. Heading for the tram stop, we walked through tree-lined but poorly paved streets. It was a desolate, rainy day, and I was once again struck by the absence of color in the Baltics; even the billboards have a way of looking windswept and gray.

In this setting, Rita, in her trim, well-pressed, bright blue U.S. Air Force uniform with her silver lieutenant-colonel leaves gleaming on her shoulders, blended in approximately as well as would, say, a giraffe walking down Fifth Avenue. Everyone stared at her. As we waited at the tram stop I noticed one small car slowly passing, the driver studying Rita. Hey, I thought, I know that guy! It's Roberts!

I have been to Latvia twice before—in 1990 and 1992—and have met a couple of dozen of my wife's relatives, including two of her cousins, brothers, Roberts and Gundars. (All Latvian male names end with an "s.")

I waved, pointing out Roberts to Rita. "That's Gundars," she corrected. I thought, but left unsaid, "Ah, all Latvians look alike in the rain," and Rita went into the street to explain to her cousin, whom she had not yet contacted, what she was doing on a street corner in June in the rain—in full U.S. military regalia.

She also explained to him why she had not yet phoned anyone; she had been working ten to twelve hours a day, helping with the preparations for President Clinton's July 6 visit. We shook hands with Gundars through the window, and with his two teenage daughters, and they drove off.

That evening the phone rang several times in the apartment. The word had spread: our American cousin, Rita, is in town. In an environment where the Communist work ethic ("We pretend to work and they pretend to pay us") has not yet been overwhelmed by the free-market concept of long hours, they had difficulty comprehending why Rita, who had been in the country about three weeks, had not yet found time to visit her family. Thus we were introduced to our first cultural clash.

Later that evening, as we were walking to the local restaurant for dinner, we had a second peculiar encounter. I was lagging behind Rita and Erika when I heard, from behind, a cheery, familiar call in a distinctly Midwestern accent, "Hello, David!"

For a split second of astonishment I thought, "There is not a friend of mine within a thousand miles." But I was neglecting the U.S. traveler's propensity to make friends easily.

When I turned around, there was John, a U.S. Army Special Forces master sergeant assigned to the Latvian military liaison team. I had met him in Rita's office that morning. A tall, good-looking guy from Michigan, he lives in the same apartment compound as we do and, like us, he was on his way to dinner. He joined us and we were four.

Every traveler in a strange land has an interesting story. Four days earlier, John had graduated from the Russian language school in Monterey, California. Three days earlier he had left Logan Airport in Boston for Europe. Two days earlier he had landed in Latvia, and the day before he had spent the day translating for the presidential advance party and the technical supervisor at the Riga airport. Three 747s were scheduled to arrive together—Air Force One with the President and about twenty-five staff members; a second, backup plane with another one hundred twenty-five staff members; and a third, press plane with two hundred journalists—in an airport smaller than, say, Duluth's.

In such a situation, where there are dozens of ways to screw up, genius, as Michelangelo reminded us, is in the details. For example, they ascertained that in all of Latvia there are only two sets of mobile airline stairs tall enough to reach the doorway of a 747. As presumably neither the President, nor his staff, nor the journalists would want to exit through their emergency chutes, and because none of these groups would likely take kindly to waiting their turn on the tarmac, something creative had to be done.

One possible solution: the arrival times could be staggered so that the press could be on the ground to cover the President disembarking from Air Force One. The departure times could also be staggered, with Air Force

One and its backup loading first. John grinned, "Of course, that means that after departure, Air Force One would have to circle over Poland, waiting for the press plane to catch up and land first in Warsaw, their next stop."

We speculated that if the circling could be scheduled during one of the more important World Cup games, half of the world would not notice anyway.

John mentioned that a second possible solution was to fly in another set of airline stairs from Finland. I fought back saying the first thing that came to mind, "But how would you get them through airport security in Helsinki?"

Spontaneous quips have gotten me into so much trouble over the last few years that I now screen all my remarks for possible political impact; a whimsical (read *unrestrained*) sense of humor can be heavy baggage these days.

One summary comment after only two days in Riga: Despite the well-publicized, and deserved, reports of chaotic conditions in Eastern Europe, the Latvians have made substantial progress in two years. Buildings are being restored, lawns are being trimmed, fences are being painted; street-corner artists, musicians, and flower-sellers provide a festive air even in the rain; and the shops are full of merchandise—much of it still out of pocketbook range for the average Latvian, to be sure. The city feels vibrant and progressive. Soon, they may even learn how to conquer the challenge of public plumbing facilities.

Whether this column qualifies as a typical "Inklings" offering on creativity and leadership could be debated, I suppose, but to me it feels as if that is all it is. To change their world, to activate what the Latvians call their "Second Awakening" (the first was in 1919 when the Baltics initially won independence) requires more creative leadership than a mere battle over market share or budget deficits. Eastern Europe is now an internationally sized laboratory for creative leadership, and I think it will be well served by pragmatic Western techniques such as performance appraisals, goal-setting, brainstorming, 360-degree feedback, self-managed teams, career counseling, and a professionally trained military that is responsive to civilian control. I intend to spend my time here with my nose pressed against the glass of this laboratory.

Now, Exactly Where Is Latvia?

As readers of my previous column know, I am living in Riga, Latvia, this fall with my wife, a Latvian American who is a U.S. Air Force lieutenant colonel assigned to the U.S. Embassy in an advisory role. As a result of this experience, and a couple of recent trips back to the U.S. where I talked about Latvia with a host of friends and professional colleagues, I have become aware of just how little most Americans know about this country. To demonstrate, here is a "Ten-question Latvian-awareness Quiz." Be forewarned: although the questions are elementary, few Westerners get even one right answer. Before I married a Latvian immigrant in 1990, I would have scored zero.

1. **Location**: Latvia is bounded by four countries and a body of water. For one point credit, name any three of them.

2. **Size**: How big is Latvia? Give an example of another country or a state in the U.S. that is approximately the same size. One point credit for any reasonable answer.

3. **Latitude**: How far north is Latvia? Name any American city at approximately the same latitude. One point credit.

4. **Population**: How many people live in Latvia? One point given for any answer within fifty percent. Extra credit question: What percentage of the people living in the country are Latvian? Two points credit for any answer within ten percent.

5. **Names**: All Latvian male first names end in the same letter. For one point, name that letter.

6. **American attention**: Who was the first American president to visit Latvia? For an extra-credit point, where did he sleep?

7. **Exports**: Name Latvia's most visible export. One point credit.

8. **Problems**: What is the minimum drinking age in Latvia? Subtract one point for every year you are off.

9. **Visibility**: Respond to any of the following: Draw the Latvian flag. Name the Latvian currency. Cite the Latvian international telephone code. Hum a few bars of the Latvian national anthem or sing a phrase from any Latvian folk song. Say "Hello," "Good-bye," "Please," "Thank-you," "One, two, three," or "I would like to buy a beer" in Latvian. Name any famous Latvian—artist, athlete, composer, military leader, scientist, politician, president, or astronomer (the last should be a giveaway for Minnesotans). One point credit.

10. **Politics**: What is Latvia's current, single most overriding political concern? One point credit.

11. For a bonus point, how do Latvians spell the name of their country?

Now, get out your red pencils and score your paper.

Answers

1. Latvia is bounded, from twelve o'clock, clockwise, by Estonia, Russia, Belarus (on some maps, Byelorussia), Lithuania, and the Baltic Sea. Sweden and Finland are each about one hundred miles away by water.

2. Latvia is about the size of West Virginia and is slightly larger than Denmark or Switzerland.

3. At a latitude of approximately 59 degrees, the country is roughly as far north as Juneau, Alaska.

4. The population is 2.7 million. Any figure from 1.4 to 4 million is acceptable. Roughly fifty-three percent of the population is Latvian; the remainder are citizens from the former U.S.S.R., mostly Russians, who have not been given Latvian citizenship—a festering conflict that has led to great stress.

5. All first names of male Latvians end in the letter "s." Some examples are: Uldis, Gundars, Alvis, Emmis, Eduards, Edmunds, and Roberts. My wife's relatives refer to me as "Davids."

6. Clinton was the first U.S. president to visit Latvia. On July 6, 1994, he flew in at 10 a.m., schmoozed a bit with the Latvian, Estonian, and Lithuanian presidents, gave a speech, listened to a wonderful Latvian women's choir sing "America the Beautiful" in front of their Freedom Monument, acknowledged the soldiers who stand eternal guard over that monument, and left for Warsaw at 5 p.m. Therefore, no U.S. president has ever slept in Latvia. No matter. The Latvians were very appreciative. (He shook hands with every single choir member.)

7. Hands down, amber jewelry is Latvia's most visible export.

8. There is no minimum drinking age. Guess what one of Latvia's major problems is. (Oops. Even though a savvy insider from the U.S. told me that there is no minimum drinking age, and even though I often see kids as young as fifteen and sixteen drinking openly on the streets, a Latvian who checked this column for me told me that "Latvia has a minimum drinking age—twenty-one." "But," I protested, "it must not be enforced." "No, of course it isn't," she said. Then looking at me slyly, knowing of my

strong disgust for how Latvia was managed by the communists, she added, "But this rule was enforced under the communists.")

9. The Latvian flag has three horizontal stripes. The middle one is white; the top and bottom stripes are purple-crimson. The currency is the *latt*, which has one hundred *santims* each, and is worth about two dollars. The country telephone code is 371. The anthem—you'll have to wait until they win an Olympic medal to hear it. (A Latvian cyclist finished well in this year's Tour de France.) The common phrases are: *Sveiki* (Hello); *Ata* (Good-bye); *Ludzu* (Please); *Paldies* (Thank-you); *Viens, divi, tris* (One, two, three); and *Alus, ludzu* (Beer, please), though in actuality a beer can be ordered in any language with a smile and appropriate hand gestures. Professor Karlis Kaufmanis from the University of Minnesota, famed, among other things, for having delivered his rapturous "Star of Bethlehem" lecture every Christmas season for the last forty years, was the only outstanding Latvian I knew until I met my spouse.

10. The current and most difficult political problem is how to handle citizenship for former Soviet residents. After the Russians invaded in 1940, they moved hundreds of Russian families here, who then had children. These children, many of them now in their forties and fifties, have grown up with no ties to Russia, yet they do not have Latvian citizenship and usually cannot speak the Latvian language. If I understand correctly, the Latvians stamp the passports of these people with a special stamp that forbids them state employment, the right to vote, and the right to own property. This is compounded by the fact that Latvia, with a higher standard of living than Russia and with wonderful seashore living and beautiful beaches, has been a magnet for retired Russian military officers, who have had portable pensions, and their descendants.

It is a serious dilemma. Understandably, the Latvians do not wish to grant citizenship to their former, often brutal, occupiers, especially since they would constitute a large voting block. Yet many of the second- or third-generation Russians had little to do firsthand with the former oppression.

When President Clinton touched on this issue in his speech here—bravely, I thought—by noting that "freedom without tolerance is freedom unfulfilled," the huge crowd in the center plaza went absolutely stone silent, even though they were otherwise exuberant in their welcome. When he said, "We will rejoice with you when the last of the foreign troops vanish from your homelands," he received thunderous applause. As with all of the other balls in the air in Eastern Europe now, it is not clear where this one will come down.

11. Latvians spell the name of their country *Latvija*.

* * *

If you scored, say, two or above on this quiz, you almost certainly have a first name that ends in "s" or you have a father, brother, or husband whose name does. To the extent that Latvia is a microcosmic study of the wrenching historic changes, good and bad, going on in Eastern Europe, it makes a wonderful laboratory for contemporary leadership events. Realistically, this same sort of "Weekly Reader Current Events Quiz" could be constructed for any of the other Baltic countries, or any of the former Soviet republics, and most of us would do as poorly. In trying to help them move forward toward a more Western democratic form of government and a higher standard of living, one of our handicaps is that we know so little about this portion of the world, which has been essentially closed to the West for the past fifty years. My major consolation is that now I can at least count to ten in Latvian and order a beer, even if I can't hum the national anthem.

Life in the Psychological Lane

The central feature of my professional career is psychological testing. Through this peculiar window I have an interesting view of life, especially when working with the varied groups that are involved with our Center.

At the Center, we are a strong advocate of psychological assessment, last year giving over 300,000 psychological surveys.

One of the major reasons for our success in this is that we provide complete privacy and absolute psychological security for the developmental process that the surveys drive. Although we are firm, straightforward, occasionally even relentless in holding up the assessment mirror for the leader to look into, we do not tear people apart. We are supportive. We are optimistic. We see glasses as half-full. Indeed, when we see glasses that are only ten percent full, we are prone to say, "Well, this ten percent provides a good starting place for you."

Following are five recent examples, taken from my travels, of what might be called "life in the psychological lane." What they have in common is a focus on psychological testing.

The first was a committee meeting of influential psychologists who were developing the national exam used to certify psychologists. More than five thousand candidates apply for certification each year, and new tests have to be continually prepared. The certification process is designed to protect the public, and the standards are high. Anyone who fails is denied the opportunity to earn a living as a therapist.

Naturally, the committee takes the assessment process very seriously, especially with the threat of litigation from failed applicants constantly hanging overhead. With each attack on the test, I am reminded of the plaintive plea reported some years ago in *The New York Times*: "It is not a higher grade I seek. I care nothing for grades. Grades are the obsession of a pedestrian society more focused on puerile rankings than on truth and beauty. However, society's gifts are bestowed on those who do well in this meaningless charade. Therefore, it is a higher grade I seek."

Because this is volunteer work, the committee is compensated by scenery and culinary adventures. The meetings are held in exotic resorts, and the after-work socializing is done over beautifully presented entrees, accompanied by mellow wines.

Which leads nicely into the next event, only a cab ride away but with a completely different group of players: a team of top commanders in the U.S. Army. During the early days of our country, the military acquired some choice real estate, and this meeting was also held in a surrealistically beautiful setting, with the ocean in front and a mountain range in the rear. The culinary adventures, however, were restricted to Danish pastries and coffee.

The commander, a man of great personal charm, and with enough stars on his collar to equip a modest-sized charm bracelet, had said to me, "I understand that you have a new team survey. How about we try that out with my team?" So we did.

The discussion had the hesitancy that appears when powerful people of different ranks are thrown together to discuss their working relationships. The commander was insistent about the need for candid discussion. Still, even when he mischievously quoted Samuel Goldwyn, "I want you guys to be completely honest about what you think, even if it costs you your jobs," he could not completely sweep away the web of concern about retribution.

Then an airplane ride home and, a few days later, several more airplanes to the Middle East, where I spent four days discussing leadership development with the Arab decision-makers who are in operational control of twenty-five percent of the world's known petroleum reserves.

As I am fond of saying, I grew up in Iowa and, therefore, am very easy to amaze, and I am in constant amazement over how useful our leadership-training techniques, including psychological assessment, are perceived to be for leaders in cultures very different from our own.

Then onto more airplanes to yet another beautiful beachfront setting, and with another jarring change of culture, this time with one hundred seventy-five marketing executives for exotic tropical liquors. Their challenge was, "Forget the lectures. We want an active experience that will help us work together better in teams," so that is what we did, but I also slipped in one survey to insure an individual touch. Supporting Ogden Nash's conclusion about the benefits of liquor over candy, the day went well. The survey results predicted that they would be enthusiastic and entertaining, and indeed they were.

During this time, I also managed to slip in two days of skiing with my good friend Tom Bouchard, a Professor at the University of Minnesota and the director of what I believe to be the most important psychological research project in history. Tom has spent most of his career searching out and psychologically assessing pairs of identical twins who were separated at birth and raised apart. He has currently assessed about one hundred thirty such pairs. Consequently, I think he knows more about genetics and psychological testing than anyone else on earth.

We talked on the ski lifts and in the lounges about means and standard deviations, intercorrelations, factor analyses, inheritability coefficients, baseball, and women. It was a welcome respite.

The final episode reeked of raw power. Because a few, select U.S. Congressmen decided that they wanted to improve their effectiveness as team players, I found myself seated at a conference table in Washington, D.C. Each of the six received, in sealed envelopes, four psychological test profiles: a career survey, a personality indicator, an interpersonal behavior questionnaire, and what is referred to as a "360-degree leadership index" (a questionnaire filled out by the Congressman and five people who have observed him in leadership situations). My colleague Bill Sternbergh and I then spent a long afternoon leading a discussion about the implications of the results. Although it was a calm, uneventful session, I had the sense of history in the making. I doubt that psychological tests have ever been used before in the halls of Congress.

Anyone who has been closely involved with such high fliers—influential psychologists, high-ranking military leaders, powerful Arab leaders, energetic marketing executives, or U.S. Congressmen—will not be surprised to learn that these people are mostly normal human beings with the same problems, quirks, and aspirations as the rest of us. They all want to leave the world a little better for their children than they themselves found it; they all smile when I quip, "If you encourage your subordinates to be creative, self-reliant, and independent, there is a grave danger that they will turn out to be . . . creative, self-reliant, and independent"; and they all identify with the stressful implications of Henry Mintzberg's finding that there is an average of nine minutes between interruptions in the life of a practicing leader.

Further, my experience has been that most of these highly successful, individually achieving people have buried within them, slightly below the surface, a persistent feeling of inferiority that quietly nags at them: "You are an impostor; you are in over your head; you don't belong in this high-powered company. These psychologists with their subtle tests are going to expose you for the fraud you are."

The major reason that I can quote that voice so well is that I also hear it muttering to me.

I was involved in one further leadership-assessment episode during this period. It was characterized by such appallingly poor performance that I cannot even discuss it here obliquely—but it did add to the rich tapestry of my life with psychological tests.

Maybe for my memoirs . . .

Nature's Way

- DEATH is nature's way of telling you to slow down.
- CHOCOLATE is nature's way of simulating the momentary impact of being slightly in love.
- TIME is nature's way of keeping everything from happening at once.
- POVERTY is nature's way of telling you you're in the wrong line of work (Craig Vetter).
- COMPUTERS are nature's way of moving enormous amounts of erroneous information around quickly and efficiently.
- LOVE is nature's way of tricking you into believing that people are different (George Bernard Shaw).
- A BABY is nature's way of reassuring us that the future is going to be okay.
- MURPHY'S LAW is nature's way of reassuring us that there are ultimate truths.
- POLITICAL CORRECTNESS is nature's way of demonstrating that good intentions are hard to implement.
- MARRIAGE is nature's way of creating delicious torment (William Shakespeare).
- NOSTALGIA is nature's way of demonstrating that you can never completely escape the place where your umbilical cord is buried (American Indian proverb).
- SMOKING is nature's way of solving the Social Security funding crisis.
- RELIGION is nature's way of comforting the afflicted.
- RELIGIOUS GUILT is nature's way of afflicting the comfortable.
- POLITICAL POLLS are nature's way of demonstrating that while figures don't lie, liars figure (Mark Twain).
- CASEY AT THE BAT is nature's way of warning us that we are all only one strike away from being a loser (Ernest Thayer).
- MARCH IN MINNESOTA is nature's way of showing Lutherans what hangovers feel like (Garrison Keillor).
- SUICIDE is nature's way of allowing us to escape the ills we have and fly to others we know not of (William Shakespeare).

- C󰀀ᴄ󰀀ɪsᴍ is nature's way of allowing academics to appear brilliant even when nonproductive (Teresa Amabile).
- Tʜᴇ Rᴜssɪᴀɴ ᴇᴄᴏɴᴏᴍʏ is nature's way of reminding us that Karl Marx never had to meet a payroll.
- The difference between ʟɪɢʜᴛɴɪɴɢ and ᴛʜᴇ ʟɪɢʜᴛɴɪɴɢ ʙᴜɢ is nature's way of demonstrating the value of picking precisely the right word (Mark Twain).
- Dɪᴇᴛɪɴɢ is nature's way of demonstrating that while fat cells may be immortal, willpower isn't.
- Tʜᴇ ᴡᴏʀᴅ *ᴇɢʀᴇɢɪᴏᴜs* is nature's way of reminding us that some words are destined to be misspelled.
- Cᴏᴄᴀɪɴᴇ is nature's way of telling you that you make too much money.
- Sɪʙʟɪɴɢs are nature's way of assuring us that our flaws might not be entirely our own fault (Glenn Hallam).
- Sᴜɴsᴇᴛs over water are nature's way of asking just what is important anyway.

Note: The source of each idea, if known, is listed in parentheses.

A Case of Etymological Thin Ice

The childhood retort of "Sticks and stones may break my bones but words can never hurt me" is not a popular sentiment these days, and most of us have learned to be careful with our words for fear of giving unintended offense. What one person might view as whimsical, if a bit coarse, another might see as sociologically insensitive, even inflammatory.

I recently encountered a case of such etymological thin ice on our office e-mail network.

A group of individuals not of the male gender decided to get together for lunch, simply for the purposes of friendship. The communal message announcing the time and place, received by all system participants, was headed, "Women's Luncheon."

I noticed the message as it scrolled up on my screen and thought briefly, "Interesting. That phraseology has a more matronly tone than my view of the double-X-chromosome-bearing members of our crew here."

The ice got even thinner in an RSVP to the luncheon message, again circulated to everyone, which said, "I can't make the Ladies Luncheon" and went on to say that it conflicted with her "Ladies bike ride." Knowing the writer, who is tanned, robust, and active, I thought it would likely be a mountain-bike ride over some challenging Colorado terrain, which is not exactly my idea of what "ladies" do in groups. Both "women" and "ladies" seemed to be inadequate terms for the spirited individuals in question.

At this point I could not resist entering the network, citing Cynthia Heimel's observation that there is no acceptable terminology for women in groups. Heimel, an ardent feminist who writes for *Playboy* (because, as she says, "They let me write about anything I want to and they pay better than *Vogue*"), points out that when you walk into a room of female friends there is no collective salutation that does not give offense: "Hi, girls," "Hi, women," "Hi, ladies," and "Hi, babes" are all either troublesome or stilted.

In contrast, as she points out, there are many choices for men: "Hi, guys," "Hi, fellows," "Hi, men," "Hi, comrades," and "Hi, mates." Each has a slightly different flavor but all are positive. Indeed, among men, even most derogatory terms would usually be seen as concealed affection—for instance, "Hello, you meatheads" or "What are you jerks up to?"

Heimel's suggestion is that, because "Hi, guys" is becoming more acceptable in many quarters, the neutering be continued until this label becomes appropriate for either or both genders.

My comments on the network stimulated more messages, including one from a female colleague who suggested that "Divas" would be a satisfactory label. (My dictionary says *diva* comes from the Italian word for "goddess" and defines it as "a prima donna; a leading woman singer, especially in grand opera.") She added, with a welcome whimsical touch, that she herself would be pleased to be addressed as the GHD (Grand High Diva).

Another writer volunteered that in an earlier chapter she had been posted to Europe in a government position with an official passport stamped in large letters, "Abroad on Government Business." When her same-sex compatriots realized that they all had such a document, they began saying to each other such things as, "I'm having lunch today with the broads."

With amused introspection, she continued, "Even today, if one of them says she will stop by, I think, 'Oh, one of the broads is coming.'"

An addition to this discussion appeared in the September 4, 1995, issue of *Fortune*; Daniel Seligman reported that the most hostile letters he has ever received came when he used the word "girls" in a previous column. (He now refers to it as the "G-word.") In musing about possible alternatives, he mentioned the recent Hillary Clinton trip to Asia when she was accompanied only by female reporters: This "came to be called the 'chicks trip.' The [press] stories say Hillary was amused, not mad, when this got into print." Seligman suggested that because of the "First Femme" support, "chick" may be "suddenly kosher."

I'm not sure. I think it is going to be a while before our CCL band puts "Chicks' Luncheon" at the heads of their memos.

Curiously, I do not see a gender-symmetrical replication of this dilemma. I cannot think of a single derogatory term applicable solely to members of my demographic class that creates any heartburn. In rummaging through my history I can think of derisive terms that have been thrown at me but none with enough potency to activate any adrenaline. At various points I have been called "hayseed," "dumb jock," "shrink," and "Yankee," but I never remember feeling anything other than amusement.

To be honest, I have been in groups of corporate decision-makers that were mockingly referred to as "the suits," a demeaning term suggesting a deferential corporate conformity where vacuums had been substituted for brains, and that bothered me—because I thought it had some validity. I seldom feel less creative than when I am power-dressed in my Hong Kong tailored pinstripes, wearing Allen Edmonds tasseled loafers, and surrounded by those who are similarly accoutered.

I suppose I could also be wounded by some specific descriptive terms, such as "inept manager," "absentee father," "inadequate lover," or "stupid investor"—partially because there is enough truth in each of them to be painful—but those terms are behaviorally based, not demographically based.

Come to think about it, there was one instance when I was really miffed by a public label associated with my demographic profile. I had just turned fifty-five and had gone to the jai alai matches near Palm Beach, Florida. In the lobby was a big sign that said, "Senior Citizens Half-price," and underneath in smaller letters, "Anyone 55 or older." I was so incensed at being termed a "senior citizen" at that early age that I refused to identify myself as one and paid full price—which, in retrospect, made me a "stupid senior citizen."

A last-minute addition: A recent *New York Times* Sunday Edition (November 19, 1995) had a timely and clever column by Natalie Angier entitled, "Where Woman Was, There Gal Shall Be." Grappling with the same issue of how to refer to contemporary women in groups, Angier dismisses the use of "women," "females," "ladies," "girls," "chicks," "dames," "broads," and "the nasty B word."

After noting that twenty-something women are now referring to their "gal pals," she comes out four-square in favor of "gal." As she says, ". . . gal has a rich and prismatic quality to it. A gal is a grown person with a sense of humor whom you'd better take seriously. A gal is a sexy subject rather than a sexy object. . . . A gal looks after herself."

I have no solution to this terminology dilemma, and fortunately it is not mine to solve. If any of you nerds (male or female) would like to offer further suggestions, or merely flame some comments, I can be reached at campbelld@leaders.ccl.org.

Memories of War...

It was midnight on the small island of Angaur (2,000 acres, population 250) in the western Pacific, and the lights had just gone off as they do every night for conservation purposes. Eight of us were marooned in a pleasant guest house by a light rain that had prevented the small Paradise Air plane from reaching us, and by the heavy waves pounding on the beach that had also grounded the small commuter boat.

Three of our party—the smokers—were out on the covered verandah with an adequate supply of Budweiser from the local store, their voices murmuring low through the open windows along with the sound of the surf. Another two, the youngest ones, were sprawled out on pads beside me on the living room floor. I had drawn one of the two rollaway beds; the other was taken by the U.S. lawyer who was counsel for the local clan chiefs, and who earlier in the day had superbly handled the historical portion of the WWII memorial service.

The two unattached senior women, both expatriates from the U.S., had spoken up for one of the private bedrooms—gender still counts for something out there—and the other private bedroom was by acclamation assigned to the guests of honor, Tom and Shirley Climie from Denver.

Three days earlier I had been opening Christmas presents with my family in Eugene, Oregon (or was it two days, or maybe four days—I cannot keep track of elapsed time when crossing the International Date Line) and I lay in the shadowy tropical night, smiling to myself, thinking, how do these things happen?

And the answer is: Fifty-one years earlier—at 8:30 a.m. on September 20, 1944—Sergeant Tom Climie, age 26, had hit Blue Beach here along with several hundred other members of the 321st Regiment of the 81st "Wildcats" U.S. Army Division. Angaur Island was being defended by a Japanese garrison of 1,456 soldiers with orders to fight to the death. In preparation for the invasion, the island had been pounded by 857 tons of 14-inch shells from the guns of the battleship Tennessee, 127 500-pound bombs dropped by planes from the aircraft carrier Wasp, and 2,000 rounds from the 5-inch guns of a flotilla of LCI landing craft.

One consequence of that bombardment is that today virtually no tree on the island is more than 50 years old.

The four-day battle was among the most vicious in American military history. According to the official published report, 1,397 (97%)

Japanese soldiers died, along with 260 U.S. soldiers killed, 1,354 wounded, and 940 "temporarily disabled."

For the month preceding the battle, 120 Palauans (Palau is the parent nation of Angaur) had hidden in a labyrinth of caves in the center of the island. When the bombardment and fighting had ended and the island was again quiet, they had emerged to meet their liberators, which included Sergeant Climie.

When our plane had landed earlier in the day, six of those cave-dwelling refugees, one man and five women in colorful island dress, were on hand to greet Sergeant Climie, along with five teenagers with flower leis for all of us. The governor of Angaur, a quiet, dignified woman perhaps five feet tall, and the Palauan Minister of State, who had come over from the main island earlier, also welcomed us. It was a cheerful reunion.

The island's airstrip, constructed by the U.S. Army Corps of Engineers after the island had been liberated, had no terminal, and we were gathered around a picnic table under a lean-to, itself under a huge spreading tree. Later that day, we would be seated under that shelter in the rain playing Hearts for a couple of hours, waiting in vain for the plane to return.

When I had arrived in Palau the day before, my local host, a U.S. psychologist who is helping me collect community survey data from the islands, said, "There is some kind of WWII service being held tomorrow on the island of Angaur. Do you want to go? I think I can get you on the State boat."

"Sure."

When the boat was canceled because of heavy seas, I was crammed into the last remaining seat in a ten-seater airplane. None of us expected to stay overnight, so we were reduced to whatever we happened to have in our carry-ons—which for me was camera and film, windbreaker, umbrella, swimming suit and towel, suntan lotion, and a candy bar, all of which but the lotion proved useful. I could also have used a toothbrush and flashlight.

Upon landing, after the initial greetings, we were loaded into a van and the open bed of a pickup truck (ironically, both Toyotas) and given a tour of the island. First, the Catholic church with the Christmas crèche still up, and then to the local cemetery with a few recent flower-covered graves and at least one grave of a Japanese soldier. With one highly visible exception, all of the tombstones were modest in size and made of concrete. The exception was a large vertical slab of polished black granite from an earlier era. On the front was a traditional inscription in German (the Germans had controlled the island from the late 1800s until World War II): "Rose Rodatz geb. Lindner, geg. 22 Mai 1868, gest. 14 Febr 1911." On the back, starkly inscribed in large German script, was a poignant, "Warum?" ("Why?").

Eighty-five years later, grief still hung in the air.

Then onto the U.S. military cemetery, which was still being maintained with the jungle growth cut back regularly, even though all of the bodies had been removed years earlier, probably for reburial in more accessible cemeteries in Hawaii or perhaps the Philippines.

Tom Climie had brought with him a copy of *The History of the 81st Division,* a large inch-thick bound volume, and it happened to have a picture of this cemetery fifty years ago. We all clustered around to see what it had looked like then. The Angaur islanders were particularly fascinated by this history book because, when turning the pages, they found a picture of some of those who had taken shelter in the caves and a few of them found themselves in the picture.

As they leafed through the book, excited, exclaiming, they came across a group shot of some young U.S. soldiers. One woman pointed to one and said something in Palauan; the rest of the locals, and the one member of our group who spoke Palauan, laughed. Later that night, in the cozy conversation in the guest house, we asked him what she had said. He laughed again, "She said, 'Oh, I remember him. We had a love affair!'"

Ah, memories of war . . .

We continued with our island tour: past the Catholic shrine on the northern tip of the island, its purpose to ward off bad weather; past the modern Shinto shrine for the Japanese soldiers who had died there; to the "airplane graveyard," off the far end of the landing strip, that contained wrecked planes that had probably been bulldozed off the runway into the jungle during flight operations. After liberation, the airstrip had quickly been constructed as a forward base for bombing runs against Japanese fortifications in the Philippines.

The planes appeared to be remnants of three or four B-24s and one Grumman Hellcat. Through the years, anything useful for an island home had been scrounged, but the wings, engines, fuselages, fuel tanks, and one gun turret were still scattered around. The iron and steel parts were badly rusted, but the aluminum skins and composition rubber fuel tanks were well preserved. The site is just off the beach, and fifty-year-old mangrove trees have grown up around the wreckage, providing an open, airy, thirty-foot canopy. The location has a quiet, semi-sacred feeling.

The final stop was at the new memorial on Blue Beach, which requires a bit of explanation. In 1994, some eighty to one hundred U.S. veterans of the fighting throughout this entire island chain (The Carolines) came over for a large fifty-year liberation celebration, Tom Climie among them. He was disappointed that there was no physical monument on the tiny island of Angaur, where some of the heaviest fighting had taken place. Consequently, demonstrating the famous can-do mentality that characterized the GIs of that era, he returned to Denver determined to do something about it.

Over the next year, working the mail, phone, and fax lines, demonstrating some of the best features of volunteer leadership—imagination, networking, and persistence—he made it happen. A large, approximately two feet by three feet, bronze plaque with an appropriate inscription had been cast; a U.S. SeaBee Civic Action Team had poured a cement foundation for the plaque on a small rise overlooking the beach; a local construction company, arm-wrestled I suspect by the diminutive governor, had cleared a field of view through the jungle from the rise down to the beach; a group of locals had set out plants and flowers around the base of the monument; and the Palauan government was hosting the memorial service, along with the help of the local U.S. expatriate community.

A beach towel had been thrown over the plaque, and Tom and Shirley undraped it. Tom said a few heartfelt words, as did the governor. There was a feeling of urgency as a heavy thunderstorm was hanging just off the beach. It hit a few minutes later, and we all jumped into the vehicles, with some of us again in the back of the open pickup. As we careened away huddled under our umbrellas, I looked back, with vast amusement, to the monument where three or four SeaBees were policing up the area, smoothing a few stones back in place, nonchalantly taking pictures of each other in the drenching downpour. They had obviously been wet before.

We sped over to the community center, a roofed, open-air building, for the rest of the ceremony: a blessing from the Catholic priest, who had been on the island for several decades; more speeches all around; a recitation of the history of the 81st Division; a Palauan chant with audience responses; and two huge tables of delicious food, entirely local dishes. The central delicacy was soft-shelled crab bodies that had been hollowed out

Memories of War... 217

and refilled with a tasty mixture of crabmeat and coconut. During the ceremony, gratitude had been expressed to the Angaur women's group for the food.

It was a mellow, engaging time.

A couple of hours later, everyone disentangled and we returned to the airstrip and waited for the plane in a light drizzle, slowly sliding into the dreary waiting and monotony that can characterize so much travel.

Later, after sundown when it was clear that the plane was not returning, we settled into the guest house. Much of the evening was spent listening to Tom's stories; short and wiry by stature, he is a natural raconteur. He told us that at one point he and his unit had been crowded into a small boat and taken to another island. "We left our duffel bags on the first island and did not see them again for ten days."

Someone asked incredulously, "You mean you lived in the tropics for ten days in the same clothes?"

"Yes," said Tom. "Our aroma became part of our armament."

Which led someone to invoke the old joke, "Listen up, troops. Today you get a change of underwear. Smith, you change with Jones; Brown, you change with Johnson...." We were experiencing the punchiness of the weary traveler.

I saw firsthand some of the generational friction over the interpretation of WWII that plagued the recent Smithsonian exhibit on Hiroshima. In response to a query, Tom was explaining why so few Japanese prisoners had been taken, and some of his stories were unpleasant, to say the least. The youngest member of our group, a wide-eyed, unfailingly cheerful, thirtyish English ecologist, exhibited considerable discomfort. Through her gasps, body language, and looks of disbelief, she managed to convey the feeling of, "But ... wasn't that against the law?"

Tom, in a gentle, diplomatic way, tried to explain the viewpoint of soldiers who have just witnessed severe atrocities, perhaps even visited on their own buddies, such as by booby-trapped souvenirs.

By implicit mutual consent, the conversation flowed into more acceptable channels. Tom had been a baker before enlisting in the Army, and when the fighting had calmed down, he persuaded the engineers to build him a large oven. "Those guys could do anything, build washing machines, fix up old trucks, you name it."

He sketched in his experiments with recipes for bread, using ingredients at hand, baking the loaves in "large Spam cans. You just slit them down the middle of the top, bend back the flaps, and you've got a great bread pan."

He continued, "I was baking them in seven- and nine-loaf batches, and they were being distributed all over. The general's mess often called down and asked for fresh bread for the general." At a distance of fifty years, you could still feel his pride in his work.

In the morning the power came back on, the ceiling fans started spinning again, fresh bananas and breakfast cake arrived along with hot water for the instant coffee in the guest-house cupboard, showers were taken, carry-ons were packed, we clustered around the rusting field-artillery piece in the front yard for a group photo, and then returned to the airstrip for the twenty-minute flight back to Palau—one of the most beautiful places I have ever been, and where I spent the subsequent week kayaking, snorkeling, diving, and preparing to use our standardized community survey to study the island residents' views of their community. At this moment, it appears that even the sixteen clan chiefs might be among the respondents.

It has been an interesting beginning for the new year.

An Inside Look at the Olympics

The Olympic games in Atlanta are now upon us, and I have been getting an inside look at them by talking with some of my colleagues, current and past, here at CCL's Colorado Springs branch.

Take, for instance, Jay T. Kearney, Ph.D. A senior exercise physiologist at the Olympic Training Center, he also works with participants in CCL's "Leadership at the Peak" course. Jay was on the 1980 U.S. Olympic team as a flatwater canoeist; unfortunately, President Carter pulled the U.S. out of the Moscow competition to show his disapproval of the Soviet invasion of Afghanistan, and Jay never had the chance to compete in an Olympic venue.

"We are setting up a support center for coaches in a fraternity house on the Georgia Tech campus. This 'coachhouse' will be a place for them to meet, relax, brief their athletes, and—with a high-tech media center—analyze videotapes of athletic performances."

He was enthusiastic about their sophisticated videotape capabilities. "We have a system where we can run through several tapes of, say, a rival basketball team, code the tapes, then the coach can request various sequences such as, for example, all segments where the center gets the ball down low.

"I actually ran that sequence on one of the other women's basketball teams, and I can tell you that their center—who incidentally is 6'8" and weighs 280 pounds—in that situation went to her left 90 percent of the time." He smiled ruefully, "Someone that big, you don't stop her from going left, but at least you know it's coming."

Being a scientist as well as an athlete, Jay T. is a walking almanac of statistics, complete with theoretical interpretations. "The 1996 Olympics will have about 10,000 athletes competing from 197 countries. Most of the athletes have been preparing from 6 to 10 years. The 18 members of the U.S. rowing team range in height from 6'2" to 6'9", in weight from 198 to 220 pounds, and have an oxygen uptake of 6 liters—normal is about 4 liters. They have all had 4 years of collegiate rowing experience and about 5 years of full-time training since, living on a grant from the United States Olympic Committee of $2,500 a year."

He gave me an insight into what it means to be "an elite athlete, an Olympic winner." As he explained it, "Over all of the events—track and field, swimming, rowing, boxing, horseback riding, shooting, and so on—

the difference between the gold and silver medal winners is about two-tenths of one percent: for example, in 1992, about 22 seconds in the 26-mile marathon. To win the gold, you have to be perfect, which means you have to anticipate everything, plan for it, train for it, and execute."

He told me the story of the kayak competition in 1992. "We worked with the kayakers in the design of their kayak hulls and were able to change the shape an amount indistinguishable to the eye but in a way that slightly reduced the drag. We also redesigned the paddle, making it somewhat like an airplane propeller in a way that increased the desirable thrust and reduced the undesirable drag. In the final competition, Greg Barton won the gold over an Australian by .004 of a second."

I also talked with Sherie Omstead, the manager of program administration here. She is a trained athlete and former director of shooting development for the U.S. shooting team. She will be in Atlanta working with the current team. A couple of comments from her stand out: "David, you want to know something interesting? In skeet-shooting competition in the first few Olympics, they used real pigeons."

Sherie also told me, "The rifle shooters train themselves to pull the trigger between heartbeats so that the slight vibration caused by their beating heart will not affect their aim."

I was skeptical, but she said, "David, I'm serious. First, they wear very stiff, very tight leather outfits that squeeze their body so much for stability that you can almost see their heartbeats through the leather; second, they train aerobically to get their heart rate down so there is more time between beats; third, they practice eight hours a day over years—like a job—with one of their goals to be able to detect their own heartbeats."

I am beginning to get some appreciation of what "elite" means.

I also dropped in on Roberta Kraus, whose office is next door to mine. Roberta, at 6'2", was an outstanding basketball player in high school and college and was an alternate for the women's U.S. Olympic basketball team in 1976. She has gone on for a Ph.D. in sports science and now, along with her work here at CCL, is heavily involved in the Olympic community, working in a variety of programs with high achievers.

"David," she said, "you would be interested in this project because it involves the use of a psychological survey with a truly outstanding team. The survey results identified a destructive team psychology, and working that out has been fascinating."

"Which team is it?"

She looked at me chidingly, "You know I can't tell you—but I can tell you that this team is going to blow your socks off in Atlanta."

I talked with one other person, Dr. John Anderson, a former Air Force Academy faculty member, a former CCL staff member, and currently president of the Center for Sports Psychology. As a sports psychologist, John works with a variety of elite performers, some Olympians but also world-class motorcycle racers and, intriguingly, some CEOs interested in improving their corporate performance.

One of John's notable achievements was as the team psychologist for the U.S. boxing team during the 1984 Olympics in Los Angeles—a 12-member team that won 11 medals. John doesn't deal much with equipment issues, training regimes, or dietary programs. He focuses on, in his words, "the most important asset athletes have—the five inches between their ears."

John of course can't reveal the names of his clients, but he told me the following story from the recent U.S. Olympic trials. "I encourage athletes to write notes to themselves about their performances and about their future training goals; then I review the notes with them.

"One young lady had listed everything she had done to get into the finals, all of her exercising, her nutritional plans, her workouts, all of the sweat and pain and exertion and self-denial that she had gone through, and then she had written, 'DESERVE a place on the Olympic team!' I had to take her aside and give her a short lecture about that kind of thinking.

"'Look,' I said, 'you don't deserve squat. Every other person in these trials has done exactly what you have done—they have exercised, they have sweated, they have gone through pain, they have given up other pleasures, they are just as deserving as you are. Saying that you deserve something special puts you in the role of potential victim, so that you can later say, "Poor me, life has failed me."

"I told her, 'You can say, I EXPECT to earn a place on the Olympic team. That's okay, that's an expression of self-esteem, of self-confidence, a stance from where you can perform better because you expect to be among the best, but let's not have any more of these victimizing statements.'"

You can perhaps understand why I sometimes feel ordinary. I have daily contact with people like these: Jay T., Sherie, Roberta, and John. They are, and they deal with, the elites. They understand the complexities and dynamics of outstanding physical achievements, and they are intimately involved in the development of outstanding talents. On occasion I feel as if I am standing with my nose pressed up against the windowpanes of their lives, yearning to take part at their level. Yet, realistically, no one is ever going to notice if my performance improves by two-tenths of one percent, even if I expect it.

~~~

Editor's Note: The June 1996 issue of *Scientific American* features an article by Jay T. Kearney, entitled "Training the Olympic Athlete." It should be of interest to anyone interested in the dynamics of high performance.

The Rhythms of Foreign Cultures

I have just returned from being embedded for several days in another culture and was once again reminded of the charms, challenges, and quirky customs found in locations other than my Midwestern hometown. As the demands on leaders become increasingly global, such comparisons become more relevant to our programs of creativity and leadership development. How important are cultural differences?

A paragraph here to set the stage: This particular episode began fifteen years ago when a charming foreign executive, relaxing in my living room, said with his characteristic twinkle, "David, I notice that you have all of these empty bedrooms." His interest flowed from a paternal protectiveness, and the upshot was that for the next several years his three equally charming and internationally sophisticated daughters used my home as a base for their American education. They definitely were not a burden to my daily life. Whether they were adequately "paternally protected" is a judgment call, but I note that one finished her BA in three years and the other two in four years, all working in their third language, a degree of educational attainment not mirrored by my own children.

On the basis of that relationship, I vacationed this year with their family and friends in what might be called "an exotic foreign culture."

The dominant dynamic, of course, was the foreign languages, and I was again almost suffocated by the sense of inferiority created by my middle-American linguistic shortcomings. To sit in an active conversational environment, listening to person A expounding in one language, with person B responding in another, with person C chiming in with whichever language was appropriate for whomever that person was responding to, with all of them turning to me occasionally in the third language, English, to tell me what was happening, is a daunting experience. To have it repeated night after night at dinner—whether on the boat, the beach, or a tropical terrace—is not conducive to a strong sense of personal adequacy.

In these international settings, I often retreat to the only defense I can muster: murmuring to myself, "Look, I speak fluently every language that was spoken within one thousand kilometers of where I grew up; no one else in this room can make that statement." One builds one's psychological defenses with whatever material is available.

Fortunately, my CCL experience has provided a repertoire of various simulations, useful for moving conversations along from bland social repetitions into personally revealing episodes. During one lull with a group composed entirely of multilingual professionals, I proposed the following dilemma:

You, along with one other undesignated person, are a member of a spacecraft that has just been hit by an asteroid. Mission Control has informed you that it will require six hours for you to return to Earth and land, and there is absolutely no way that that time can be shortened. Further, they have informed you that you have only eight person-hours of oxygen left in your craft and that there is absolutely no way that this oxygen can be supplemented or that your rate of consumption can be lowered.

In surveying your resources, you find a survival kit with three objects: a powerful sleeping pill, a .45 caliber revolver (loaded), and a Swiss Army knife.

Your companion, assessing the situation, quickly swallows the sleeping pill and goes to sleep.

What would you do?

Universally, no matter the culture, this quandary always produces a flurry of initial reactions, all focused on somehow denying the facts.

"A really clever engineer could find some way to get us down earlier."

"A good physiologist could figure out some way to lower our temperature and reduce our rate of oxygen consumption."

A relentless reality eventually forces its way through, with almost everyone agreeing on the arithmetic death sentence: only one person can survive and the person who is awake must make that choice. The conversation then usually shifts to morality, justice, philosophical decision-making, and, often, black humor.

Thus it was with this group. After initial denials, the conversation focused on the potential differences between morality, reality, and justice. The usual variations for decision-making were discussed: Russian roulette, coin flipping, or polling the international audience who would surely be watching on CNN. How to decide who should survive? Some individuals were more pensive and constrained than others, suggesting that they might be having thoughts they preferred not to share.

One husband answered abruptly in a language that I did not understand; his wife replied equally abruptly. Their body language and hand gestures were dramatic, so I was not surprised when the translation came:

He said, "Obviously, you take the revolver and plug the other guy right between the eyes." She said, "That's the kind of mentality that I have to live with all the time."

When the discussion turned to "Who is this undesignated companion?" the humor began, with various strategies being created, depending on whether the other person was a stranger, a close colleague, a former superior, or perhaps an ex-spouse.

To this point the dynamics of the discussion followed closely those of dozens of other group discussions I've watched, and I have concluded that, in general, the rhythms of group processes are universal.

One noticeable difference between the current U.S. culture and the one in which this conversation took place is that the latter is less uptight about what might normally be considered issues. Reflecting this, a witty and lively artist, whose works are hanging in many prominent homes and galleries worldwide, finally said, in merry frustration, "Well, I would certainly try to wake up the other person to at least have some fun before the oxygen deadline when one of us had to die!"

Given the general hilarity and related suggestions that this comment elicited in a variety of languages, I am certain that I missed much in the translations.

In the several times that I have led U.S. compatriots through this exercise, not one person has ever suggested that his or her final hours might well be spent in such hedonistic diversions, but then I am usually working with executives, not artists.

As always, the conversation finally sputtered out with no one wanting to accept responsibility for a definite decision and, as usual, many of the participants fully expected to be saved by a "school solution," perhaps involving the Swiss Army knife in some peculiarly innovative way.

Finally, with cultural differences and similarities noted as reflected by the space capsule impasse, we moved on to the next dilemma: "You are a collector of Chinese art, and your friend has just returned from Japan with a gift for you, a vase for which he paid $89 . . . ."

After working through numerous such episodes in a wide range of international settings, I am convinced that the similarities across different cultures in the manner in which moral dilemmas are discussed are far greater than the differences. The conversations that swirl around the issue of who should die and who should choose are not very different whether the setting is around a pot-bellied stove in the middle of America or on a white sand beach under swaying palm trees near the equator. Just as lungs, livers, and spleens work precisely in the same manner no matter what the culture or language, so perhaps do moral compasses. Leadership development programs focused on universal principles such as vision, empowerment, alliance building, the establishment of trust, innovation, goal setting, and feedback of results are likely, I believe, to be universally applicable.

Civic Art at Sunrise

Because of the nature of my work, and perhaps because of my personal inclinations, I spend a lot of time wandering the streets of strange cities. I like to do it early in the morning, both because I am drawn to sunrises and because the air is usually fresh then and also because I have noticed that there are fewer hooligans out and about at that time.

My starting point is often a hotel lobby, and although I believe in maps and guidebooks, I am prone to navigate randomly, to some extent because of lazy expediency but also because I like surprises. This strategy has led me to see more than my share of warehouse districts and railroad yards, but it has also turned up a fair number of out-of-the-way historical plaques, diners, and art galleries—not to mention civic artworks of various kinds, such as monuments, statues, and public sculptures, which I really like. One of the real red-letter days in my life was the first time I stumbled across the Picasso Poodle in Chicago.

Occasionally I become a bit discouraged when I view the urban landscape that we have created in this country, especially in comparison with some of the truly beautiful cities of the world, but there is some cause for optimism. Chicago has other public beauties besides the Picasso sculpture. Minneapolis has a wonderful outdoor sculpture garden attached to the Walker Art Museum just a short stroll from the Hyatt Hotel, and in the lobby of the Hilton Hotel there is a spectacular life-sized bronze casting of a string quartet. Even Houston, not a city I usually associate with art, has added some intriguing public sculptures in its downtown center.

Because of my involvement with leadership and organizational politics, I am always curious about how the civic attraction came into being, and I note that those details are never reported on the accompanying plaque. Although we know something about the background and psychology of artists who create inspiring art, we know very little about the dynamics of art committees, acquisition budgets, and political acceptance, other than it is usually a rocky road.

Such issues jumped to the top of my head recently when I stumbled onto an amazing, new, and wonderfully inspirational public piece of art I had never known of before. I looked at it in astonishment: it is an engraved granite wall ninety-six feet long, three stories high, weighing sixty-three tons. I thought: "How in the world did this ever get conceived? How did it make its way through the inevitable labyrinth of government committees, some of whom surely had budgetary constraints? And how did it finally survive legislative scrutiny?"

The wall, constructed of "Sunset Red" Texas pink granite, is a tribute to public education; it forms part of the outer wall of the Public Education Building on the state government mall in Raleigh, North Carolina.

Dominating the wall, in engraved letters that are huge and black, is a vertical statement three stories high, taken from a poem by North Carolina poet Fred Chappell entitled "Child in the Fog":

> YOU ARE
> A CHILD
> YOU ARE
> SUITABLE
> TO BE
> AWED

Across the length of the wall in letters perhaps ten inches high, up about two stories above the ground, is inscribed a translation of an Arabic proverb: "Learning in old age is writing in sand but learning in youth is engraving on stone."

The remainder of the wall is filled with an eclectic collection of educational quotations, pictures, and symbols. The words "to teach" and "to learn" are captured in Cherokee Native American script; a diagram shows how granite is formed; a musical staff displays a melody written by John Coltrane; some lines of poetry are quoted from George Moses Horton, an African American slave who taught himself to read and eventually published three volumes of poetry; some text in Braille tells you about the wall you are touching; a quotation from North Carolina educator Charles McIver reads, "Nothing except ignorance is more costly than education"; and a colorful line drawing from a kindergartner pictures a one-room schoolhouse complete with students and a belfry, the kind of drawing that often graces refrigerator doors.

The wall is altogether delightful and inspirational. In the plaza around its base are some smaller bench-sized blocks of granite with a variety of inscriptions; on one, Reynolds Price—the well-known novelist who teaches at Duke University in nearby Durham and who attended Broughton High School in Raleigh—describes his English teacher, Phyllis Peacock: "A magical teacher—a combination of effortless command of the subject, the discipline of a field marshal, the theatrical skills of classroom mastery, and, most crucial, a fervent belief in the life-or-death importance of her subject."

The wall is signed by the artist, Vernon Pratt, and by his editorial collaborator, Georgann Eubanks, who chose the quoted material and wrote descriptive text. They have become stars in my firmament; but as always, no credit is given to the unsung heroes and heroines who surely steered this creation through the shoals of organizational and budgetary processes. A pity.

Perhaps the most dramatic feature of the wall is the record of a speech on education delivered in 1912 by Charles B. Aycock, then a former governor of North Carolina:

> Open wide the schoolhouses and give every child the opportunity to develop all there is in him.
>
> You are going to educate your girl; I know you are. You are going to sit up all night to educate her; going to economize; going to be stingy to educate her. Maybe you want her to be a musician. Well, I am going to tell you, you can send her to all the schools; you can let her burn the midnight oil; you can let her study under great musicians until she is almost blind; you can send her to the conservatory of music; you can send her abroad until her whole soul thrills and feels the glory of her gifted music, but she cannot make music to people who do not understand. You cannot talk to an audience that cannot hear. . . .
>
> When I was governor I made speeches all over North Carolina. I canvassed the State for four years on behalf of the education of the children of the State, right straight along. Sometimes on Sundays, they would ask me down to the churches to talk, and I always talked about education . . .

At this juncture, according to the engraving on the wall, Aycock fell dead at the podium.

That we can produce such enlightened celebrations of education in these days of constrained budgets gives me hope, for I share the belief of Jonathan Daniel, a columnist whose words written in 1941 are also engraved on the wall: "As far as I can see, schools everywhere are not lanterns but mirrors. I think they will always be as good or as bad, as stirring or as easy-going as North Carolinians are." This sentiment is relevant far beyond the boundaries of North Carolina.

Stop by if you happen to be in Raleigh, and see this wall. It will likely cause you to reflect upon your own education, and you might offer up a belated mental thank-you to those extraordinary teachers who had such an early impact on you. Actually, a copy of this column with a short warm note would probably make their day.

Excerpt from the poem "Child in the Fog" is from *Source: Poems* (Louisiana State University Press) ©1985 by Fred Chappell.

A Mid-Career Leadership Curriculum for High-Potential Leaders

Many leading organizations have established a leadership course for individuals deemed to have the potential to rise to the top ranks. Examples include Motorola, General Electric, IBM, and Caterpillar in the corporate world and the American College of Life Underwriters, the various military command and general staff colleges, and the Federal Executive Institute in the nonprofit world.

The courses have a wide range of names: The President's Council, The Mid-Management Forum, The XYZ Corporation Leadership Lab, or perhaps something like The Starved Rock Program or The Hamilton Park Seminar, denoting the conference center where the program was conducted.

The programs vary over many dimensions: content, duration, location, means of selecting attendees, size and quality of the staff, degree of intensity and demand on the participants, and involvement of the organization's top leadership. At the extremes, they range from a day-long program conducted in a company warehouse with the participants sitting on folding chairs to a twelve-month course heavy with homework and class projects, conducted in a university-like setting with comfortable hotel rooms and well-equipped classrooms. My experience suggests that one to four weeks in a comfortable conference setting with a first-rate faculty consisting mostly of "hired gurus" is the most typical.

Among the most impressive settings is General Electric's Crotonville, New York, campus, just off the Hudson River about fifty miles north of New York City, a facility created by clustering together the grounds and mansions of several private estates and then adding appropriate classroom and residential facilities. The facilities for the American College of Life Underwriters were created in a similar fashion on the outskirts of Philadelphia. Creating such an institution is definitely an act of organizational faith because the people who dream up and drive the founding are often not around when the institution finally becomes viable.

The classes generally range in size from about twelve participants on the low end to perhaps eighty to one hundred on the high end. The selection process varies over organizations but is usually based on some combination of reward for meritorious service and an acknowledgment of future potential. Historically, this meant that until well into the 1980s the rosters were almost exclusively populated by thirty-five to fifty-year-old white males.

I recently had a couple of conversations with representatives from young, rapidly expanding corporations that are just beginning to establish such a course. At one informal luncheon, I was expounding on my ideas of what a curriculum should look like; my companion was scribbling on the back of a napkin. At one point, looking up, grimacing, he said, "You know, this would be a lot easier if you would write down some of these thoughts," which led me to write this column.

As I told him, I think the curriculum of a high-potential program should cover five general topics: (1) fly the flag, (2) teach the company, (3) train the individual, (4) build networks, and (5) invoke the arts and sciences.

Fly the Flag

Attendance at these programs is virtually always seen as a stimulating, motivating, rewarding, career-enhancing episode—that is, as a feather in one's cap—and the course should be conducted in a manner to cultivate that perception.

One excellent way to accomplish this is for either the CEO, the president, or the chairman of the board to formally open, or perhaps close, each program, making a few appropriate comments emphasizing how seriously the company views this opportunity. An even better way is for one of these individuals to show up during the course for a lengthier interactive session, say, dinner and a Q&A session afterwards. Every young manager at General Electric likes to be able to say, "Well, when I was having dinner with Jack Welch at Crotonville a few weeks ago, I asked him about that very point and he said . . . "

An extension of this, but not a replacement, is to invite a marquee name, perhaps a member of the board or a leading outside expert in the company's technology or a visible community figure, say, a Colin Powell–Henry Kissinger–Warren Buffet–Anne Armstrong type (or any of a few thousand other equally fascinating people one notch below this group in fame) to speculate about something relevant to the company and its future. The presence of such horsepower emphasizes that the organization takes this educational experience very seriously.

Teach the Company

Some of the instruction should focus on the company. The range of possible subjects is wide, including such mundane topics as accounting, computer, or inventory systems; or more interesting ones such as company history, the latest technology, or global operations; or perhaps really spicy subjects such as pay, promotion, bonus, and stock option policies. The specific content should be drawn from whatever list of hot topics the current top leadership thinks is important, and at least a few of the presentations should be conducted by the organization's own high-level executives. This again emphasizes the importance of the course and also, not an incidental benefit, requires these executives to get their act together so as not to look stupid or ill prepared in front of this high-potential audience. I have seen executives with high six- or seven-figure salaries sweating bullets backstage, apprehensive about going on before "this den of young attack tigers."

Train the Individual

A substantial portion of the course should be focused on individual development, spotlighting skills that are useful across a wide range of leadership settings—such as making presentations, interviewing, and problem solving—and interpersonal skills useful for managing others.

The area of assessment for development is one on which CCL has centered much of its attention; consequently, I am highly biased toward including assessment tools in a leadership course as a means to guide instruction. We have learned that individual assessments, using a variety of psychological tests, surveys, and simulations, provide a powerful means of encouraging leaders to look at their leadership actions and their impact on others.

One of the most effective recent additions to high-level leadership training courses has been the 360-degree assessment and feedback procedures whereby individuals are provided with highly specific, standardized results showing what the impact of their leadership style has been on those around them. The higher the level of executive assessed, the more potent are these activities because high-level people get so little honest, straightforward, constructive feedback in the normal course of events.

Emphatically, these assessment activities must be conducted in a thoroughly professional and engaging manner or the participants will become cynical and unruly. If the participants are truly drawn from the "best and the brightest" of the organizations, they will almost certainly be highly self-confident, action oriented, impatient with fuzziness, slightly disdainful of academic approaches, and thoroughly turned off by anything they perceive as mushy or touchy-feely.

The payoff is that when individual assessments produce results that participants see as relevant to their day-to-day demands, the assessment results are often perceived as the most useful portion of the course.

Build Networks

Inevitably, the feature of the course that will be most memorable for the participants is the opportunity to interact closely with a range of other organizational members, that is, to make new friends and to build networks. Consequently, this feature should be exploited.

Two factors are important here: first, the quality and diversity of the other members of the class and, second, the degree of interactivity created by the instructional activities. Regarding the former, participants should be drawn from both the broad spectrum of the organization's activities—such as production, distribution, marketing, accounting, and research labs—and the broadest possible geographic locations. In addition, a wide range of demographic categories should be included. I believe that at least three to five percent of the class should be "far out" people who can add spice to the mix; they might include representatives from the company's advertising agency, or major customers, or local community leaders, or artists or scientists of one stripe or another.

On the second point, the interactivity, the course activities should go way beyond simply putting people together in small discussion groups or organizing golf foursomes; there should be sophisticated interactive activities spread throughout the duration of the course so that individuals really get to know each other at a personal level. Any first-rate training staff should be able to create these opportunities.

One of my most memorable observations was watching a four-star admiral, with a dramatic military career, interact closely with a young, highly talented African American poet, with an earring in an unlikely place, working on a project to produce a television script for an event depicting "creative leadership." They moved from initial and symmetrical dislike, to grudging admiration, to something approaching fondness over the course of the project; and they certainly became better educated about, and more tolerant of, a portion of our world for which they had earlier had only disgust.

Invoke the Arts and Sciences

A few excellent presentations drawn from the world of ideas help people imagine wider horizons when they return to their regular lives. The possibilities are virtually endless. I have seen a wide array of superb presentations, from the jazz trumpeter who demonstrated how different "leaders," such as Louis Armstrong, have changed the nature of music; to the mathematician who held an audience spellbound on the topic of infinity; to the English professor who speculated on Shakespeare's views of leaders; to the genetically oriented psychologist who talked about identical twins raised apart; to the geographer who demonstrated how our graphic view of our neighborhood changes our behavior; to the sports psychologist who spun tales about and drew conclusions from a career of advising high-performance athletes. All created a sense of personal involvement and wonderment about future possibilities.

Such experts do sometimes need to be educated about the demands of high-level leadership audiences. The presentations must be fast paced with good audiovisuals. The friendly professor with rumpled tweeds, using grease pencils to write on crinkled overheads, doesn't fare well in these settings.

A Final Thought

Although I, and other members of my profession, would be hard-pressed to produce irrefutable scientific data documenting that such courses are cost effective, observation and anecdote strongly suggest that these experiences have a strong impact on the attendees. They do change, both in thinking and in action. Their world has been expanded, they have learned what they do well and where they might have some modifiable flaws, they have closely observed other people of quality, and they have been stimulated to consider what future changes they might make, both personally and organizationally.

Regrettably, only a very small fraction of our top leaders will ever have such an opportunity. How would our world be different if every top-level corporate executive, university administrator, military officer, government official, religious leader, educator, and community leader from every country on the globe had such a mid-career expanding experience?

Down-to-Earth Life and Leadership

I grew up in rural Iowa in the thirties and forties, close to the land, close to reality. I was born at home, as were my two sisters. We milked our own cows, gathered our own eggs, pumped our own water. There was still a blacksmith shop, where horses were shoed, on Main Street, and every day a coal-fired steam locomotive made a round trip up from Creston, which was on the main Chicago-Denver C.B.&Q. rail line, with the local freight.

Every week or so my mother would say to me, "David, go out in the backyard and catch a rooster. Cut off his head. I need to fry him up for dinner." "Running around like a chicken with its head cut off" was not just an expression for me.

Although I don't miss the arduousness of that life—chicken from the freezer is considerably easier than chicken from the backyard—I do miss the clarity, the unambiguity of down-to-earth reality. The life I lead now feels elevated and often contrived. There are few natural causes and effects. When it is cold outside, I am not cold. When it is hot outside, I am not hot. When it is raining outside, I am not wet. Nothing down to earth in that.

Which is why I enjoyed myself so much recently when I spent a long evening with two former big-city cops. Both were delightful storytellers, and afterwards on the long ride home I kept laughing to myself at their recollections, thinking, "These guys spent their careers working close to life."

For example, each of them had delivered several babies. My eyes widened at that. One related, "Yeah, I'll never forget the first one. I was a rookie cop, riding around with a veteran. We were sent to a building to help a sick woman. When we walked in, someone hollered from upstairs, 'Get up here quick. She's having a baby.'

"I thought to myself, 'Now wait a minute. We're supposed to be dealing with someone sick; nobody said anything about babies.'

"We went upstairs, and sure enough, there she was on the bed definitely giving birth. My partner took one look and said, 'You take care of her. I'll call an ambulance.' And he was out of there.

"I took off my shirt—I didn't want it to get bloody—and I'm thinking, 'Yeah, well, check for a breech birth, to make sure that it's coming out the right way,' but I just had enough time to get my hands out in front of me and, pop, I'm holding a baby. I looked it over. It seemed fine. So I cleaned it off, using some water they'd brought me."

He laughed. "You know, it really is like in the movies. Somebody always does bring you water and towels.

"I laid the baby carefully on the mother's stomach, as they'd taught me, and then I looked down and out came another one.

"I barely got my hands there in time and, pop, I'm holding it.

"I cleaned it off, laid it up beside the first one, and said to her, 'You got any more in there?'

"She said, 'I don't think so.' "

Listening in amazement, I asked, "Wasn't she in pain—real agony?"

"Nah," he laughed again. "These were her seventh and eighth kids, and she was not a small woman."

Leadership in Action

As always, because CCL is the prism through which I view life, I was interested in the thoughts of these guys on leadership and management.

"Yeah," said the other cop, "let me tell you about this so-called leadership stuff. At one point the higher-ups in the department decided that they were going to improve response times, get the police on the scene faster, make the citizens happier, so they had us watched, fed us some fake calls, then timed us to see how fast we got to the scene of an alleged incident.

"Now, that sounds good. You always want the police to arrive as soon as possible, right? But let me tell you about response times for a cop. There's a lot of situations in which you don't want to be in too much of a hurry. Let's say that you get a call that there's a fight going on over in Louie's Bar. Now of course you know Louie's, and there's nothing there but trouble. If you get there too quick, maybe the fight's still going on—in which case, if you barge in, somebody's likely to get hurt, maybe even you; or you might have to make an arrest, which takes you off the street for the rest of your day and maybe the night too. You don't want to get there until everybody's been pulled apart, lying around all bloodied up and out of energy.

"So what you do is pull up in front of Louie's with your siren on, your lights flashing, and check out the joint through the window. If it looks as if mayhem is still being committed, you drive on slowly, around the

Down-to-Earth Life and Leadership   239

block, maybe looking for a place to park your cruiser 'so that it will not impede the normal activities of ordinary citizens' "—this last spoken as if he were reading from a procedures manual.

"You come around again, lights and siren still going so that maybe the warriors inside will think that reinforcements have arrived.

"Finally you go inside, moving slowly. No John Wayne stuff here. You help sop up the blood, maybe call an ambulance, ask around, 'What happened?' Of course nobody knows anything. Which is good.

"So you ease out of there, letting the locals work it out themselves."

After a pause, he added with a distinct glint in his eye, "You let the good citizens solve their own problems." Then, grinning, "You *empower* them to deal with their own issues."

After more stories about his experiences, I asked, "How did you do all of this for thirty years without becoming completely cynical?"

He smiled at me, full of cheerfulness and good nature but with an underlying seriousness, and said, "You do what you have to do to get by."

Hi Ho, Silver, Away

My favorite story of the evening was about thinking on your feet.

"I always wanted to be a mounted policeman," one of my companions said wistfully. "I thought that would really be the life. I applied more than once, but I never made the list.

"I had a friend, Ollie, who did though. One day he's riding around, not much going on, kind of bored. So he decides to take in a movie. He heads into a dead-end alley behind a theater, ties his horse to a drainpipe, and goes in for a couple of hours.

"When he comes out, he finds a car parked across the alley entrance, blocking him in. He goes over to check it out, and he can tell from the department oil-change sticker on the dash that he has been trapped by an inspector from headquarters.

"He looks around. No one in sight. The guy is probably somewhere nearby taking a break. So he assesses his options. He knows he can't get the horse to jump over the car; he briefly considers trying to get it to crawl through the back seat, but that's obviously no good. Finally, he goes back and unties the horse and says, 'Come on, Silver, we're going to the movies.'

"Ollie opens the rear door of the theater and pushes the horse inside, then leads him up the aisle past some very surprised moviegoers.

" 'Don't worry, folks. Don't panic. We've got a problem here but the local constabulary has the situation well in hand. Please remain quiet and stay seated.'

"And he leads the horse out through the lobby, mounts up, and rides off to the other side of the precinct."

Home on the Range

When everyone had stopped laughing, he looked at me. "You know, I still would like to have a horse. Maybe I should move out there where you guys are, out in Colorado. You still have some open spaces, don't you?"

He mused, "Maybe sixty or eighty acres, a mountain view, a couple of horses, a few dogs, maybe my own skeet range, blue skies, clear air, no babies to deliver, no response-time monitors . . ."

I looked over at his wife, who was listening with an open expression, not one of disinterest, perhaps thinking, ". . . and a small garden."

And it occurred to me that they, too, longed to get closer to a different reality.

Jugando con Palabras en Español

I was fortunate to grow up in rural Iowa with both a mother and a grandmother who loved language. My grandmother would recite poetry by the hour, especially Wordsworth, and my mother was always playing word games. For example, when I remarried later in life, at the wedding reception—which was reasonably posh, with tuxes and all—she passed out little slips of paper with the following poem, explaining, "David always liked this sort of thing."

> Seville der dago
> Tousan buses inaro
> Nojo demis trux
> Summit cowsin summit dux.

This heritage has continued to stimulate me, especially when I recently decided that I had to get serious about learning another language. Our world is becoming ever more global, and at CCL we are spending more time in international activities. So, for a flurry of personal and professional reasons—not the least of which is my constant sense of monolinguistic inferiority—I have been tackling Spanish.

It has been slow going. Some recent research on brain activity suggests that after age ten or twelve, complete and accentless fluency in another language is essentially impossible; sadly, I am a couple of generations past that point. My experience agrees with the research. I note with frustration that I can hear a Spanish word seventeen times and not recognize it on the eighteenth.

To keep up my motivation, and for the learning that it provides, I have retreated to my family's approach and have been playing with the Spanish language—*jugando con palabras en español*—both spoken and sung. Although the learning is still slow, the enjoyment is high. Proverbs, maxims, adages, and poems are fun, and—an unexpected benefit—they provide a window on the Spanish-speaking mind.

If French is the language of love, then Spanish is the language of passion. It is especially rich with references to sex, death, dancing, blood, bones, fighting, and the devil, with sentiments ranging from ethereal to tragic and from pathos to comedy—especially the low country humor of the sort that we were familiar with in Iowa.

In the spirit of increasing the intercultural awareness of those in leadership roles, and also for the simple love of language, I will repeat here some sayings in Spanish that I have recently come across. They come from a wide range of sources: books of proverbs, dictionaries, newspapers, many from conversations with Spanish-speaking people who know of my interests. Some are quite old; others were coined on the spot. I have appended my translations, and where necessary I have added a few words of explanation.

Más vale pájaro en mano que cien volando. [Better a bird in the hand than a hundred flying.]

No es lo mismo hablar de toros que estar en el redondel. [It's not the same to speak of bulls as to be in the bull ring.]

Hay más tiempo que vida. [There is more time than life.]

Quien con la esperanza vive, alegre muere. [Who lives with hope dies happy.]

Viviendo y muriendo bailamos con la vida. [Living and dying we dance with life.]

Las acciones de las mujeres en la vida de las naciones son lo que constituye la poesía de la historia. [The deeds of women in the life of nations is what creates the poetry of history.]

La cosa más maravillosa del amor es lo especial que nos hace sentir. [The most marvelous aspect of love is how special it makes us feel.]

El hombre es fuego, la mujer estopa; llega el diablo y sopla. [The man is fire, the woman straw; along comes the devil and blows.]

Esto me está aburriendo como una ostra. [This is making me as bored as an oyster.] This is perhaps my favorite. What a great phrase. Mutter it under your breath at your next business meeting. Don't quote me.

No vendas la piel del oso antes de haberlo matado. [Don't sell the bearskin until you have killed the bear.]

El mejor torero es el de la barrera. [The best bullfighter is in the box seats.]

Aunque la mona, se vista de seda, mona se queda. [Even though a monkey is dressed in silk, it is still a monkey.] Note that because of cadence and rhyming, the Spanish is often much catchier than the English translation. A Chilean friend reminds me that Spanish is not monolithic. *Mona* does mean "monkey," but in Spain and much of Latin America it means "beautiful" and in Colombia it means "blonde"; in Mexico it means "coward." To complicate matters, *agarrar una mona* apparently means "to get drunk."

Cuando esta vibora pica, no hay remedio en la botica. [When this snake bites, there is no remedy in the drugstore.] This comes from a Mexican gentleman who is describing a sword hidden in his riding crop.

Todos nacemos llorando y nadie se muere riendo. [We are all born crying and no one dies laughing.]

El santo que no está presente no tiene vela. [The absent saint gets no candle.] You have got to be there to protect your budget.

En el país de los ciegos el tuerto es rey. [In the country of the blind, the one-eyed man is king.]

La ira es locura, el tiempo que dura. [Anger is a short madness.]

Quien tiempo toma, tiempo se sobra. [The busiest people find the most leisure time.]

Me muero por una cerveza fría. [I'm dying for a cold beer.] Good to add to your repertoire.

Él que algo quiere, algo le cuesta. [He who wants something has to pay for it.] Another way of saying "No pain, no gain."

Bailar bien o bailar mal, todo es bailar. [Whether you dance well or whether you dance poorly, it's all dancing.]

Let me close by saying,

Yo soy del pueblo. [I'm just a country boy.]

P.S. You would have solved my mother's poem more quickly if you understood the implied transportation of waterfowl: "See, Willie, there they go, / Thousand buses in a row. / No, Joe, them is trucks, / Some with cows in, some with ducks."

Notes from a Road Warrior

While unpacking from an overseas trip on December 29, 1997, I made a quick telephone call and found that I had flown 96,990 miles in 1997 on my favorite airline. Damn . . . there are many benefits to breaking 100,000 in terms of upgrades, ease of reservations, and other little niceties that help diminish the pain of constant travel—but I was 3,010 miles short, with only two more days in the year.

"Well," I thought, "I'll fly to San Francisco and have lunch with my son." (The benefits in eventual free tickets would more than make up for the cost of the flight.) But that would result in only 1,600 more miles.

A little creative thinking and another telephone call produced an invitation to be a houseguest over New Year's Eve in Hawaii (3,300 miles). The recipients of the call had earlier been houseguests of mine, so the act was not as brazen as it first appears. Consequently I experienced the incredible firecracker binge that hits Honolulu every New Year's Eve. I learned that fireworks are legal in Hawaii only from 9:00 p.m. to 1:00 a.m. on New Year's Eve and that families save up all year for this pyrotechnical spree.

When boarding the flight from Colorado Springs to Denver (90 miles) on December 31, from the New Year's Eve camaraderie on the plane I noted at least three other people were doing what I was doing, logging more miles. One person lacked only 100 miles, so he was flying merely to Denver and back.

In Denver, boarding the flight to San Francisco, I found it was the same story. More road warriors getting their 100,000-mile tickets punched at the last minute. What a life.

Now, 100,000 miles translates into at least 200 hours in the air, the equivalent of five working weeks—which is a conservative estimate because it does not include time spent waiting to board, time sitting on the runway because of congestion, or time circling an airport waiting for a thunderstorm to move on; nor did it include the 25,000 to 30,000 miles traveled on other airlines.

In earlier days I used to be fairly productive on airplanes, working on projects, editing manuscripts, planning the future. Now, for whatever reason, I am more zombie-like; I usually just zonk out or maybe retreat into what are called around our office "airplane novels"—Tom Clancy, John Grisham, Robert Ludlum.

However, I do write paragraphs of observations as they pop into my mind while I'm waiting, for example, for the plane to be de-iced. Here are some of my musings. There is no flow here, only the same sort of disconnected thinking that travel produces.

• Why can't I find colorful luggage? I want a bright red, patterned, extremely durable, highly visible, unique suitcase that I can see all the way across the terminal. Yet the typical bag is black, brown, or gray. In fact, most baggage carousels have signs saying something like, "Check your name tags. Many bags look alike." And that's right. They do.

Why? In contrast, go to a ski area and look around. You can ski all day long, interacting with hundreds, even thousands, of skiers, and you will continually see bright, colorful clothing and equipment—reds, yellows, oranges, blues, purples, greens, plain and fluorescent—never with a duplicate ski jacket, backpack, hat, or even skis.

I have an extremely durable black hard-sided suitcase with excellent wheels and handle. It has served me well, yet it is not uncommon for there to be two or three identical bags on the same flight. In self-defense I have plastered mine with a Broncos sticker and some colored tape.

Why should I have to do that? I wish someone like Head or Rossignol would take over a luggage company.

• There is at least a five-to-one ratio between the productive levels of the best and worst people in the world. Learn to recognize the top performers early. Work for them if possible, hire them as subordinates, and hang around them as peers. Their habits rub off; so does their glory and maybe even some cash. (According to an article I read recently, Microsoft has produced six thousand millionaires among its employees in Seattle.)

• No matter what your contingent preparations, weather will sometime affect your plans. One of the more important presentations of my career was shortened from an hour to five minutes because of an East Coast snowstorm. ("We've got to get out of here.") The project never recovered.

• As people ascend the leadership ladder, they tend to cut themselves off from those who will tell them unpleasant truths. At least 50 percent of the people I have known well in top leadership positions have a reputation among their subordinates for killing off messengers. Curiously, not a single one believes that about themselves. Most of them operate as did Samuel Goldwyn: "I want you people to tell me the truth even if it costs you your job."

• If you have no particular passion for the specifics of what you do, you might as well seek out the most lucrative position available, because dollars will likely be your only reward. However, paradoxically, if you have little passion for what you do, you will probably never make much money.

• Why doesn't the corporate world use music more for motivational and inspirational purposes? The military understands its value; there are military bands all over the place, and the best of them have truly professional musicians in their ranks. Church leaders understand the value of music; in fact, for centuries the church was virtually synonymous with music. Universities devote entire departments, even separate schools, to music. The intellectual, philosophic, spiritual, and motivational ends are apparent in these settings. Why not in a corporation? Indeed, corporate CEOs often invoke a symphonic analogy to explain what they do. "My job is to come up with a score (a vision) so that our talented performers are all reading from the same music." Why isn't there an IBM symphony, or a GE traveling chorus, or—given their quasi-Scandinavian Minnesota location—a 3M polka band?

• Most people make up their minds about the people they meet in the first four minutes, which can be an unnerving fact if you are about to embark on a full day of employment interviews or a blind date.

• When you achieve a leadership position with some power and influence, you will soon be introduced to lawyers and the legal process, and you will inevitably become frustrated, even furious, when you realize that there are times when you must pay more attention to a lawyer's advice than to your own instincts.

• Why doesn't the world recognize the enormous need for energy and physical durability in a leader? I have sat through what seems like a zillion discussions of what leaders are and of what leadership requirements are needed in any particular organization. I have seen dozens of idiosyncratically produced lists of the necessary characteristics to succeed in corporation ABC or agency XYZ. None of them has ever included physical stamina and energy. Yet the typical leader's day is chaotic with demands—wearying jet-lagged travel, long meetings, conflicts and confrontations, a variety of diets and sleeping arrangements, and unpredictable crises. Perhaps this is why both early military and athletic experiences so often show up in the biographies of leaders.

• Speaking of athletes, why aren't athletes who use a set of muscles disproportionately in their trade, such as baseball pitchers or tennis players, grotesquely deformed? Why isn't Pete Sampras lopsided?

• If the world were truly fair, the seats on airplanes would systematically vary in the amount of legroom provided, starting with seats in the rear of the plane for, say, six-foot-six passengers and working their way forward to seats for, say, five-foot passengers. Then boarding would be by height, with the taller passengers boarding first. They would immediately go to the rear of the plane, expediting the boarding process. The result would be a much fairer distribution of available space. I know, I know, this is another one of my truly great ideas where the details still have to be worked out.

• The most universal motivation for wanting to be in charge is the wish to be relevant.

• I note that while flying the equivalent of almost seven working weeks last year, I did not meet a single person that I will ever see again. Even the extraverts tune out while in the air.

Nor, for the record, were there ever any crises. While flying about as many miles as five times around the globe, I never experienced a single white-knuckle fear or really even any severe discomfort—except for lack of legroom. I really do wish that someone would do something about the legroom.

Are We Connecting?

We are accelerating into the greatest communication explosion in history. With more impact than movable type, the international postal system, and the Dewey decimal system taken together, it will combine telephone, radio, computer, television, and satellite technologies; the global positioning system; the almost inconceivable range of detection, monitoring, and activation devices; and large-scale sophisticated database-management programs. In a few short years, the world as we know it will drastically change, especially in the ways in which we connect with each other and use information.

We have been moving toward this development for the last several years, with all sorts of psychological implications. For example, procrastination has now been honed to a science. Before the establishment of FedEx, if you were responsible for, say, the development of an agenda to go into the program for a professional meeting, you had to get that agenda into the mail several days early to allow for delivery time, and because the agenda was typed on a manual typewriter, using carbon paper for multiple copies, it had to be drafted at least a day or two before mailing to allow for inspirational changes; consequently, you thought in terms of a week or two before a deadline.

Then along came self-correcting typewriters, copying machines, and overnight delivery services, and you could now procrastinate until the day before the deadline, knowing that immediately revised materials could reach the printer overnight; you thought in terms of a day or two before the deadline.

Then came the word processor and the fax machine, allowing more delay; the final draft could be created and sent in a few minutes. You could now think in terms of an hour or two before a deadline.

Then came e-mail, which made it possible for everything to be done at once, allowing procrastination up until a minute or two before a deadline.

I have been fascinated by such unintended psychological consequences of the new technologies. Another example: No one predicted, when the Internet was developed mainly for military purposes, that one of the major advantages of international connectivity would be to facilitate more complicated social engagements. For instance, six scientists with mutual interests became aware that they were all going to be attending the same professional meeting in Sydney, Australia. They were from Amsterdam, Auckland, Colorado Springs, London, Sydney, and Toronto—that is, from six countries on five different continents or islands.

In earlier days it would have been daunting to the point of impossibility to arrange a luncheon date by mail; the planning and interrelated communications would have taken several months and would likely have been stiffly formal. The letters would have been typed by secretaries and addressed to Professor This and Doctor That. Even by telephone it would have taken several days, given the challenges of different time zones and the typical telephone-tag dynamics. But with e-mail it required only a simple message to multiple addresses, "How about lunch at the Hilton on Wednesday?" and the confirmations came in within twenty-four hours, in easy communiqués like, "Jolly good, mate."

The accelerating rate of technological change will broaden the impact of these advances even more, something that I have been pondering but with very little optimism that I, or anyone else, can predict what the psychological future will be.

Let me remind you of where we are going. Soon, say in five to fifteen years, each of us will have some gadget constantly with us, perhaps strapped to an arm or maybe hanging off our belts like an engineering slide rule of the 1950s or maybe on our heads like eyeglasses, that will keep us immediately in contact with an electronic world. It will combine the following features:

- Instant two-way television contact with everyone on the globe who has a similar gadget
- Instant access to a wide array of monitoring devices—such as television cameras positioned to cover everywhere from Red Square to our grandchildren's cribs or transmitting chips embedded in anything that anyone cares about tracking (expensive cameras, antiques, cars, or teenagers, with the chips in the latter monitoring physiological indices such as blood pressure, anxiety levels, food intake, and caloric expenditures)
- Instant indexed access to any stored information anywhere on earth, including the contents of all major libraries, museums, telephone books, air/train/bus schedules, newspapers, magazines, former TV programs, legal records, and public and private financial records and transactions—in short, everything publicly and personally known and knowable, the personal category presumably password protected

It is impossible to present any coherent, comprehensive analysis of how our lives will be changed by these interlocking technologies. The dynamics are too complex, interrelated, and unpredictable. The success of any current futurist will be more determined by his or her fluency and showmanship than by predictive accuracy. Simple but dramatically important questions can simply not be answered—such as, "What will be the nature of warfare?" "What kind of genetic interventions will be possible?" or, "What will happen to love?"

Futuristic speculations, however, are fun. Here are some of mine.

Privacy as we know it will soon be gone. Your specific location at any point in time and all of your transactions will be knowable. I can imagine the following beginning to a conversation: "Honey, I tried to locate you this afternoon between 2:00 and 4:00 to remind you to pick up the dry cleaning. I noted that your transmitter was turned off—and that you had a credit card charge at the Exotic Boutique and Lounge at 3:15."

There will be no good reason for us not to be continually reachable by our family members and employers, nor any good reason for our personal financial transactions to be beyond the reach of our partners or, indeed, the police.

It is worth noting that the bombings at the World Trade Center and the Oklahoma City federal building were solved by electronic "paper trail" sleuthing. Such solutions will be commonplace when all transactions everywhere are immediately available.

Personal and family relationships will be enhanced. The amount of daily communication between me, my siblings, and my adult children, all living in different cities, has soared because of the Net. Enabling exchanges are common (for instance, "I have a two-hour layover in the San Francisco airport next Friday; want to have a drink?" "Sure") as are the inevitable cellular telephone calls ("I'm stuck in traffic on the interstate and will be late").

The advent of low-cost, continual, two-way television exchanges will lead to relationships that are constrained only by imagination. For example, imagine a dining-room table surrounded by chairs that are occupied by plywood human cutouts with seventeen-inch monitors for faces. Every Sunday morning, by a prearranged tradition, you could dial up the appropriate people and have an interactive family brunch with Aunt Sue from Minneapolis, Aunt Sally and Uncle Ted from Omaha, Drew and AnnMarie from San Francisco, and even Jim and Heather who are on vacation in Salzburg and thus having breakfast with you in their late afternoon. And the nursing home could dial in for Grandmother to join the group, even though she has never conquered this technology.

People will meet, fall in love, and get married via the Net (Drew and AnnMarie met via match.com) and perhaps consummate their relationships by means of embedded, voice-activated physiological chips without ever meeting physically. According to an article I read recently, the two most common current uses of the Net are for pornography and financial transactions, and future technologies will likely serve both of those needs even more creatively.

The range of current "gee whiz" applications is impossible to digest, from the tracking of entire truck fleets right down to their tire pressures, to the monitoring of the health of trees on golf courses by satellite ("The maple by the sand trap on the fifth fairway needs some fertilizer"), to the tracking of convicted felons using electronic ankle bracelets. A futuristic world is already here, and it requires hardly more than a glass of wine or two to imagine the next developments.

For example, whimsical as it sounds, I can seriously envision a judicial policy whereby all repeat sexual offenders would have an activation chip embedded that would beep like a garbage truck backing up whenever the repeater became physiologically aroused, thereby warning everyone in the vicinity.

One of my favorite futuristic fantasies is this: By typing a detailed profile of yourself into your transmitting gadget (your interests, your hobbies, your demographic characteristics, your experiences, whatever is important to you) and activating the "scan within one hundred yards" feature, you could be alerted, wherever you were, to the presence of any other similarly described individual in your immediate environment. Imagine walking up to a stranger in the concourse of Chicago's O'Hare airport and saying, "I understand that you also grew up in the rural Midwest, your mother was a music teacher, you like Mozart and barbershop quartet singing, you lust after Julia Roberts, Richard Feynman is one of your idols, and you ski and play squash. Would you like to have a cup of coffee and chat?"

And of course the extension to "DWM, N/S, mature, mischievous, ISO Julia Roberts within a hundred yards" is obvious. What a world we live in, and we haven't seen anything yet.

Whatever Happened to the Skyhook?

In February 1966, *Science,* perhaps the world's most prestigious scientific journal, published a short report entitled "Satellite Elongation into a True 'Sky-Hook.'" In two pages dense with scientific tables and formulas, the authors suggested a remarkable idea—basically that a satellite could be suspended roughly 25,000 miles above the earth in a synchronous orbit, with a cable dropping down to the earth and a balancing cable sticking out of the other side into space, thus creating a stable, permanent skyhook.

The authors were John D. Isaacs, Hugh Bradner, and George E. Backus from the Scripps Institution of Oceanography at the University of California in La Jolla, and Allyn C. Vine from the Woods Hole Oceanographic Institution in Massachusetts.

The editor of *Science* was nervous enough about the paper to introduce it with this unusual editorial note: "The authors have made a very interesting suggestion in this paper. One referee described the 'Sky Hook' as 'a delightful idea and a grandiose scheme for a future technology.' However, the reviewers were concerned about the problems of stability and felt that these might make 'Sky Hook' impracticable. The majority recommended that we accept this paper [for publication] in spite of their reservations."

At that time, just eight years after the launching of Sputnik, we were not yet familiar and comfortable with some of the central concepts, such as positioning a satellite in a manner to achieve a balance between gravitational and centrifugal forces to allow it to hang in space with no further expenditure of energy, and such a proposition appeared to be science fiction in the extreme. Actually, in 1998 it still does, especially with some of the further implications that Isaacs and his colleagues suggested.

If I understand their suppositions—and that could be debatable—they further noted that if a weight, say a thousand kilograms, roughly the size of the Volkswagen Beetle, were gently shoved out of the satellite, riding the cable that points out into space, centrifugal force would soon take over, accelerating its movement until by the time it reached the end of the 25,000-mile cable it would have achieved launch velocity and would be slung into space with the expenditure of virtually no energy. Thus a free launch platform.

Even more wondrous, if a smaller line were attached to the thousand-kilogram weight and dropped down to the earth along the opposing cable, it could be attached to a payload, and as the thousand-kilogram weight was being launched into space by centrifugal force, it could effortlessly pull the payload up the other cable to the satellite, again with the expenditure of very little energy.

It appears to be a win-win situation all around.

The two major problems seemed to be the issue of stability referred to by the reviewers, especially where the cable entered the earth's atmosphere, and the necessity for the cable to be constructed out of a material approximately twice the strength of the strongest known material, which in 1966 was diamond.

To overcome these problems, the authors expanded their thinking to a wider universe: "The conditions on some other bodies of the solar system appear to be less demanding. . . . From the surface of Mars, the Martian satellites, the backside of the earth's moon, some of the Jovian moons and rapidly rotating asteroids, the system probably would be capable of launching large masses to any point in the solar system without excessive demands on materials." Their thoughts conjured up images of giant space slingshots, hurling people and materials from one planet to another.

That was fascinating enough, but there was more to come. Almost two years later, in November 1967, *Science* published a reaction letter from Vladimir Lvov of the Novosti Press Agency, Moscow, USSR. In a congenial but scientific manner, Lvov pointed out that Konstantin Tsiolkovski, "the Russian pioneer of astronautics," had sketched out the basic scheme for this "cosmic lift" in 1895, though apparently without providing the detailed analysis of Isaacs and his colleagues.

However, Lvov then went on to point out that a "Leningrad engineer," Y. N. Artsutanov, had published a more detailed analysis in *Komsomolskaya Pravda* in July 1960, and Lvov reported that Artsutanov, in his suggestion for a "heavenly funicular," had anticipated many of the factors described by Isaacs et al. In short, he had upstaged them.

Lvov added optimistically, "Such a project may possibly get underway by the end of this century."

At the time of his letter, the Cold War was white hot as the United States was bombing North Vietnam, an ally of the Soviet Union, on a daily basis, and in that environment Lvov's conclusion was a model of scientific diplomacy: "Our attitude toward [Artsutanov's] priority is devoid of chauvinism or nationalism. We welcome international ties in science and believe that the 'sky-hook' project affords a good opportunity for the cross-pollination of ideas in science."

Isaacs and his American colleagues were (almost) equally diplomatic in their response. First, they acknowledged that "the article clearly demonstrates that Artsutanov proposed the 'sky-hook' development some six years before our paper appeared in *Science*," but they could not refrain from adding, "Artsutanov's article presents none of the calculations or results on cable diameters, strength, energetics, traffic capacity, and a number of other factors to which Lvov alludes. Presumably Lvov has also had access to . . . [other unreferenced] studies." They did end diplomatically with the "hope that Artsutanov derived as much excitement and enjoyment working on the idea as we did."

I have a disquieting habit of tearing out interesting articles while reading, and throwing them into an ever-expanding file labeled merely "Stimulation," though by now it is not a file but more like a filing cabinet. In preparing to downsize from a large home to a more manageable condo, I was recently leafing through a career's worth of stimulation and came across these articles, and they now occasion me to ask, Does anyone know whatever happened to the skyhook or the heavenly funicular? It is almost the end of the century, and I want to know what is going to happen next.

To this end, I ran a draft of this column past a neighbor, Major Bruce Chesley, who, with a Ph.D. degree in astronautics from the University of Colorado, is on the faculty of the U.S. Air Force Academy. He alerted me to a couple of Web sites (see below) where NASA has reported some experiments with satellite cables, or *tethers* as they are called because they are often used to tie two satellites together or to hang something outside a satellite. As with any scientific experiment, there have been some wins and some losses, the latter caused to some extent by the instability problems predicted earlier. However, NASA scientists have reported that they successfully deployed a twelve-mile tether, far short of the 25,000 miles required by the calculations of Isaacs et al., and it was hardly a large cable of diamond. In fact, it was 0.75 mm in diameter, approximately the size of dental floss. Still, their results appear to have validated Tsiolkovski's speculation over a century ago about the possibility of a "cosmic lift." Perhaps their most surprising new finding was that because the tether was continually cutting through the earth's magnetic field, it generated an electrical current. Their calculations suggest that a sixty-mile tether could generate 15,000 volts, which could be used either for power in a space station or to move a satellite into a higher orbit without using any fuel hauled up from earth. Again, once in orbit, free power.

Clearly, one hundred years later, the final chapter on the skyhook, Artsutanov's heavenly funicular, is yet to be written. It may prove to be one of the delightful surprises of the next millennium.

NASA Web Sites

http://amsd-www.larc.nasa.gov/seds
http://sets16.sprl.umich.edu

Wall Street Rules That Have Made Some People Rich . . . Sometimes

Approximately twenty years ago, during the late seventies, I gave a presentation to a group of managers at an East Coast conference center. When I went to the room early in the morning to check the setup, I found a leftover handout from the previous day. It had the following rules on it. It was neither dated nor signed, and had no identifying information of any kind.

1. Nobody has been right three times.
2. Turnarounds take seven years.
3. Buy in haste, repent in leisure.
4. Sell the stock when the company announces a new corporate headquarters.
5. Sell the stock when it runs off the top (or bottom) of the chart.
6. When everybody likes a stock, it must go down. When nobody likes a stock, it may go up.
7. Sell your losers and let your runners run.
8. Never confuse brilliance with a bull market.
9. More stocks double than go to zero.
10. The market is a random walk up a 9.3 percent grade.
11. If anybody really knew, they wouldn't tell you.
12. The best thing about money management is that it's indoor work with no heavy lifting.
13. A stock well bought is a stock half sold.
14. It's a long, long time from May to December, but no longer long enough for a long-term capital gain.
15. In a bull market, be bullish.
16. The bottom is always 10 percent below your worst case expectations.
17. There are no customers' yachts.
18. Risk is what's left over after the bad news hits.
19. All growth is temporary.
20. A bright and energetic self-starter can make all the mistakes in this business in five years. With fools and sluggards it can take a lifetime.
21. You only need two research sources on a stock if one is a bull and the other is a bear.

22. An outstanding portfolio always contains an outstanding stock.
23. Analysts write long research reports when they don't have time to write short ones.
24. Nobody is smarter than the guy who gave you your last winner.
25. You never understand a stock until you're long (or short).
26. Some stocks will beat you every time.
27. The more heavily someone is supposed to be taxed, the greater that person's power to avoid taxes.
28. The best telephone message is, "Ask him to call me before the close."
29. None of the old rules work anymore, but then they never did.
30. Never throw good money after bad.
31. Never dip into capital.
32. A lot of things aren't worth knowing.
33. A penny saved will depreciate rapidly.
34. Half of your portfolio is cyclical, but you don't know which half.
35. You will never be the first to hear.
36. Growth will bail you out . . . if you live long enough.
37. There is no such thing as inside information.
38. Sell at the opening. Buy at the close.
39. You can make a silk purse out of a sow's ear, but it's not worth the effort.
40. Don't apologize for acting on your instincts if you have spent years developing them.
41. Money management is 10 percent inspiration and 90 percent perspiration.
42. The stock doesn't know you own it.
43. You can't spend relative performance.
44. The trouble with managing money is that everybody once made a successful investment.
45. Sell when the research file gets full.
46. A portfolio that goes down 50 percent and comes back 50 percent is still down 25 percent.
47. There are no one-decision stocks.
48. All really great money management organizations have had three partners.

49. Never own it if the corporate title includes "Universal," "Global," or "Intergalactic."

50. If you have a great thought and write it down, it will probably look rather stupid ten hours later.

51. You can be 200 percent wrong when you switch.

52. You'll never know who your friends are until you've had two bad years in a row.

53. A good portfolio manager never asks a question unless he knows the answer.

54. A guy who has all the answers doesn't even understand the questions.

55. The trouble with the stock market is not that it is controlled by mathematical factors or that it is controlled by nonmathematical factors but that it is controlled by nearly mathematical factors.

56. The trouble with this generation of analysts is that they have never lived through a bull market.

57. The trouble with economists is that they have never had to meet a payroll.

58. If all the economists in the world were laid end to end, they wouldn't reach a conclusion.

59. An economist is a guy who is fascinated with numbers but who doesn't have enough personality to become an accountant.

60. All the news that fits, they print.

61. If the industry leader is overpriced, don't buy the dogs.

62. There will always be a two-tiered market.

63. Price is fundamental; it's the only thing you know for sure about a stock.

64. Whoever has the gold makes the rules.

65. Middle age is when you are doing more things for the last time and fewer things for the first time.

66. Middle age is when every new feeling you have is probably a symptom.

67. If God had meant money managers to fly coach, He would have given them narrower posteriors.

Clearly, this was someone's idiosyncratic (read *undisciplined*) collection of proverbs, aphorisms, quips, quotes, adages, and epigrams. And this someone was obviously male and a money manager.

At the time, the economy was recovering from the 1973-1974 recession—the Dow Jones was probably about 600—and the man and woman on the street had not yet learned to be fascinated by the market and its gyrations.

Perhaps the strangest feature of these statements now, when approximately 50 percent of the U.S. households own stock, is how up-to-date they seem. Even the humor seems topical.

With the rules' final emphasis on middle age, one cannot help wondering how the collector, whoever he is, is faring in the nineties. Did he turn conservative in the seventies downturn, put his personal money in bonds for old age, and thereby miss most of the recent boom? Or did he stay current and hit it big with Wal-Mart, Microsoft, or Dell, and is he now savoring some warm-water, secluded location with his yacht and a satellite system for leisurely trades?

We will never know, a tantalizing yet somehow satisfying outcome.

Twenty-five Years—Seemingly Quick as a Heartbeat

I recently celebrated my twenty-fifth anniversary at CCL, an occasion that calls for reminiscing and realignment. The reminiscing comes below; the realignment is that this will be my last Inklings column, mainly under the theory of "quit while you are ahead."

Following are the major themes that come to mind when I think of how life at CCL is different today from the way it was on my 1973 fall arrival.

Growth. When I resigned my professorship at the University of Minnesota to take over CCL's professional activities—first as vice-president, research and programs, and ultimately as executive vice-president—CCL had a total staff of about twenty-five people, a 35,000-square-foot building in Greensboro, and a budget of roughly $750,000. Today we have a staff of five hundred; we occupy approximately 285,000 square feet spread over Greensboro (190,000), Colorado Springs (72,000), San Diego (15,000), and Brussels (8,000), and we have a budget of roughly $60 million. In addition, we have a widely spread web of adjuncts, licensees, and affiliates, ranging over several continents. We have grown from a closely knit family in which we not only knew each other but also knew each other's spouses and children. Today we need name badges, especially when we meet staff from campuses other than our own and from the outlying operations. Still, the growth, though turbulent at times, has been highly gratifying, and it has allowed us to take on challenges that would have been unthinkable in the past.

Diversity. CCL's staff has traditionally been separated into exempt (professional) and nonexempt (support staff). In 1973, the professional staff was 100 percent white males; the support staff, excluding the housekeeping staff, was 100 percent white females. In a recent reorganization, in a dramatic shift, we wound up with an executive team of seven vice-presidents, only one of whom is a white male; the rest of the team is comprised of three white females, two African-American females, and one African-American male. The president and four senior fellows are white males.

Overall, our demographic breakdown is 70 percent female, 30 percent male; 81 percent white, 19 percent nonwhite.

Although at any given time, progress has undoubtedly seemed painfully slow to the nonwhite, nonmale contingent—who have suffered an unconscionably large number of personal and professional slights and barriers—from the perspective of history this much change in a relatively brief time is striking.

The increased diversity has been beneficial in many ways. We are now more representative of the general population, we have tapped talent pools that were heretofore unavailable to us—for example, we now offer leadership training for women conducted solely by women, and likewise African-American sessions conducted solely by African Americans—and we have credibility in a wider range of demographic categories.

Also, it just "feels" more equitable.

There are some mild downsides. My instincts tell me that we are now a somewhat more political organization in that more decisions are now questioned on the basis of perceived gender or racial slants and, in a lighter tone, humor has been a definite victim. I do not dare insert here an example of 1973 humor to illustrate how supersensitive we have become about using whimsical constructions involving ethnicity, gender, religion, race, occupation, national or regional origin, physiology, anatomy, hair color, age, and on and on. Even lawyers are demanding compassionate treatment.

Still, in general, the dramatic shift in diversity feels upbeat.

Technology. How can our newest employees, many of whom are in their twenties, comprehend the CCL world of the 1970s, which had no voice mail, e-mail, fax machines, copiers, FedEx, electric staplers and erasers, ATMs, word processors, spreadsheets, laptops, audiocassette players, VCRs, scanners, Weather Channel, remote controls, point-and-shoot cameras, CDs, and scented Magic Markers? When I arrived twenty-five years ago, CCL had neither a 35 mm camera nor an overhead projector, depending for instructional use on blackboards and an occasional 16 mm movie. Secretaries still took dictation in shorthand on steno pads, and we used lots of carbon paper.

With the array of new technology, our current productivity gains feel enormous; we routinely pull off projects that would have simply been impossible twenty-five years ago, such as conducting complex programs in several parts of the world simultaneously, with immediate support from home.

Expansion of leadership programs. Twenty-five years ago the focus on leadership programs was generally restricted to the military; a few major corporations such as AT&T, GE, and IBM; and a few youth-oriented organizations such as the Scouts, 4-H, Future Farmers of America, and

Junior Achievement. Community programs, such as Leadership Atlanta, and foundation programs, such as the Bush Foundation Leadership Program in Minnesota, were just starting to appear.

Today the expansion almost constitutes an explosion. Numerous corporations have established some sort of "XYZ Corporate Leadership Forum," most branches of the military have expanded their offerings in both number and sophistication, and even high schools have leadership programs. Virtually every civic area has some leadership development activity designed to bring citizens together around governmental and societal issues—for example, Leadership-Greensboro, Leadership-Iowa, Leadership-Montgomery County, Leadership-Evansville, Leadership-Columbus, Goals for Memphis, and Citizens Goals for Colorado Springs. The Blandin Foundation in Grand Rapids, Minnesota, is in its second decade of conducting state-of-the-art leadership programs for small Minnesota communities. The Jepson School of Leadership at the University of Richmond has been founded to provide both academic and service-oriented leadership opportunities for undergraduates, culminating in a bachelor's degree in leadership studies.

I could fill the rest of this column with other examples. Perhaps the most remarkable and potentially most important new program is the Global Leadership Initiative organized under the umbrella of the United Nations by Adel Safty, former director of the International Leadership Academy. In two sessions, over the past two years, Safty—a visionary, multilingual Egyptian—has brought together emerging leaders from around the world to grapple with the personal and organizational issues of leadership and to interact with distinguished international leaders. Part of his program has included CCL's assessment-for-development approach, conducted by Stan Gryskiewicz and other CCL faculty. As this program moves forward, it may prove to be not only an effective training program for leaders but also an interpersonal forum for identifying and dealing with issues of international tension.

Though these four changes—growth, diversity, technology, and the expansion of leadership programs—are the most vivid, several other shifts over the twenty-five years are also worth noting, although some of them are admittedly superficial.

Fads of leadership. For reasons that I do not understand, leadership and managerial training run constantly through fads. Here, for example, are some that come to mind from over the past twenty-five years, a few of them still active: managerial grid, situational leadership, assessment centers, sensitivity training, EST (Erhard seminars training), decision making, the risky shift, brainstorming, guided imagery, left brain/right brain, transactional analysis, I'm OK/you're OK, the one-minute manager, TQM (total quality management), quality circles, ropes courses, the seven habits of highly effective people, diversity training, in search of excellence, emotional intelligence, and paint-ball sessions.

Each of these approaches, often driven by a creative zealot, has had something to offer, and even the ones that have faded have usually left behind a useful residue: for example, brainstorming taught us to nurture, at least briefly, even the craziest ideas; sensitivity training taught us the importance of paying attention to others' perceptions of our behavior; and ropes courses taught us that we can succeed even when terrified.

Why though, I ask, do we need the fads? It is as if chemistry professors came together and said, "Why can't we find something more exciting to teach than the periodic table of elements? Our students are bored with that." Is there no basic technology of leadership that remains constant over time, technology that needs to be mastered by aspiring leaders?

CCL's process of personal assessment for development, a psychological testing approach created twenty-five years ago by Robert Dorn, our first director of training, has been durable over all this time and is becoming ever more widespread and sophisticated. This year we will process something over 400,000 surveys. Still, many times I have awakened at night in a heavy sweat thinking, "*Mi Dios,* what if leadership itself is just another fad? How will we meet the budget?"

Smoking. In my executive role at CCL, no single issue consumed more personal energy in the early days than smoking. I had arrived from Minnesota, a health-conscious state that had recently passed the Minnesota Clean Indoor Air Act, which banned smoking indoors in public places, to find that in North Carolina, tobacco was still king. Most people smoked, and they smoked anytime, anywhere. I remember my shock at finding that people sitting beside me in movie theaters were smoking. CCL instructors smoked in the classroom while teaching. We sold cigarettes in the cafeteria, and people smoked while going through the food line.

When I tried to impose some constraints, I was looked upon as a wild-eyed Yankee who was trying to take away a God-given right. Progress was slow. It was not until roughly 1990 that CCL finally went smoke free, and then only after a citywide referendum showed that even a majority of Greensboro residents favored smoke-free zones. Confrontations around smoking are my least favorite memories of those early years.

Styles. Rummaging through twenty-five years of photos of CCL parties, conferences, weddings, and other social events reminds me of the style cycles we have been through, especially hair length and tie width for men, skirt length and heel height for women. We are also older (sigh), probably eat more junk food, and are generally less active physically; larger waist and hip measurements are likely reflected in those changes. On the positive side, we are now more ecologically aware and are killing far fewer little polyesters to dress the male staff.

People. Finally, of course, I think of the people. Although it feels syrupy and completely predictable to say it, the most dramatic memories concern the people. CCL attracts interesting individuals, both as staff and participants, and the nature of our activities guarantees that we will have intense and, though brief in the case of participants, gratifying interactions with them. I cannot imagine a more interesting, satisfying day-to-day life than my social and professional interactions with my colleagues and our guests. In the long run, friendships matter, perhaps more than anything else—except health.

So it has been a fascinating time, and I feel favored to have been part of this growing, thriving, important institution. Although this is my valedictory column, it does not signal the end of my CCL involvement, merely a shift to other activities. I thank my constant readers for their letters, notes, and lately, e-mails, and wish you well. May you deserve good leaders, and find them.

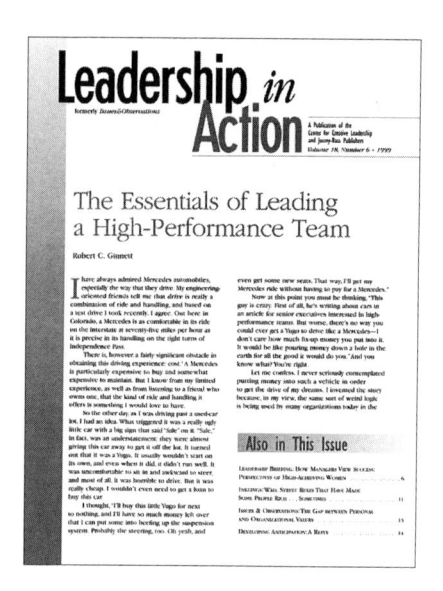

Leadership in Action

*A quarterly publication of the
Center for Creative Leadership and
Jossey-Bass Publishers*

Martin Wilcox, Editor

Leadership in Action is a bimonthly newsletter that aims to help practicing leaders and those who train and develop practicing leaders by providing them with insights gained in the course of CCL's educational and research activities. It also aims to provide a forum for the exchange of information and ideas between practitioners and CCL staff and associates.

The annual subscription price for *Leadership in Action* is $99.00 for individuals and $124.00 for institutions. To order, please contact Customer Service, Jossey-Bass Inc., Publishers, 350 Sansome Street, San Francisco, CA 94104-1342. Telephone: 888/378-2537 or 415/433-1767; fax: 800/605-2665. See the Jossey-Bass Web site at www.josseybass.com

CENTER FOR CREATIVE LEADERSHIP
New Releases, Best-sellers, Bibliographies, and Special Packages

NEW RELEASES

IDEAS INTO ACTION GUIDEBOOKS
Becoming a More Versatile Learner (1998, Stock #402) .... $6.95 *
Ongoing Feedback: How to Get It, How to Use It (1998, Stock #400) .... $6.95 *
Reaching Your Development Goals (1998, Stock #401) .... $6.95 *

The Center for Creative Leadership Handbook of Leadership Development (1998,
Stock #201) .... $65.00 *
The Complete Inklings: Columns on Leadership and Creativity (1999, Stock #343) $30.00
A Cross-National Comparison of Effective Leadership and Teamwork: Toward a
Global Workforce (1998, Stock #177) .... $15.00 *
Executive Selection: A Research Report on What Works and What Doesn't (1998,
Stock #179) .... $30.00 *
Feedback to Managers (3rd Edition) (1998, Stock #178) .... $60.00 *
High-Performance Work Organizations: Definitions, Practices, and an Annotated
Bibliography (1999, Stock #342) $20.00
International Success: Selecting, Developing, and Supporting Expatriate Managers
(1998, Stock #180) .... $15.00 *
Leadership Education: A Source Book of Courses and Programs (1998, Stock #339) .... $40.00 *
Leadership Resources: A Guide to Training and Development Tools (1998, Stock #340) ... $40.00 *

BEST-SELLERS
The Adventures of Team Fantastic: A Practical Guide for Team Leaders and Members
(1996, Stock #172) $20.00
Breaking Free: A Prescription for Personal and Organizational Change (1997,
Stock #271) $25.00
Breaking the Glass Ceiling: Can Women Reach the Top of America's Largest
Corporations? (Updated Edition) (1992, Stock #236) .... $13.00 *
CEO Selection: A Street-smart Review (1994, Stock #164) .... $25.00 *
Choosing 360: A Guide to Evaluating Multi-rater Feedback Instruments for
Management Development (1997, Stock #334) .... $15.00 *
Eighty-eight Assignments for Development in Place (1989, Stock #136) .... $15.00 *
Enhancing 360-degree Feedback for Senior Executives: How to Maximize the Benefits
and Minimize the Risks (1994, Stock #160) .... $15.00 *
Evolving Leaders: A Model for Promoting Leadership Development in Programs (1995,
Stock #165) .... $15.00 *
Executive Selection: A Look at What We Know and What We Need to Know (1993,
Stock #321) .... $20.00 *
Four Essential Ways that Coaching Can Help Executives (1997, Stock #175) $10.00
Gender Differences in the Development of Managers: How Women Managers Learn
From Experience (1990, Stock #145) .... $35.00 *
A Glass Ceiling Survey: Benchmarking Barriers and Practices (1995, Stock #161) $15.00
High Flyers: Developing the Next Generation of Leaders (1997, Stock #293) $27.95
How to Design an Effective System for Developing Managers and Executives (1996,
Stock #158) .... $15.00 *
If I'm In Charge Here, Why Is Everybody Laughing? (1984, Stock #205) .... $9.95 *

If You Don't Know Where You're Going You'll Probably End Up Somewhere Else
(1974, Stock #203) .... $9.95 *
The Lessons of Experience: How Successful Executives Develop on the Job (1988,
Stock #211) $27.50
A Look at Derailment Today: North America and Europe (1996, Stock #169) .... $20.00 *
Making Common Sense: Leadership as Meaning-making in a Community of Practice
(1994, Stock #156) .... $15.00 *
Making Diversity Happen: Controversies and Solutions (1993, Stock #320) .... $20.00 *
Managerial Promotion: The Dynamics for Men and Women (1996, Stock #170) $15.00
Managing Across Cultures: A Learning Framework (1996, Stock #173) .... $15.00 *
Maximizing the Value of 360-degree Feedback (1998, Stock #295) .... $42.95 *
The New Leaders: Guidelines on Leadership Diversity in America (1992, Stock #238A) . $18.50 *
Perspectives on Dialogue: Making Talk Developmental for Individuals and
Organizations (1996, Stock #168) .... $20.00 *
Preventing Derailment: What To Do Before It's Too Late (1989, Stock #138) $25.00
The Realities of Management Promotion (1994, Stock #157) .... $15.00 *
Selected Research on Work Team Diversity (1996, Stock #326) $24.95
Should 360-degree Feedback Be Used Only for Developmental Purposes? (1997,
Stock #335) .... $15.00 *
Take the Road to Creativity and Get Off Your Dead End (1977, Stock #204) .... $9.95 *
Twenty-two Ways to Develop Leadership in Staff Managers (1990, Stock #144) $15.00

BIBLIOGRAPHIES
Formal Mentoring Programs in Organizations: An Annotated Bibliography (1997,
Stock #332) $20.00
Management Development through Job Experiences: An Annotated Bibliography
(1998, Stock #337) $20.00
Selection at the Top: An Annotated Bibliography (1997, Stock #333) .... $20.00 *
Succession Planning: An Annotated Bibliography (1995, Stock #324) .... $20.00 *
Using 360-degree Feedback in Organizations: An Annotated Bibliography (1997,
Stock #338) .... $15.00 *

SPECIAL PACKAGES
The Diversity Collection (Stock #708; includes 145, 173, 177, 236, 238A, 320) $85.00
Executive Selection (Stock #710; includes 157, 164, 179, 180, 321, 333) $85.00
Guidebook Package (Stock #721; includes 400, 401, 402) $14.95
HR Professional's Info Pack (Stock #717; includes 136, 158, 169, 201, 324, 334, 340) $100.00
Leadership Education and Leadership Resources Package (Stock #722; includes
339, 340) $70.00
New Understanding of Leadership (Stock #718; includes 156, 165, 168) $40.00
Personal Growth, Taking Charge, and Enhancing Creativity (Stock #231; includes
203, 204, 205) $20.00
The 360 Collection (Stock #720; includes 160, 178, 295, 334, 335, 338) $75.00

Discounts are available. Please write for a Publications catalog. Address your request to: Publication, Center for Creative Leadership, P.O. Box 26300, Greensboro, NC 27438-6300, 336-286-4480, or fax to 336-282-3284. Purchase your publications from our on-line bookstore at **www.ccl.org/publications**. All prices subject to change.

*Indicates publication is also part of a package.

ORDER FORM

Or e-mail your order via the Center's on-line bookstore at www.ccl.org

Name _____ Title _____

Organization _____

Mailing Address _____
(street address required for mailing)

City/State/Zip _____

Telephone _____ FAX _____
(telephone number required for UPS mailing)

Quantity	Stock No.	Title	Unit Cost	Amount

CCL' Federal ID Number is 237-07-9591.

Subtotal _____

Shipping and Handling _____
(Add 6% of subtotal with a $4.00 minimum; add 40% on all international shipping)

NC residents add 6% sales tax; CA residents add 7.75% sales tax; CO residents add 6.1% sales tax _____

TOTAL _____

METHOD OF PAYMENT (ALL orders for less than $100 must be PREPAID.)

❏ Check or money order enclosed (payable to Center for Creative Leadership).

❏ Purchase Order No. _____ (Must be accompanied by this form.)

❏ Charge my order, plus shipping, to my credit card: ❏ American Express ❏ Discover ❏ MasterCard ❏ VISA

ACCOUNT NUMBER: _____ EXPIRATION DATE: MO. ____ YR. ____

NAME OF ISSUING BANK: _____

SIGNATURE _____

❏ Please put me on your mailing list.

Publication • Center for Creative Leadership • P.O. Box 26300
Greensboro, NC 27438-6300
336-286-4480 • FAX 336-282-3284

5/99

Client Priority Code: R

fold here

PLACE
STAMP
HERE

CENTER FOR CREATIVE LEADERSHIP
PUBLICATION
P. O. Box 26300
Greensboro, NC 27438-6300